Hildegard of Bingen
An Integrated Vision

Anne H. King-Lenzmeier

A Michael Glazier Book

THE LITURGICAL PRESS
Collegeville, Minnesota

www.litpress.org

A Michael Glazier Book published by The Liturgical Press

Cover design by Ann Blattner. Illustration: *Hildegard and Her Assistants*. Liber Divinorum Operum, c. 1240, Lucca, Biblioteca Statale.

1   2   3   4   5   6   7   8

Library of Congress Cataloging-in-Publication Data

King-Lenzmeier, Anne H., 1953–
    Hildegard of Bingen : an integrated vision / Anne H. King–Lenzmeier.
      p. cm.
    "A Michael Glazier book."
    Includes bibliographical references and index.
    ISBN 0-8146-5842-3
    1. Hildegard, Saint, 1098–1179. I. Title.

BX4700.H5 K56 2001
282'.092–dc21

00-052044

To my family and friends

Contents

Contents

Figures and Illustrations

1. The original enclosure at Disibodenberg.
2. Engraving of the Rupertsberg in the seventeenth century. Collection of Dr. Werner Lauter.
3. Part 1, Vision 2, *Scivias*.
4. Part 2, Vision 6.
5. Part 3, Vision 11, *Scivias*.
6. Vision 1, *De Operatione Dei*, Bibliotheca Statale di Lucca.
7. Musical Notation: definition of neumes.
8. Musical Notation: *porrigat* in Hildegard's composition.
9. *Lingua Ignota. Analecta Sanctae Hildegardis,* vol. 8 of the *Analecta Sacra*, ed. J.-B. Pitra (Monte Cassino, 1882) 497.
10. Isidore of Seville: the cardinal directions and their properties. My translation from the original diagram of Isidore of Seville, *De natura rerum* 11; *Patrologia Latina*, vol. 83, p. 976.
11. Physica: Characteristics of the natural world (my adaptation and translation).

Acknowledgments

This book would not have been possible without the support of the following institutions and persons:

The University of St. Thomas, whose travel grant and semester sabbatical allowed me to travel to Germany to visit the Abtei St. Hildegard, consult archives in Wiesbaden and Cologne, and in Belgium to consult the manuscripts at the archives in Brussels.

The Sisters of the Abtei St. Hildegard, for a week of learning about Hildegard's way of life and their hospitality and support.

Studium, a place for scholars to work and live, created by and with the support of the Sisters of St. Benedict of the College of St. Benedict, St. Joseph, Minnesota. Were it not for the six-week opportunity given me by this wonderful place to work, the original draft of the manuscript would never have been written as quickly nor as well. I thank in particular Sr. Dolores Super, O.S.B., who administrates this program, as well as the other scholars working with me in *Studium* at the time. I also thank the members of the community of the Monastery of St. Benedict for their kindness, support, and inclusion into the Benedictine cycle of life and prayer which has truly enriched this book. I have been nourished and sustained by their prayers.

Rev. Michael Naughton, O.S.B., of The Liturgical Press for encouraging me to take on the project of this book and for his extraordinary patience with the vicissitudes of this writer and her manuscript; Mr. Mark Twomey for trusting his judgment and giving me the extra time needed to complete it; and Mrs. Colleen Stiller for her careful oversight of the process of making the book actually arrive in print successfully.

Dr. Werner Lauter, without whom I never would have seen Disibodenberg or the remnants left of the Rupertsberg; who has been a staunch supporter of my writing since the beginning; who tirelessly works to give scholars the benefit of his life-long association with Hildegard in many ways, not the least of which are his authoritative bibliographies, contained in three volumes, of everything written about Hildegard.

Those colleagues and friends who consented to go through the initial reading and later editing of the manuscript after its various drafts, and who made many helpful critiques and suggestions. I thank in particular those who read through the whole manuscript: Rev. Michael Joncas, Ph.D., University of St. Thomas; Dr. James Callahan, University of St. Thomas; Dr. Peter King, Ohio State University; Ms. Sarah Spencer, M.A., University of St. Thomas; and Liza Ramberg, M.A., University of St. Thomas.

Thanks also to those who answered questions about their specialties on short notice: Dr. Susan Verdi Webster of the University of St. Thomas on art history, Dr. Mona Logarbo of the University of Michigan on Latin paleography, Dr. Anna Greco on translation problems, Thomas Lenzmeier, M.A., on computer formatting.

Introduction

Hildegard von Bingen, once an obscure figure in twelfth-century history and theology, has today captured the imagination of scholars and the general reading public alike. What is the reason behind this new-found celebrity? What makes this German Benedictine nun, the "Sibyl of the Rhine," such an attractive figure for people at this time?

First, Hildegard's impressive array of talents contributes both to her rediscovery by scholars and to her broader appeal. Her range is impressive: she is a musician, a theologian, a prophetess, an artist, a biologist, an herbalist, a healer, a correspondent, a playwright, a preacher, a cosmologist, an interpreter of the feminine in the human and the divine, and a leader of her religious community.

Second, although Hildegard lived in a world whose assumptions were radically removed from our own, she speaks to us today through the centuries as an important voice for concerns we share. These include seeing both the particular and the universal in creation, rediscovering the complementarity of gender imagery, and showing that the feminine can be used creatively in relationship to the divine and the human. She is eminently practical, yet passionate in her concern for what her visions tell her is the right course to follow. In short, she appeals to us on a variety of levels. As we shall see, some of this appeal is as much implicit as explicit, since her life and works are so much a part of a complex whole that the pull toward her we feel may be both a conscious and an unconscious process.

Third, her works are now becoming ever more available to us. Hildegard literally disappears from history and the record until the nineteenth century; although her feast day was still kept and celebrated in Germany, no systematic effort had been made to hear her voice in the intervening centuries. Her rediscovery was almost accidental, occurring when scholars came across fragments of and references to parts of her work.

Scholars first rediscovered Hildegard through differing avenues of her achievements. Musicologists began to analyze her unique use of melismatic chant forms; from specific interests in her musical compositions, commentaries on the unique structure of her body of work, the *Symphonia,* emerged. Linguists rediscovered her as perhaps the first playwright of the age: her work dramatizes the virtues and the history of salvation in the *Ordo virtutum.* Although this play is set to music, it dramatizes the struggle of virtue against the Devil and is anticipatory of many of the medieval morality plays. Both the artistic and the theological communities, their imaginations fired by her theological-visionary works, have explored and debated their import. Having experienced visions since she was a child, she felt God calling her to depict and to reflect upon a set of visions she received after the age of forty-two. These visions are depicted and explicated in the *Scivias* (Know the ways of God), the *Liber vitae meritorum* (Book of the Merits of Life), and the *De operatione Dei* (The Works of God). They are dramatically and at times disturbingly portrayed in both art and text. While there is general agreement that Hildegard did indeed closely oversee the drawing of the visions, several conflicting sources are available that portray the visionary pictures as Hildegard dictated them, so there is continual debate concerning their content, origin, and meaning. Furthermore, the manuscript that was most likely illustrated under her direct supervision was lost in Dresden in 1945. Theologians have seen her from a variety of standpoints: as a twelfth-century feminist foundress, as a holistic healer and representative of creation spirituality, as a Benedictine steeped in the liturgy, as a prophetic preacher and teacher, as a mystic whose works are both theological and spiritual. Those interested in medicine have been curious about her theories of biology and the cosmos, her use of herbs, and the possibility of migraine as a source of her extraordinary visions. There is continuing fascination with her images of the feminine divine and with all of her feminine language and imagery. Often these images contrast with her notions of the male and female person as noted in her biological works and correspondence. Her vision of the feminine is a unique contribution, and it is a startling one for her time; for many, it is one of the most important facets of Hildegard of Bingen, perhaps the central idea of her work.

Hildegard has not been discovered in technical journals alone, however. Her wide-ranging talents, her versatility in adapting to circumstances, her spiritual insights, and especially her visionary paintings, her music, and her cosmic approach to creation have given her an appeal to a much wider audience. Her visionary paintings appear in several works, the most popular of which is the *Illuminations of Hildegard of Bingen,* a work in which Matthew Fox has popularized Hildegard as the holistic "wise woman" who recognizes the surpassing goodness of all creation, using her paintings to illustrate the possibilities of meditating with her thoughts in a contemporary setting. Various musical groups have recorded her music, beginning with classical ensembles and emerging recently as a popular figure in the album *Vision.* In this recent work, promoted by Angel Records, she has been made the heiress to the rediscovery of Gregorian chant; her original settings are intertwined with and interpreted by the work of a contemporary composer and arranger, Richard Souther. Many authors have written books guiding people to pray in Hildegard's words and to meditate on her reflections. Some have written fictionalized accounts of her life, such as an autobiography or a diary. Many have seen her as a champion of the feminine, particularly the feminine as envisioned in God; they have found her phrases and her illustrations liberating in an androcentric culture, both in her own time and in ours. Particularly in Europe, there are those who are seriously reconsidering her methods of healing and understanding the human body, following her precepts as a guide to natural, holistic health. As we can clearly see, she appeals to a wide range of interests and audiences. Some of those audiences are quite separate from one another, which lead us naturally into the structure and concerns of this book.

With her growing popularity among both scholars and the general public, it has become essential to look at Hildegard as a whole. She is penultimately someone who responds to her own personal setting and place in time. In technical examinations of the facets of Hildegard's work and personality, this can render the talents she offers us virtually impenetrable to the non-specialist; some of the articles directed toward literary criticism of her work and musicological concerns are only read by a Hildegard specialist from another scholarly discipline with the greatest of care. Nevertheless, there have been accessible scholarly works that have seen Hildegard as a whole and have been read by many interested in this striking woman's life. Among these are books such as Barbara Newman's *Sister of Wisdom* and Sabina Flanagan's *Hildegard of Bingen: A Visionary Life.* At this time new source materials are being made available rapidly, enhancing our understanding of Hildegard. There is an ongoing and recent translation of her letters into English, previously only available piecemeal in German and Latin. There are new translations of her musical texts and poetry, considering the relationship of text to composition, and many recordings of her music with fresh and differing interpretations. Publications of her visionary and non-visionary works in English, translated from either the original Latin or the German, are now being made more widely available—the English-speaking audience has relied primarily on her writings in the *Scivias* until recently, of which there are now several versions available in print. In this veritable renaissance of Hildegard studies and sources it is all too easy to lose our way in the maze. It is necessary to build on the solid work of other scholars and writers who have contextualized Hildegard for us, but we do well to try to preserve both the foreign qualities of her world and her time in history while simultaneously making her as accessible to modern sensibilities as possible without compromising who she truly is. This is our pivotal concern and the primary methodological approach of this book.

This book intends to explore Hildegard von Bingen with the intent of integrating her life with her personality, thus introducing her to the reader interested in the "big picture." Because of her array of abilities and the considerable written record of her works that we possess, it has been all too easy to choose the "part" or "interpretation" of Hildegard that appeals to either the individual scholar or member of the general public. Because she has much to offer it is only within the context of a balanced and integrated approach to Hildegard as a person who lived a complex and varied life that we can begin to understand her. It is the purpose of this work to consider Hildegard as a whole person, not just the sum of her parts, and to place her within her own century and context. Only then will her contributions for the contemporary world be discussed. It is essential to attempt to create a framework for discerning who Hildegard was from who different people might *want* her to be. Claims to know the "authentic Hildegard" come from both scholars and popularizers, writers and readers alike. Each of these claims has its own degree of validity and must be judged on its own merits.

Why is this so crucial? To be true to Hildegard the historical person we must insist that what is said about her is factual, even though interpretation is necessary. Many excellent books and articles have been written about Hildegard that claim a particular voice for her, fascinating and accurate in their use of the sources at their command; one such work is Barbara Newman's excellent *Sister of Wisdom*. These types of books have made great contributions to our understanding of this multifaceted woman and her talents. However, there are others who claim Hildegard as their own, *without* having the support of the source herself in a consistent fashion. A prime example of this are the works of Matthew Fox, who chooses his texts from Hildegard with an eye to how he himself wishes to think of her, as a representative of creation spirituality. She does indeed have a knowledge and love of creation, but it is much more complex and far more pessimistic about human nature than Fox's works would lead the reader to believe.[1] How are most people to discern the difference, especially when it is this type of book that is easiest to grasp and to popularize? What will lead them to realize they are being led in the direction a contemporary author prefers to go, even if it misrepresents Hildegard's own intricate and compelling personality?

This book intends to gather together the many strands of data we have about Hildegard, accenting what makes her such a compelling figure for the modern reader while retaining the integrity of her own peerless voice, yet making it accessible to readers without scholarly background. Hopefully, it can serve as both an introduction to Hildegard and a corrective for simplistic interpretations of a sometimes maddeningly complex and gifted woman whose legacy is a multitude of works.

What is it that is so singular about Hildegard? We need to look at what her contemporaries considered to be her unsurpassable gifts; therefore, the metaphor I will employ throughout emerges from the circumstances of her life. Like musical polyphony, where one line of music connects, harmonizes, and prefaces the next strand, Hildegard's life is polyphonic. To cut her apart from the totality of her life and work is not only to put the part before the whole but to actually misrepresent who she is as a person. For Hildegard, each activity flowed into another and yet another. Her ability to bring coherence to all these talents and activities is her special genius. Her experience of contemplative life and Benedictine prayer is pivotal for understanding the woman, the theologian, the musician, the healer. For Hildegard, all life is lived in the constant presence of the Living Light, of God. The Living Light speaks in prophecy and in visions; is praised and experienced in liturgical music, both created and sung; is served in the needs of the human heart and the human body as they are ministered to by the community. Hildegard claims that her work is *given* to her, shown and revealed by that Living Light that has been her constant support and companion.

Her life exudes a "mystical polyphony." By this phrase I mean to imply that while, ironically, she does not compose polyphonic music, she lives a life in which overlapping and interwoven strands make the piece a whole. In the non-technical sense her experiences are *polyphonic,* which is to say they *possess a dense texture and a multivalent sense of meaning.* This metaphor of mystical polyphony will be the method by which this book integrates Hildegard's life and work. After all, even though her own music is not polyphonic in the musical sense of the term, polyphony actually *did* begin in the twelfth century and was used by other composers. She might not mind this characterization; she lived rather than composed polyphonically, with many strands coming together to make the whole tapestry of who she was in her lifetime and who she is for us today.

Exploring the Method: Mysticism, Spirituality, and Polyphony

One cannot merely characterize Hildegard as living a "mystical polyphony" without giving equal weight to both terms. She is a talented, multilayered figure whose integration stems from her spiritual life. The interwoven strands that make polyphony such an apt metaphor with which to approach the figure of Hildegard are thus conditioned by her spiritual development. In order to understand clearly what this means, we have to explain the concept of spiritual journey as it relates to the theme, and to examine what makes Hildegard a mystic rather than just a spiritual leader.

In spiritual formation and development it has long been taken as a given that one begins with a simple desire for God, and that then this simple desire, fulfilled by God, takes the shape of an ever increasingly complex spiritual path. Over the course of a lifetime, a mature simplicity is grasped, at first in glimpses and then more consistently. To return to simplicity it is necessary to go through the tangled and at times perplexing phases of spiritual life; the simplicity to which one returns is not the original simplicity but one refined by fire and depth. This is also what we mean when we describe God as "simple," as Aquinas does: it is not that God cannot and does not encompass all that exists or might exist; instead one comes to realize simply that God IS. Hence, God is simplicity itself, but one we can only come to understand gradually (if at all) through exploring all the complexities of God's creation and revelation, the mysteries of incarnation and salvation, of beginning and ending. This spiritual progression is our journey toward God, or in Hildegard's terms, toward the Living Light. In this life, she notes, we experience the shadows of the Living Light; when we complete our journey we shall be bathed in the Light Itself.

Hildegard's works and her life are intensely incarnational and revolve around the scope of salvation history as it is located in the cosmos, which is encompassed by and ultimately identified with God's light. The metaphor of spiritual journey from the simple through the complex and returning to simplicity is one that is mirrored in Hildegard's life. This fits well with the polyphonic character of that life, for ultimately it is in the nexus of the strands she weaves that Hildegard becomes a human representative of what mature Christian simplicity looks like. By concentrating on these images and metaphors it will be possible to do justice to the wide variety of talents and experiences Hildegard possessed without losing the center: the melodic line, the simplicity around which the complex harmonies develop. For this reason the approach here is thematic rather than purely biographical. Many good biographical sources are already available, and while it is important to tell the story of her life, it will unfold here polyphonically, although we must separate the strands and knit them back together as we proceed. It is also an investigation of her unique contribution to our growing awareness of what "mysticism" can mean in different times and settings. Yet Hildegard cannot be understood as having a mystical *corpus* that can be separated from her life and other works. Because they claim "visionary" status, three of her theological-mystical books are usually set apart: the *Scivias,* the *Liber vitae meritorum,* and the *De operatione Dei.* Yet they are set within what I call the "polyphonic" character of Hildegard's mysticism. For taken from the context of her life as a whole and the rest of her works, they are almost impenetrable. How are we to understand the complex visions, the voice of God, the implicit exegesis of these works without considering why they overlap one another, adding to the central theme or melody of each vision? It is helpful to take into account what *else* was going on as she was writing these books. There were many other things going on simultaneously with the writing of the theological-mystical visionary works, and there is a mutual impact. For Hildegard there is a kind of "double vision": even when she was receiving visions and revelations from God, she insists that she remained aware of her surroundings and the everyday tasks that occupied her. She rejects the notion of her visions as "ecstatic," thinking that this means being taken out of herself and out of time. At all times she remains awake to both the cosmic and the daily dimensions of life as she is living it. This is why her background and history will be discussed in the first chapter: to give the reader a feel for the person in her historical time and respecting the cycles of her life, which provide a context for her ideas.

Because of Hildegard's insistence that she is awake and aware while receiving the visions, we need to consider what could be an awkward question: can we rightly call Hildegard a mystic? What do we mean by *mysticism* in her case? Many would say that Hildegard is a visionary rather than a mystic per se, one who lived a spiritual and holy life, receiving visions from God yet not having specifically a "mystical" relationship with God. Such a claim presupposes a certain definition of a mystical relationship with God. Yet it remains a legitimate question nonetheless. Hildegard, while talented and diverse, does not seem to fit some of the frameworks of spiritual development common to others called "mystics." Her adamant refusal of the ecstatic is one example: many would classify mystics as having a characteristic union with God that draws them up out of the everyday experience of time and space. Even someone who meets these criteria, however, is suspicious of this as the primary criterion. Teresa of Avila, for example, saw her own raptures as a preface to the more advanced and calm stage of union with God, where she remained constantly aware of God's presence by her side at all times (intellectual union). Another distinction often made is that of the "visionary" versus the "mystic"—this is judged by the fact that visionaries in and of themselves do not necessarily pursue the quest for interiority and an inner life with God that progresses through characteristic stages. In Hildegard's case, I think it is legitimate to respond that although her life is an active one, her constant awareness of the presence of God in creation bespeaks both an interiority and an exteriority characteristic of both mature spirituality and mystical insight and experience. It is true she does not dialogue with her visions in the way we have come to expect of many mystics in their quest for union with God. Perhaps part of the reason is that for Hildegard, from her earliest years, she has not known a time without these visions of the *lux vivendi,* the "Living Light." Her whole growth and formation have been a form of dialogue with her visions about the meaning of her life and mission. While we experience her insistence upon the words of her visions as the voice of God directly, Hildegard's many expressions of the Living Light as working in and through her are also intertwined with her own voice. She is not as introspective as other mystics appear to be, but the very confluence and separation of the two voices, hers and God's, indicate an inner awareness and sensitivity to her interior journey as it relates to the Voice that prophesies through her speech. While we will return to this subject in greater detail, it seems sufficient to state at this point that Hildegard can legitimately be called a mystic in the narrower sense of the word—avoiding the idea that everyone is a mystic—because of the interiority that must precede and be constantly involved in the discernment of her exterior writings and pronouncements. She was not as interested in writing about her interior life as she was in conveying what that interior life meant for the community of Christians as a whole. Hildegard would probably regard self-exploration in the middle of dangerous spiritual times as a luxury she, above all others, could not afford. Moreover, when she became fearful, afraid, or dwelt too much upon what she was receiving in authentic visions, she would collapse from ill health and suffer constantly as a result. So she is a mystic of a different stripe: like others, she has both the interior life with God and the expression outwardly in charity; unlike others, the outward expression is not just in charity but in prophecy, sharing her inner exploration as it unfolded during her lifetime. This is all the more reason to see her as living a polyphonic life and for the term "mystical polyphony" to capture the essence of what Hildegard is all about.

In summary, Hildegard's mystical polyphony will enable us to see the great diversity and unity in her works and in her life as she lived it. Central to her mystical polyphony is the setting of her life, which gives the parameters—metaphorically and musically, the key—within which the compositions of her life were constructed. It is here that we need to note the importance of bipolar tensions in Hildegard, which are often overlooked by modern authors. This tension of opposite extremes are typical of the understanding of the history of salvation in a twelfth-century context, bipolarities that for Hildegard nonetheless remain securely incarnational in the many senses of the term. One of the most profound misunderstandings of Hildegard today is to see her only as an affirmative cosmological prophetess; she concerns herself equally with the forces of darkness and evil that surround and threaten humankind, moving people to sin and damnation rather than to grace and salvation. This tension between the praise and affirmation of that which is created and yet the dangers lurking in the created world and in time is one of the crucial bipolarities in Hildegard's overall scheme of reality. Another would be the bipolarity and conjunction of the masculine and the feminine, as differing but essentially complementary forces that make up the true image of God when they are found in the correct balance.

To enhance and clarify the theme of mystical polyphony as the metaphor guiding us through an exploration of Hildegard of Bingen, see the two charts appended here. The first chart is a schematic chart of some significant dates in her life, overlapping one another so it is possible to see the density of her activity at certain times of her life. It also resembles the concept of polyphony by showing more clearly the different lines of melody harmonizing to make the one sound at a given time. The second chart is divided into three sections, representative of the three major phases of Hildegard's life and work: the early years, the productive middle years, and the synthetic-prophetic final years. This, for the sake of metaphor, corresponds to the themes of a musical composition: **(a) (b) (c)** in melodic structure, with a figured bass note of *vision* tying the piece together throughout. A visual representation of the overlapping strands of her life shows how they are intertwined, even when we are considering them separately throughout the chapters of the book.

The first chapter will take up Hildegard's mystical polyphony by exploring the forces that shaped Hildegard's development throughout her life, stressing her historical context, her personal history, and the setting in which she lived and wrote. This will provide indispensable background for seeing how her many talents are interwoven within the confines and demands of her lifetime. In this chapter we will also include a more traditional listing of dates and events of significance, entering into them in greater detail than possible in either of the charts.

In the second chapter we will move on to consider the specifically visionary treatises. These are the theological trilogy mentioned previously: the *Scivias,* the *Liber vitae meritorum,* and the *De operatione Dei.* This is an exploration of her mystical polyphony in the explicitly visionary theological works. Yet her approach goes beyond writing theological tomes; included will be a discussion of these works as they fit into an integrated view of Hildegard, considering them with and not separately from the other occurrences in her life while she was composing them. Like the musical score, however, these three works do come full circle to present a complete account of Hildegard's revelations as she communicates them to the reader or listener: the Word revealed, the Word embodied, the Word at work toward final completion.

Then it will be time in the third chapter to consider her musical vision in depth, for Hildegard uses music in a deeply mystical way. For her, music is a reflection of the heavenly sphere and a way in which we can be a part of it in this life. Yet the music she writes and sings in praise of the Living Light is not meant to stand alone or to be her creation alone. It is the fruit of her union with God and her vision of Christian life. It is significant that her musical compositions were written throughout her life and are well-known even before her prophetic abilities; music is the core of her expression of the incarnational form of human life and our link, through the incarnate Jesus Christ, with the divine. The bulk of her musical compositions is gathered together in a body of work called the *Symphonia,* a symphonic series of praises of God that were given to her and expressed through her, as were the visions. This revelatory character is also apparent in the musical and literary work *Ordo virtutum,* which we will examine in detail as an expression of Hildegard's eschatological and cosmic vision of Christian life and destiny. The *Ordo virtutum* has the distinction of being part of Hildegard's musical vision set in combination with her dramatic and literary gifts.

In the fourth chapter we will consider the vast array of her nonvisionary works, including the "unknown language," the *lingua ignota,* which she created for reasons as yet unclear to us; her lives of the saints and founders; her commentaries and theories about the natural world, linked to her cosmology (the microcosm and the macrocosm introduced in the visionary works). All these together form a part of her mystical vision as it expresses itself in reflection and in action.

The fifth chapter will look at Hildegard's prophetic gifts and voice. She is called the "Sibyl of the Rhine" because of her voice as a prophetess, one who speaks of and for God. Here we will examine her relationships with others: in the communities in which she lived and governed, "in the world" by correspondence or encounter, in her encounters with authority, and in her claim to be an authority in her own right. Her authority always depended on her prophetic voice; it is characteristic of Hildegard to insist on distinguishing the voice of the Living Light given to her directly and her own voice in interpreting to others the significance of her visions or pronouncements. Hildegard is astonishing in her calling as a twelfth-century prophet: a sickly, enclosed, contemplative Benedictine woman who proclaims in the strongest imagery and language the failings of her "effeminate age"!

The conclusion will try to draw what has gone before it into an integrated vision of the mystical polyphony that Hildegard represents. What makes her unique as a mystic, and what does she share with others? How is Hildegard's mystical journey a paradigm for other mystical journeys? I will argue that her progression from a certain simplicity to a complex polyphonic vision and back to a mature, integrated simplicity represents the spiritual journey of the Christian in a very classic sense. In this way, the *pattern* as well as the *content* of her life and work demonstrate why she is a powerful figure for spiritual seekers today and not just in the twelfth century. Because of its polyphonic character, Hildegard's mystical life involves more than just herself and her talents. I will attempt to draw forth the major elements that integrate her life and work, to summarize and interweave what has gone before in previous chapters, and to indicate in what way she is a mystic paradigmatic for other mystics who share her polyphonic temperament and spiritual path. This concluding chapter will demonstrate Hildegard's uniqueness among the mystics while presenting the universal appeal of her mysticism. We will see that her opus shows balance, unity, complementarity, and a stress on the gospel, a life and an opus that served as an inspiration and a challenge for the twelfth century and now for us at the beginning of the twenty-first century.

Chronology of Hildegard's Life

1098	**1106**	**1112–15**	**1136**
Birth	*Enclosed*	*Professed*	*Death of Jutta*

1141	**1146/47**
Begins	*Letters*
the Scivias	*to Bernard*

1147/48	**1150**
Reading at Trier	*Move to*
Inspired to move	*Rupertsberg*

1148
Letter from Odo;
songs already well-known

1151–1158
Composition of Physica
and Causae et Curae

1151–52 **1154** **1155** **1158–1163**
Scivias *completed;* *Ingelheim* *Settlement of* *Composition of*
Richardis leaves. *lands/governance* Liber vitae
　　　　　　　　　　　　　　　　　　meritorum

Richardis dies 1152

1158–1161
First Preaching Tour

[1159: Schism]

1160 **1163**
2nd Preaching Tour; *Begins to write*
goes to Trier De operatione Dei

1161–1163 **1165** **1167–70**
3rd Preaching Tour *Eibingen* *H. falls ill again*

1170
Life of St. Disibod *written*

1170–71 **1173–1176**
4th Preaching Tour *Volmar dies;*
　　　　　　　　　Gottfried replaces him

1173/74
Completes De operatione Dei

1175
Correspondence with Guibert of
Gembloux

1176
Gottfried dies

1177
Guibert of Gembloux
acts as secretary

1178
Interdict imposed

1179
Interdict lifted;
Hildegard dies

Three Phases of Hildegard's Life and Works

The Early Period: 1098–1136

1098: Hildegard is born at Bermersheim, Alzey. Said to be the tenth child of Hildebert and Mechtilde, she was certainly the youngest; "tenth" may be a play of words on "tithe." She was pledged by her parents at birth to the service of God.

1106: When she was eight years old, she was given into the care of Jutta of Spanheim, a noblewoman living as an anchoress attached to the monastery of St. Disibod. Probably Hildegard also went through the rite of an anchorite, although it is possible she was pledged as an oblate.

1112–15: At some point during this time, Hildegard took the veil from Bishop Otto of Bamberg; professing virginity. As more women joined Jutta and Hildegard, they transformed the anchorage into a small cloistered convent that followed the Benedictine Rule.

1136: The death of Jutta and election of Hildegard as leader of the cloister in her place. Her elevation to *magistra* (title used). This marks the beginning of Hildegard's leadership, which would last until her death.

The Active Life: 1136–1158

1141: Hildegard, upon hearing the call from God, begins to write the *Scivias* with the assistance of Volmar and Richardis.

1146–47: Wrote to St. Bernard of Clairvaux.

1147–48: The Synod of Trier, where Pope Eugenius III read her work aloud, having heard of her from Bernard. Hildegard received official approval and was given apostolic license to continue her work.

1148: A letter from Odo of Soissons (extant) confirms that at this time Hildegard's musical compositions were already known and admired.

1148: Hildegard receives a vision telling her to move from Disibodenberg and found a new convent at the Rupertsberg. This vision/command was the subject of much argument and dispute. Only in

1150: were the nuns (about 20) allowed to move.

1150s: Considerable correspondence carried on with a variety of persons of differing ranks. During the late '50s she visited Barbarossa at Ingelheim at his request.

Prophecy and Synthesis: 1158–1179

1158–61: First series of preaching tours, despite illness, going along the river Mainz to Bamberg.

1158–63: Writes the *Liber vitae meritorum.*

1159: *Beginning of 18-year schism with the election of the first of three antipopes.* Since this is a dispute between Barbarossa and the reigning pope, Alexander III, Hildegard says little, seeming neutral.

1160: Takes the second tour, which includes public preaching in the city of Trier.

1161–63: Third preaching tour, northward to Cologne and Werden.

1163: Frederick Barbarossa grants her written and perpetual imperial protection for the Rupertsberg, addressing her as *abbatissa.*

1163: Hildegard begins to write the *De operatione Dei.*

1164: *Election of 2nd antipope.* Hildegard writes a scathing letter to Barbarossa about the schism.

1165: Founds the daughter convent at Eibingen, across the Rhine. Writes Henry II of England and Eleanor of Aquitaine.

1151–52: *Scivias* completed. Richardis elected as abbess of Bassum and leaves, much to Hildegard's sorrow and despite her efforts. Richardis dies in October of 1152.

1151–58: Begins the *Physica* and *Causae et curae,* works on science and healing.

1155: Hildegard was granted free and exclusive rights to the Rupertsberg property by Frederick I.

1158: Bishop Arnold of Mainz becomes the spiritual protector of the Rupertsberg and of St. Disibod, regulating both temporal and spiritual matters; St. Disibod is to provide spiritual guides, with the approval of the nuns.

1167–70: Suffers from severe illness. Despite this, in

1169: Hildegard warns Barbarossa at the election of a *third antipope* that God will strike if it isn't resolved.

1170: Writes the *Life of St. Disibod* and completes her fourth preaching tour to Swabia.

1173–74: Volmar dies in 1173; mediation required for a replacement, since the abbot does not cooperate. Gottfried appointed, finally. Finishes the *De operatione Dei.*

1176–77: Gottfried dies, having completed part one of the *Vita.* Guilbert of Gembloux, with whom she had corresponded since 1175, replaces him in 1177.

1178: Rupertsberg placed under interdict when Hildegard refuses to exhume a man claimed as excommunicate;

1179: after many letters and pleas, the interdict is lifted. Hildegard dies on the 17th of September, 1179.

I

Shaping Forces

For most of us it is the time in which we live and its circumstances that go a very long way toward shaping who we are and who we become. It is an easy thing for us to forget this fact when we study the past, or instead to go to the alternative extreme and pay such careful attention to time and place that we never get any further than the setting. If we ourselves are aware of how much our century and environment make us who we are, we need to emphasize how much more accurate that is when looking at the past. Until the twentieth century, with its modes of rapid transit and its ability to shrink distances to the point of envisioning a global community, people by and large were determined in their lives by geographical, social, and cultural constraints that we can now barely imagine. As we travel back in time to the twelfth century, Hildegard's world, we need also to be aware of the all-encompassing nature of the religious awareness of the inhabitants of the Middle Ages. In the medieval world, the world was created, sustained, guided, and inhabited by God. It is an intensely religious worldview that was not confronted with modern questions such as the separation of subject and object, whether we can speak meaningfully in God-language or not, and how it is possible to be tolerant in a pluralistic setting and yet have the courage of our own convictions. The worldview of the twelfth century was not entirely univocal, but compared to ours it certainly appears that way. Only if we recognize that this is the atmosphere in which medieval persons responded to the events of their lives, large and small, can we begin to grasp the issues with which Hildegard dealt in a way that makes her story meaningful for us. This might appear to be contrary to our purpose of seeing Hildegard in her significance for us today. Indeed, the exact opposite is true. To take a person from her natural environs and transport her without heeding the specificity of her life does her no justice and simultaneously makes it *harder* to see the contemporary relevance of the person. This is the case because the person has not been understood before she has been interpreted in a way quite alien to her own cultural and temporal setting.

This is not to claim it is easy or even possible for any modern person, writer or reader, to put themselves in the medieval mindset. Far from it. There are too many things that separate us from the past, too many complicated issues of how we are to interpret history, too many questions about whether the intent of an author or artist can really be accessed and understood. In fact, part of Hildegard's fascination for us may come from the alien quality of her works, the "otherness" of her world. Nevertheless, it is pivotal to begin our acquaintance with Hildegard by showing where it is she came from: in time, location, class, and education. Only then will we begin to perceive how the incarnate spiritual journey and the strands of polyphony come together and finally emerge out of the facets of her personality and her formative environment.

A Sense of Place: Society and Surroundings

Hildegard came from a noble family in the area of Bemersheim near Alzey in Rhenish Franconia, what we call the Rhineland today. We know little of her parents save that their names were Hildebert and Mecthilde; they apparently were of the nobility, although not of the highest nobility. Unlike the set structure of the feudal system that had taken hold in England and France, in Hildegard's "Germany" the structure was in place, but the ranks of nobility were rather more fluid than elsewhere. Technically, the kingdom of Germany was composed of five or six great duchies and came under the jurisdiction of the Holy Roman Empire. This allowed for more local autonomy and shifting allegiances than in the areas that had been greatly affected by the barbarian invasions. The highest rank of nobility, the *primores,* comprised dukes, margraves, counts, and barons who held hereditary titles. The *ministeriales* originally were not free men; they earned their lands and their rank from royal service and so were a class of nobility who earned their right to prominence through power and service. Between these two was the class Hildegard most likely came from: the nobility born as free men who held large tracts of land in their own right but did not possess hereditary titles of distinction. The very fluidity of the class system plus the constant uncertainty of imperial politics would have a major influence on Hildegard and her family.

Hildegard is generally reported to have been pledged as a "tithe," or gift to God, a not uncommon practice of the day. So when pledging their last and possibly tenth child to God, it was of concern to her parents that Hildegard go to a religious setting in which she would associate with

2

persons of similar background and rank, and they looked for a suitable place where their daughter might be placed. Later Hildegard was criticized for taking only those born of noble families into her convent. This was the customary practice at the time, and Hildegard's sense of class and station was part of her identity and stability. To be part of a social order was to be part of a human community as it had been determined by God; there was nothing shameful to the medieval mind about openness regarding class distinctions.

Sometimes when a child was pledged as a tithe, their destiny was reconsidered later; but this was not the fact in Hildegard's case. The *Vita,* the story of Hildegard's life composed by the monks Gottfried and Theodoric, suggests that even at an early age she possessed two qualities that would have suited her for a religious vocation. The first was her spiritual sense from a very early age: they record her as being unusually holy (but this is likely in the history of one esteemed as a saint), and also they record Hildegard's account of seeing a vision as early as the age of five, in which she could tell the time of a calving and the exact colors of the calf. Not knowing this to be a special circumstance, she apparently told her nurse; she frightened and impressed the household with her prescience.[2] In an autobiographical fragment Hildegard takes it back to an even earlier time:

> You human one, hear these words and speak them not according to your meaning but mine, and, animated by me, speak in the following manner of yourself: "At my first formation when God brought me to life in the womb of my mother, together with the breath of life, he impressed these visions in my soul. For in the year 1100 A.D. the teaching of the Apostle and the glowing righteousness which he had laid down as fundamentals for both Christians and the clergy began to slacken off and become shaky. At that time I was born, and with sighs I chose God for my parents. In the third year of my life, I saw such a great light that my soul trembled, but, because of my youth, I could not speak about it."[3]

Of course, this is the reflection upon her life that Hildegard is speaking of in her old age, and the *Vita* was composed near the end of her life and completed after her death. However, we get the sense both from her biographers and from Hildegard herself that the spiritual sense of vision was her destiny, something as normal to her as breathing. The normalcy of visions for Hildegard would create difficulties for her in the intervening years when dealing with others, for whom they were decidedly *out* of the ordinary. The second quality, not nearly as impressive, was often one that entered into the consideration of parents pledging their children at a particularly early age: Hildegard was a frail and sickly child and was to intermittently but continually suffer from illness—if not actual frailty—throughout her adult life. Lest we be too harsh on Hildebert and Mechtilde, such a child was often thought to be close to God by virtue of the projected length of life or, more likely, by the need for "special circumstances" in which to flourish.[4] People were and are considered to be particularly in touch with the spiritual and divine spheres when they hover between life and death, health and illness. All of this is speculation but would not be unlikely given the circumstances and the precocious visions.[5]

According to Hildegard, at the age of eight she was taken to live with a noblewoman who, having rejected all offers of marriage and renouncing the world, was living at the monastery of St. Disibod as an anchoress. Jutta of Sponheim was from a distinguished noble family and could have married well; she was not promised to the religious life as Hildegard was but chose it gladly. At the age of twenty-one Jutta embraced the life of an anchoress, the most austere form of enclosure, for the purpose of promoting dedication to God in prayer. The anchoress was considered as literally dead to the world: part of the process of enclosure was to go through the actual funeral rites and to end them with the anchorite being enclosed for life in the anchorage, never to leave it again. While this does resonate with the austerity Jutta practiced throughout her life, the timing may not be as clear as the *Vita* wishes to portray it; at the time of the supposed enclosure Disibodenberg was in the midst of a reconstruction and rebuilding of the older site, founded ostensibly in the seventh century. In the biography of Jutta, this early age of entry is contradicted, as it claims she led a religious but unvowed life with a widow until the monastery was ready to receive her. Hildegard may or may not have lived with her at this time; in any event it places Hildegard's actual entry into Disibodenberg closer to the age of twelve.[6]

In addition, there is conflicting evidence about whether others were enclosed at the time Jutta was, although we are certain her reputation for holiness drew others to join her later. She is referred to in later documents as "Blessed Jutta" and appears in at least one calendar as a saint. It was by popular acclaim Jutta was revered as "blessed" and as a particularly holy woman, and it is doubtful that at the time Hildegard, her student, was expected to surpass her.[7] In Hildegard's *Vita*, Jutta is described in this way:

> God showered streams of graces on this lady to the extent that her body got no rest because of her vigils, fasting, and other good works until she finished her earthly life through to a good ending. By heavenly signs, God also made her reward public.[8]

4

It is a matter of some debate about whether Hildegard entered her life with Jutta going through the traditional rites of an anchorite or whether she entered as an oblate.[9] In the current Abtei St. Hildegard she is portrayed as an oblate, being handed over into the care of Jutta and several others by her parents. The rite of oblation, particularly when the destiny of the child was an anchorhold, may have had a finality about it that was clear to all in anchoritic enclosure. Yet the effect of going through the actual funeral rites of an anchoress would be bound to have a much stronger effect on an impressionable child. How she entered may well have had some effect on her in later life, but all we can do is conjecture about it, since we know little for certain. We know little of her early life except the major events: her entry into the anchorage under the tutelage of Jutta; the fact that Jutta attracted other young women to the religious life as well; and by the time of Hildegard's profession around the age of fifteen, the anchorage had become a small convent living in accordance with the Benedictine Rule, which was the practice of the monks of St. Disibod.

Natural Surrounding and Religious Inspiration

Before continuing with her biography, however, let us return to the question of her surroundings. Why pause at this point in the story of her life? Precisely because it is not really a pause but rather an emphasis. Here we come to an extremely important point in understanding who Hildegard was and was to become. From a formative age Hildegard lived at or around Disibodenberg as an anchoress and as a nun. Although complete enclosure was the rule in an anchorage there would have been at least one window; normally there were three, one into the church, one for food and necessities, and one for hearing visitors and giving them counsel.[10] It was not uncommon in the early Middle Ages for the strictures on seclusion to be somewhat more relaxed than the *Anchoritic Rule* would lead us to believe. If we take into consideration the claims that Hildegard entered later, or during the reconstruction of the abbey, she would have had much wider access to the world around her, especially the natural world. Judging from the evidence of Hildegard's later use of imagery, which clearly came from close contact with the outdoor surroundings in which she lived, and also by the size of the enclosure as it can be seen and measured at the ruins of Disibodenberg (see fig. 1), it is likely that Hildegard and Jutta had more freedom of movement than was common to the anchoritic life. Certainly this would have been the case once the anchorage became a small convent attached to the Abbey of St. Disibod.[11]

It is virtually impossible to convey the sense of place at Disibodenberg: even in ruins it still feels like holy ground, a place in which many

FIGURE 1

people lived, prayed, and worked. The land is lush with trees, plants, ivy, and grass. From the soil and the rocks a moistness exudes that is not the dampness of mold or mildew but instead smells more like fresh spring water. The monastery itself was located on a site between two rivers, the Nahe and the Glan, which accounts for the richness of its natural surroundings. There were good building materials of rock to quarry, and the monastery was under renovation of one type or another while Hildegard lived there. Although in ruins and uninhabited now, it retains the beauty of its setting and a vivid sense of life, vitality, and sheer greenness rarely seen elsewhere.

One of Hildegard's guiding images will be that of *viriditas,* literally meaning "greenness." It will be her synonym for all the life-giving qualities of God's spirit in matter, both human and non-human. Whether or not she was familiar with patristic literature—and she probably was not—her imagery of the life-giving power of God in the natural world is one that resonates with the voice of Justin Martyr. Justin, in order to attempt to explain Christianity to the pagan philosophers of the second century, adapted a concept first used by the Stoics: that of the *"logos spermatikos."* In his use of the term he is referring to the germinating Word (Logos), the fire of creation that spreads like wildfire and is the life-giving force that permeates the earth. He differs with the Stoics in the use of the term *logos,* which for Justin is a reference to God's eternal Word, the Son who became incarnate in Jesus Christ. Hildegard is also very incarnational in her metaphors and, like Justin, chose a familiar image around her in order to convey this idea. While he drew on the philosophers, she drew on her surroundings. Seeing Disibodenberg, one can understand why she chose this as an overriding image: it could hardly have been disregarded in that environment. She will use this sense of the lushness of her surroundings constantly in the imagery of her writings, her compositions, her letters, and all of her works: it is a pivotal image for her. Paradise is akin to the flourishing growth of gardens, using the Latin words *viriditas* and *sudare/humiditate* (moisture). While the imagery is delightful, *viriditas* is not a word easily rendered into any other language without losing the "feel" and rhythmic repetition of the original. The translator of her *Letters* describes it this way:

> Perhaps the most notable example of [her creative use of Latin] is her use of *viriditas,* a word never far from Hildegard's reach. This *viriditas,* the despair of translators, this "greenness" enters into the very fabric of the universe in Hildegard's cosmic scheme of things. In Hildegard's usage it is a profound, immense, dynamically energized term. The world in the height of the spring season is filled with *viriditas,* God breathed the breath of *viriditas* into the inhabitants of the Garden of Eden, even the smallest twig on the most insignificant tree is animated with *viriditas,* the sun brings the life of *viriditas* into the world; and (in the spiritual realm) the prelate who is filled with [weariness] is lacking in *viriditas,* the garden where the virtues grow is imbued with *viriditas,* the neophyte must strive for *viriditas,* and the holy Virgin is the *viridissima virga.* Hildegard can even speak with aplomb of a saint as the *viriditas digiti Dei,* "the *viriditas* of the finger of God," as she does of St. Disibod.[12]

This passage that shows how Hildegard's use of *viriditas* is both engaging and extremely frustrating. How do you translate a word that, through a variety of uses, is the pivotal point of her thought? Especially when its literal rendition turns out to be "greenness" or "verdure" or something else that entirely lacks the spectrum of resonance of the original Latin word? Throughout our consideration of her works it will be translated in several ways to try to grasp the fullness of its intent and to avoid literal repetition, which might detract from it. Nonetheless, it loses something in any translation. As the cornerstone of Hildegard's word imagery it is also linked with the words mentioned previously for "moisture." In Hildegard's way of thinking it is *viriditas* and *humiditas* together that bind the living world together; without them all would dry up and turn to ashes.

Although the Rupertsberg was her own foundation and site, the land around it is quite distinctive from that around Disibodenberg, despite the fact that they are separated only by about fifteen miles. Since today the town of Bingen is built over the remains of the Rupertsberg, we have to use older engravings and descriptions to regain a sense of the landscape in Hildegard's time (see fig. 2). Although along the river Nahe, as was St. Disibod, the convent was built on a high place where St. Rupert was reputed to be buried. Mount St. Rupert had possibilities, but the landscape was not so lush and green as Disibodenberg. Although closer to the Rhine, the location was not on the river, and the country was poorly developed. Hildegard clearly notes the contrast between the two sites in her later reflections:

> For a long time my eyes were darkened; I was no longer able to see the light. I felt that my body was bent over from such a load that I was not able to get up, and I lay down with severe pains. I suffered this precisely because I did not want to reveal the vision which had been shown to me: that I, together with my sisters, was to move from that place where I had been consecrated to God and go to another place. I suffered in that way as long as I remained in the place where I was. As soon as my sight returned, at once I felt relieved, but I was not completely freed from weakness. However, when my abbot and the brothers as well as the people of the vicinity learned about the change of place and its significance—that we wanted to move from the fertile fields and vineyards away from a beautiful area to a dry area—they were in amazement. . . . Just as the children of Israel caused Moses's heart to be heavy, so in my case people shook their heads at me and said: "What use is it that noble and rich nuns are moved away from one place where they have everything to a place where there is need?" We however hoped that the grace of God who had shown us this place would be with us.[13]

While Hildegard has other rhetorical reasons for using the Old Testament parallelism and emphasizing the trauma of moving away from the monastery that dealt with human components, it is clear that she herself saw and experienced the contrast in the landscape. It was her price to pay for independence and for following her visionary command. After the move several of her nuns would leave the Rupertsberg, chiefly because of the conditions of hardship in starting a foundation on land that was stubborn in the attempt to cultivate it and live off its fruits.

When discussing the setting of Hildegard's life, it is important to remember that land was not merely a commodity. It had value in terms of social prestige, but its real value came from agricultural cultivation and hunting grounds. Land provided all the necessities of life: food, drink, clothing, building materials. To sustain oneself, one lived on and from the land. So for Hildegard this change of place was not a rudimentary one of having a less fortunate view. It was a radical act of faith, literally

FIGURE 2

"uprooting" herself from her formative landscape, which reflects so power-fully in her imagery. Instead of drawing on the moist, living greenness of Disibodenberg for sustenance, the task would become the moistening and "greening" of the Rupertsberg. This *viriditas* was a gift of God and became inseparable from her expression of her visions, theology, and songs given to her in visions and using the metaphors and realities of the lushness of the land on which she was raised.

Liturgy and Learning

Aside from the physical setting of Disibodenberg, Hildegard was shaped by the society she now entered. Jutta was her *magistra:* her teacher as a child and her superior as she grew older. The monk on whom she depended for much of her life, Volmar, would have been just slightly older than Hildegard and came to be friend, spiritual director, and advisor for her. It is likely that she learned her letters and her Latin from Jutta through recitation of the psalms and participation in the Liturgy of the Hours. Reciting and learning the psalms was a common way of teaching children about the biblical text and helping them learn to read with appreciation. When we speak of Jutta as Hildegard's teacher, it is not meant to have the academic connotation we might assign to it. She would have functioned more nearly as a spiritual mentor: Jutta modeled a way of life for the child Hildegard, whom she taught and guided into the woman she would become. Both Jutta and Hildegard would have learned Latin as the common language of the Church and the liturgy; Jutta, having entered at a more advanced age and being from a noble family, may have had even more education than we might suspect. Although later Jutta was overshadowed by Hildegard's fame and accomplishments, it is unlikely that these would ever have come to the fore without the help of Jutta, since it was only her *magistra* to whom Hildegard confided about the visions she saw. This was perhaps because it was said that Jutta herself had prophetic visions, though none are recorded; this would be another point of continuity between teacher and pupil.[14] Later, Jutta in her wisdom suggested consulting Volmar about her unusual companion and pupil. We can see some of Hildegard's reflections on this process of formation from an autobiographical section in her *Vita:*

> For out of fear of people I dared not tell anyone what I had seen in visions. But the noble lady, Jutta, to whom I had been committed for my education, noticed it, and confided it to a monk well known to her. . . . I confided this to a monk, my teacher, who due to his good monastic habits and sincere efforts, was quite distinguished, and he was averse to busy pryings into other people's conduct and listened obligingly to my strange story. It astounded him, and he enjoined me to write down these visions so he could consider their true character and origin. When he recognized that these visions were from God, he consulted his abbot and thereafter assisted me most willingly.[15]

We can note several things about this reflection from Hildegard's *Vita.* First, it is clear that although she is older at the time Jutta referred her to Volmar, he had functioned as a teacher for Hildegard too, even before the question of the visions arose. Second, it is Jutta's guiding hand and presence that helped Hildegard understand what exactly this visionary gift she had might mean, and she wanted to be assured that this was indeed God's presence and will being made manifest in this young pupil. Jutta herself was extremely ascetic, something Hildegard will later reject in her own practices; despite the influence of her holiness and austerity on Hildegard, we need to consider that Hildegard absorbed some teachings readily and rejected others, at least later.[16] We must also remember the constant presence of the monastic community of St. Disibod surrounding them, whether or not they had a great deal of contact with the monks outside of the anchorage in particular. By the time Hildegard left Disibodenberg after twenty-four years, they would have amassed a large library and the monks at least would have been on easy speaking terms with the surrounding nobility, who endowed the monastery and provided vocations.

Having spoken in the previous section about the significance of space and surroundings, we must remember that time was not measured by artificial light or clocks. Rather, the rhythm of the seasons and the measure of light and darkness for the hours of the day and night marked time for the medieval person. It is a schedule both dependent upon and in harmony with the natural surroundings. From her entry into the anchorage, Hildegard's life would have been organized around the seasons of the year and the practice of prayer. Hildegard's experience is thoroughly permeated by a sense of the liturgical rhythms of Benedictine community, especially with its focus on the sacramentality of worship and of life itself. For her, the eucharistic liturgy and the celebration of the liturgical Hours would have played a central part in her formation. Moreover, they would be as natural as breathing: her entire life is formed in the two worlds that meet in the sacraments, the visible and the invisible. In developing her ideas about cosmology and her theology we can clearly see how steeped she is in knowledge of the Scriptures as learned through prayer and liturgical celebration; she also exhibits a massive knowledge of the world around her, including practical remarks about the weather, plants, and herbs. Although her knowledge of all these things would have grown considerably throughout her lifetime, it is logical to assume that the awareness of them as essential to life began at an early age. But how much learning can we claim for Hildegard when she is so insistent about being uneducated herself?

Much stress is placed on the fact that Hildegard described herself as "a poor, uneducated female." In point of fact, it really means what she means by *indocta*. She naturally would not have been educated in the universities of the time or even schooled in Latin and reading in the same way that men of her time were taught, both in order to learn their letters and to preserve knowledge that had been passed on for generations. She carries this insistence about her lack of education even back to Jutta, saying that it was a "formally uneducated lady" (Jutta) who taught her to write,[17] despite the fact that there is some evidence Jutta's community was considered a *scola* by some![18] But Hildegard's lack of what we might call a "formal education" certainly does not indicate she is unaware of the language and literature surrounding her. Indeed, although Jutta's first concern may have been to instruct her pupils in the Psalms, ascetical practice, and the Rule, she also undoubtedly had the women in her small convent read sermons and treatises as part of their training.[19] Hildegard's first and foremost reason for wishing to claim to be "ignorant" or without education is probably to assure others that her visions are directly from God, the Living Light, with no interference from Hildegard, God's willing but frail vessel. Yet scholars are convinced—in varying degrees—that Hildegard may have not been educated in a traditional way but that she was conversant with much more of the learning available in the twelfth century than she is willing to admit. Peter Dronke, a very careful scholar, probably takes it the furthest in his claim that she was not only acquainted with the major works of the Fathers of the Church but also with classical philosophers such as Lucan and Cicero.[20] Others make the more moderate claim that in a Benedictine environment she would have read the authors of medieval times and the Fathers, in excerpts if not in complete form. In reading her *Letters,* of which about four hundred are available to us, it is clear she uses subtle expressions and plays on words, which would not convince us of her ignorance of learning and letters. Indeed, the converse is true. Hildegard's multilayered style of reference in the wide variety of her writings tends to convince us that she did indeed have an appetite for learning and was familiar with a variety of sources upon which she could draw. Her writing indicates this was no "formal education," for while she can fly to rhetorical heights and use expressions of great poetry, she also can be simplistic and pedantic in her phrasing and exposition.

To understand why this issue is such a primary one in speaking about the shaping forces of Hildegard's life, we have to take into account three things. First, the modern concerns that spur scholars to investigate the extent of Hildegard's learning; second, the medieval setting for acquiring knowledge; and third, the issues of gender concerning both Hildegard herself and her later commentators. This last may seem to be a side issue, but it is of utmost importance in approaching Hildegard herself; it also, ironically, shows us that the response to Hildegard is virtually as "polyphonic" as she is, when it does not dissolve into cacophony!

Modern scholars have a great deal at stake in wanting to know exactly how much education Hildegard received. Some are preoccupied with the visions themselves: if we do not accept divine visions as authentic, then how could she have known some of these things or spoken with such clarity? Many in the twentieth century have been more concerned with discrediting the divine as the source of Hildegard's competence than in finding out the actual state of her education. Lest this seem an overly simplistic rejection of this position and an endorsement for her totally divine "education," we must insist that it is natural for those in a secular context to struggle with these issues more than her medieval admirers and detractors. Because of this contemporary gulf between faith and reason, which makes the idea of direct divine inspiration so very difficult for the modern mind, it has allowed us to further investigate the educational resources Hildegard may have had at her command. To earlier authors as to Hildegard herself this would seemingly contradict the veracity and authority of the visions and prophecies she claimed were given to her directly from God. It remains a matter of lively discussion about how much of Hildegard's own creativity and capacities went into the writings that are claimed to be divine in origin. This is a topic we will pursue in the next chapter in greater detail. Other modern authors are concerned with what is often called "the modesty *topos*," a traditional formula by which the author claims to be merely the vessel of something far more important than his/her individual self. In Hildegard's case this is related to the question of gender, and for feminists especially the modesty *topos* is a form of disclaimer that allowed Hildegard a voice in an androcentric society. Thus, if she *were* a woman of great learning, she would hardly go about claiming her expertise as something to be reckoned with.

The medieval setting for acquiring knowledge is quite different from the modern setting. We take for granted certain standards and ideas of literacy, and we use the written word to communicate with others. But in ancient and medieval times communication and education were often passed on orally rather than in writing. We tend to overlook the importance of oral tradition and the greater use of memory before printing and the written word became predominant.[21] Reading aloud was common before the printing press. Even those who were well educated often distinguished between reading silently to oneself and "normal reading," which would have been murmured or spoken. We find this attested to in Augustine's *Confessions:* first he is impressed and overwhelmed that Ambrose can spend so much time reading silently; then later when he hears the voice telling him to take up and read Paul's gospel, he explicitly mentions that he read silently to himself.[22] Augustine is much earlier in time than Hildegard, yet one could argue that in Augustine's time, before the fall of Rome, there was actually greater access to the written word than in medieval times. Certainly Augustine himself would hardly have claimed to be "unlearned" or "ignorant" and unlettered! Wordplay itself was a form of entertainment as well as educative, and oral traditions were important for understanding oneself and the world. While we cannot place ourselves in the mind of the Middle Ages, we can indeed attempt to recapture something of the environment and the setting, radically different from our own. Edward P. Nolan summarizes this point for us cogently:

> In the current debates regarding medieval literacy and education, I find both terms often far too narrowly construed, resulting in a set of exclusionary definitions that must be met by a "literate" individual that are not

in fact historical, socially, or civilly realistic or responsible. There is far more to literacy than the mere ability to read and write down letters of the alphabet in a discourse intelligible to one's neighbors. And there is a great deal "less" to literacy than a complete training in all available genres of writing and a demonstrated ability to replicate all these modes. . . . [W]e probably should be able to ask of the literate that they reflect in their thinking, speaking, and whatever kinds of exposition they engage in, the rich interplay of words and images that are common to the culture in which they live. In order for us to become more aware of, and sympathetic to, the medieval social reality, we need to recuperate a way of reading that has all but disappeared from our current sense of things.[23]

Hildegard is claiming to be uneducated in the way of the universities of her day, but it certainly would not have prevented her from being "literate" by the standards ascribed above.[24] Indeed, her fondness for double meanings, for echoing the Scriptures—especially the Old Testament, Paul, and John—in her letters and her writing in general apparently confirm the supposition that Hildegard, by the standards of her time, was not only literate but gifted.

In all likelihood, Hildegard's education was based in the learning of the Benedictine community that surrounded her. She began her literacy with the Latin of the Church as expressed in psalmody, liturgical prayer, and reflective readings. In this way, we could conclude that by the time she took over as *magistra* at the time of Jutta's death, she would have had considerable exposure to church tradition. Whether Volmar helped to educate her more broadly than would be usual for a woman in Hildegard's situation, or if conversation with him and the other monks of St. Disibod would have furthered her comprehension of received wisdom inside and outside church sources is something we will never know. We can only deduce from her writings and the ways in which learning took place in the twelfth century that she was nowhere near as uneducated as she claimed to be. She later expressed disapproval of the emerging "scholastic" way of learning, assuming it to be presumptuous in its idea that the human mind can grasp the ways of God (her interpretation), and this too could have influenced her desire to be seen as "uneducated" when to be "educated" was to tend toward sin and evil.[25]

The third and final consideration about Hildegard's attitude toward learning that is a prerequisite for drawing conclusions about her formation is that of gender. We must be exceptionally cautious in dealing with issues of gender in Hildegard: since the feminine holds such an important place in her visionary imagery and she herself can be said to write in a "feminine" way, we are in danger of placing modern expectations and constraints on this twelfth-century woman. Hildegard was not a twelfth-century feminist. Furthermore, what is troubling to some feminists is her attitude toward the relationship of the male and female in some of her writings, which is contrary to the picture of a liberated, confident prophetess who dares to use the feminine divine in her imagery and exposition. To be scandalized about such an apparent contradiction says more about our assumptions than it enlightens us about Hildegard. In point of fact, it may very well obscure how very striking her use of feminine imagery is, how unusual her claim to prophecy was. For a splendid account of Hildegard as a voice for the feminine and the Wisdom tradition, which uses female imagery for God, and untainted by the need to put her into modern categories, there is no better source than Barbara Newman's *Sister of Wisdom*. Newman is able to see Hildegard's unique qualities without subsuming them into an agenda foreign to her personality.[26] However, we should not go to the opposite extreme of assuming that this woman visionary is somehow only tangentially a female voice and can be subsumed into a long tradition of allegorical imagery of the feminine. Hildegard may inherit this knowledge of the allegorical, but she is totally unique within the tradition of her day. It is far more appropriate to place Hildegard in the context of the twelfth century than to place her in some form of female mystical tradition, of which she may well be the first outstanding representative.[27]

Even if we do not separate her from the big picture, how exactly did Hildegard receive her distinctively "feminine" voice and use of symbols? She was surrounded by a male monastery and in a small community of women, so one would not expect such a resounding use of feminine language, thought patterns, and imagery. The key may possibly be in her visions. Aside from the divine inspiration Hildegard claims for them, the imagery that accompanies the visions may have preserved her own feminine voice. While male scribes could edit and reword what was spoken and written, the priority of her startling images enables the voice of the female seer to remain unedited and unexpurgated.[28] This could be indicative of a culturally conditioned style, in which Hildegard's protestations of a lack of knowledge make greater sense. She does not think or speak in the traditional "male" model of her time, a model that stressed exegesis and analysis of texts. Rather, she begins with images, visionary or homely, and then weaves a form of story or commentary around them. This suggestion that Hildegard is part of a tradition of a peculiarly "feminine poetics" may explain a great deal about both her style and her creative independence within that style. At times Hildegard's visionary text seems impenetrable or incoherent if taken literally. It resists interpretation beyond its own imagery; the words are descriptive of the image rather than the other way around.[29] Her use of such a style, then, might not be a conscious one but one naturally inherited from her cultural milieu and possibly from other women writers preceding her.[30] Alternatively, the proposition of a feminine style of writing could be a modern interpolation. Whatever its origin, an analysis of Hildegard's style of writing and her use of the feminine give us an insight into her motivations and characteristic approach to life.

Moreover, in considering her style we should observe carefully that the claim to be a "poor, ignorant woman" also strengthens her claim to divine visionary insight. For just as the prophets of the Old Testament were called by God to speak God's words and message to the people of Israel, so Hildegard feels herself to be called in a similar way to speak to the Christians of her time. Hildegard had to struggle with the visionary impulse, which she did not make public until she was almost forty-two; she doubted her commission to speak. Once she felt affirmed and confirmed that the visions were indeed those given to her by God, then nothing stopped her from relaying them to others. She was often compared to the towering female figures of the Bible, such as Deborah, as a precedent for a woman claiming the authority of prophecy and leadership.

While these may be some satisfactory answers to her "feminine" style and the confidence and creativity with which she employed it, the question of the overriding use of female symbols in her writings is not so easily traced to her formation, especially since we know so little of her early life except through the *Vita,* the *Acta,* and the *Letters.* Hildegard could claim the feminine images she uses by right of inheritance; the symbols she uses are traditional ones within the language of the Church. A number of them are symbols that were more commonly used in the twelfth century, belonging to a sapiential tradition that drew widely on the Wisdom literature of the Bible. In these books there is a greater use of personified symbols: Wisdom, the Church, Mary, Virginity, Eve, and sometimes the cosmos, which were portrayed in feminine form.[31] However, her use of feminine imagery and symbols is a theme that will be interlaced through all the chapters of this book. It is not the intent here to do a thorough analysis of Hildegard as a feminine or feminist voice but rather to see how much of it we may attribute to the shaping forces of her life and times.

We can conclude from this discussion that Hildegard was, in fact, more learned than she claimed to be, though she certainly was not educated formally or in a traditional twelfth-century way. While she does not meet contemporary definitions of literacy clearly, she certainly meets those of the Middle Ages. Much of her formation and learning came from the ecclesial and monastic setting in which she was raised and which had a significant effect on both her learning and her perception of the way learning should be put to use. Always learning is treated by Hildegard as a part of the larger whole of God's creation, purpose, and will for humanity. This is true whether we are considering her visionary writings, her other copious written work, or her practical advice in letters and medical commentaries. The history of salvation, determined already by God, was a common theme of the twelfth century. It is within the scope of this determined historical process that Hildegard placed herself and the Christians of her time. We do well to remind ourselves at this point of the chronology of Hildegard's life and the purpose behind looking at the forces that shaped her, despite our lack of resources about this time. Hildegard lived as an anchoress with Jutta for six years, and as a nun for all the rest of her life. The period of tutelage under Jutta, Volmar, and other sources and persons cited are pivotal to her character: by the time of Jutta's death, Hildegard was thirty-eight years old, a mature woman who then became a *magistra* in her own right. She did not speak publicly until after she was forty-three at the earliest. Nevertheless, even before the visions became a focus for outside attention, Hildegard had many other priorities and concerns.

Music and Light: The Meeting Place of the Human and the Divine

Music is hardly something that can be separated from the impact of the liturgical cycle on Hildegard. However, it warrants a section of its own at this point, because it is in and through music that Hildegard first began to express the polyphonic style for which she would become famous. The music of the liturgy was chant, not polyphony. What is polyphonic are the themes of her music rather than its structure, which remains in chant form. She does have a distinctive chant form, however, which first becomes evident in the liturgical music she began to compose sometime during her earlier years, since it reflects an overlapping set of concerns and motivations characteristic of her mature accomplishments. We know from her history that by 1148 her songs were well known enough for Odo of Soissons, writing from Paris, to mention the admiration he had for her musical compositions. She probably began to compose music sometime in the 1140s, while still at Disibodenberg, and continued after the move to the Rupertsberg. We will devote an entire chapter to a discussion of Hildegard's music and its importance. For now, our primary concern is with where music fits into the polyphonic tapestry of her character formation.

Hildegard had a natural love of the liturgy, principally as it was expressed through the singing of the liturgical Hours. It is clear from both her musical compositions and the way she speaks about music and liturgy in her letters and other sources that song in praise of God is another form of divine expression. Thus music and vision, the auditory and the visual, are closely linked in Hildegard's perception of the world, possibly experienced simultaneously. While we have mentioned her visionary experiences, it is most suitable when speaking of the sung praise of God to also discuss her perception of the blinding Light of the Godhead she experienced. Hildegard felt the interface between the realms of the divine and of the human. Both her visions and her music were, for her, glimpses of the celestial, the heavenly, a foretaste of what was to come. Both her visionary and musical expressions are simultaneously incarnational in the broader use of the word and also in the more restricted sense of the incarnation of the divine and the human in the God-man, Jesus Christ. How is this the case?

From her earliest years Hildegard describes her visionary experiences as ones in which she is "bathed in Light." On reflection, she would eventually call this "the Living Light"—meaning God—and speak of her experience of the "shadow" or "reflection" of the Living Light. She is not in an ecstatic state; moreover, she considered this state to be so normal that she assumed when she was a child that this type of "double-vision"[32] was characteristic of all the people around her. Her confusion and embarrassment on discovering that this was not at all common kept her from discussing the experience of the Light, but it hardly stopped her from having these experiences. In a way, the sense of seeing two things simultaneously from an early age gave Hildegard a unique insight into the meaning of the Incarnation. Since she saw the daily events of her life, the mundane and created realities with which she lived, overlaid by a celestial light and vision of overwhelming glory coming straight from the heavens, she could see how the divine and human natures of Jesus could coexist. Although acutely aware of the sinful parts of human nature since the Fall, this capacity to see the spheres of heaven and earth simultaneously gave her an intuitive grasp of the harmony that *could* exist between these spheres. They came together in the person of Jesus Christ; they existed in creation before the Fall; and they would once again be reunited after the Last Judgment and divine fulfillment of the created world. Until such a time would come for humanity, it was necessary to come into contact with the Living Light in whatever way possible. One way for her was the revelations of the Light, but she recognized that this was an individual gift, although later she would be compelled (her words) to share these insights with the Christian community at large. However, in praising God in the liturgy, and most especially through song, people could come into contact with the Eden they had lost, the risen Jesus among them, and find once again the promise of salvation in eternity. Her innate grasp of the structure of the Christian worldview combined with the power of revelation in the Holy Spirit is apparent in Hildegard's compositions: she works within the confines of the chant form, and yet there is a great deal of fluidity in her interpretation of them.[33]

Hildegard's musical compositions, both in text and score, reflect this anticipation of the coming of the divine to be present in the world, in those who praise God. Since liturgy and music would have surrounded her in her formative years, it is likely that the connection between liturgical music and her experiences of the Light eventually helped interpret each other for her. Both were mediums in which the human and the divine meet. We might also conclude this is the case in her attitude toward virginity: it is virgins praising God who are most likely to recapture some of the innocence lost by Adam and Eve and to be transported into celestial realms. Her unique view of this privileged status conferred by musical praise would bring her criticism from others when she was head of the Rupertsberg, since on certain feast days she apparently allowed the nuns to wear special clothing and crowns as a sign of their virgin status.[34] We are unsure of the exact setting in which this was permitted. It is possible they were costumed for the performance of Hildegard's morality play, the *Ordo virtutum,* but also equally possible this was a custom for special feast days when singing and praise of God were the central activities of the convent.

For Hildegard, it was a vital necessity to look toward the union of the visible and invisible worlds that surrounded and embraced the cosmos. She is both singular in her experience of dual vision and in her methods of conveying the union of these spheres. Conversely, she also shares a common view with her contemporaries in certain attitudes toward the relationship of the two. What she shares in common is an assumption that may apparently be contradictory when first encountered by the modern reader but that, taken as a whole, can be seen to make sense. All that exists is of God, so the totality of being comes from the divine. God has foreseen the outcome of history and has predestined it.[35] That belief in predestination results in a strong conviction of the power of God over the devil, a confidence in the ultimate triumph of Jesus Christ, the importance of the redemptive role played by the Virgin Mary, and assurance of the coming of a divine judgment that will justify the virtuous and condemn the wicked—a time when the true Church will be glorified. Thus the invisible world is one that is far above us and beyond our scope and grasp, since the world we live in is shaped by fallen human nature. This world of the visible and palpable falls far short of God's intended destiny for it: evil and the devil are constant threats to the salvation of souls; the Church in its purity is attacked from without and within; and conditions are not as they should be. Hildegard will dramatize this separation of the divine invisible realm and the worldly visible realm in her musical drama, the *Ordo virtutum,* later on. And yet even when she sets these worlds in opposition there is always the interpenetration of that which is visible to all and that which seems invisible. God's power and presence resound throughout God's creation, especially in the creation of humanity made in God's image and likeness. Thus we do not really *belong* to either world as we live out our earthly existence, for this world in its fallen condition is not what God intended for creation, man, and woman; and the heavens are our foreordained destiny, the promise of fulfillment to come, which is glimpsed in the works of the virtuous and the faith of the spiritual heirs of Christ. Hildegard's unique language of the "reflection of the Living Light," as seen in the world described above, captures in a single phrase the tension between the visible and invisible, a tension that is meant to be and can be overcome in moments of spiritual awakening and insight or in songs of praise. We may not see the fullness of the Living Light, but the shadow or reflection is always there. We find that she uses the light imagery that so permeates the New Testament as a language that gives voice to her own experience of the Light; she also molds it to her own theological exposition when, for example, she claims that in paradise Adam saw not the actual divinity of God but with his eyes beheld the brightness that proceeded from God's face, giving him a genuine knowledge of the true God.[36]

In Hildegard's work we find the linear history of a person's life and the history of salvation curving into a circular pattern. We are meant to return from whence we came with the help of the incarnation of the Savior: the perfection of creation in the beginning will once again be made into a reality at the end, and we will have come full circle. In this way we attempt to imitate the angels, whose praise circles around God and the cosmos and whose celestial songs resound throughout the heavens.

The World Outside

The visible world in which people lived was the canvas on which their lives were painted. It was important to Hildegard, especially later in her life, to make sure that the world outside the cloister was considered in the picture of the world in which she lived. Particularly in her letters and later in her preaching tours she would show a great concern for the errors and heresies of her time. Catharism is an example of the urgency she felt toward those being led astray: we have the entire text of her sermon against them.[37] The Cathar heresy, widespread in Hildegard's area in the Rhineland in the late 1140s and the entire 1150s,[38] was dualistic in character. As a version of the Manichean heresy, which others had battled before, the Cathars saw matter and the material world as evil, the spirit and the spiritual alone as good. Jesus therefore could not be incarnate—he must have been an angel. For Hildegard, the attitude of Catharism insults all of God's creation and its intended goodness, and in particular is repulsive in its attitude toward the Word of God Incarnate. Although the realms of heaven and earth can be distinguished, the Scriptures teach us that they are not divided and totally separate. While Hildegard's personification of the devil and evil spirits sometimes strikes the modern reader as gruesome and negative, she means for this reaction to occur. What she does *not* intend is to set up the devil against God in some sort of dualistic religious hierarchy. To do so would reduce the power and majesty of God; it would make the incarnation of the Son inconsequential; and it would reduce the scope of the work of the Spirit to chosen individuals, the "spiritual selves." Hildegard's vision of the world, like that of her contemporaries, who held orthodox views of Christianity, is deeply sacramental. The invisible and the visible meet and join ever so briefly, but constantly, in this world when our eyes are searching for signs of God's presence. But how did Hildegard come to be shaped in such a way that her convictions about this were unshakable? Obviously, this was not the case for everyone at the time.

Ever since Hildegard was born, her area of the world was in a state of constant upheaval. The First Crusade had ended a year after her birth; the Second Crusade would get off to a bumpy start in her lifetime. Kings were struggling for power in Germany, and politics was both complicated and corrupt. When Hildegard took the veil and professed her virginity, she did this in a ritual presided over by Bishop Otto of Bamberg. Now, St. Disibod came within the province of the diocese of Mainz, so it was the archbishops of Mainz who were present for all solemn ceremonies, such as Hildegard's profession. The Archbishop of Mainz undoubtedly would have been happy to preside, save for the inconvenience of having been imprisoned by Henry V, the Holy Roman Emperor at the time. From the eleventh century and into the twelfth, opinions regarding the relationship between religious and secular power came into direct conflict with one another. Bishops had traditionally been treated as members of the nobility in Germany and often came from noble families. The kings and emperors, in turn, thought that bishops should be appointed by them and ruled by them, as were all the rest of their subjects. This brought them into continual conflict with the popes, who jealously guarded their jurisdiction over the Church hierarchy. The famed "investiture crisis" of the eleventh century was the most prominent example of the conflict over who should wield control over the clergy. Despite numerous

21

battles won and lost, compromises reached and abandoned, the political and religious climate of the time was one of strife, strain, and tension. Hildegard managed to live during a time that would see popes who could not live in Rome because of antipapal uprisings, popes set up against antipopes promoted by secular authorities for their own purposes (approximately twelve popes and ten antipopes in her lifetime), and a general cry for reform of the Church, including the papacy. The twelfth century was the beginning of a spiritual revival, despite or perhaps in response to these circumstances. In the flowering of twelfth-century spirituality questions abounded about how the Church, the state, and the individual should live out their lives before God.

It is possible that a degree of Hildegard's certainty amid the tumult came from two inviolable sets of structure in her life: the social and ecclesial orders. For Hildegard, God had ordained a certain order and structure in the world. She had no difficulty accepting the concept of hierarchy inside the Church and outside of it; indeed, she embraced it as a means of stability and an expression of divine calling. Hildegard counted on this divine order to counteract the confusing wiles of the devil and the forces of sin and evil in her time. It is probable that her own noble birth, coupled with her association with other members of the nobility in her religious life, enabled her to have a firm acceptance of this view of the world. In addition, her concern for the visible and invisible as meeting in an embodied way in this life was dependent on a sacramental Church, which could make God's Word incarnate for all. She accepted the need for a structured religious rule and hierarchy; the former most likely was natural to her from her formation in a Benedictine double monastery, and the latter accorded with her idea—and that of many other medieval thinkers—that hierarchy is necessary in order for virtue to flourish and vice to be stamped out. Her notion of hierarchy, however, is one based on the ideal hierarchy: she had little patience for the misuse of office, secular or ecclesial, and believed God had even less patience with those who would "foul the nest" of his grand designs for humankind.

Hildegard was not a passive woman, but she did have a highly developed sense of order and appropriate place, which is clearly exhibited in her writings and her letters. This did not mean that when she disagreed with her superiors or with the churchmen of the time that she would not speak out against them in favor of her views; but she always did this in accordance with what she believed the Living Light guided her to do and say, and within the scope of legitimate church authority. We have only to look at two of the most painful events in her personal life, the transfer of her beloved nun, Richardis, to another abbey against her wishes and the interdict put on the Rupertsberg late in her life, to be able to see the depth of her personal convictions yet her preference for working through the channels of appropriate authority. In both cases, which we will speak about in detail later, she waged a war of correspondence, pleading, and visionary exhortations beginning with the first step on the ladder of authority and going on to the highest appeal available to her. Obedience was essential to the Benedictine spirit, and Hildegard understood obedience as a discipline of being responsibly receptive to what the natural hierarchical order had to say. Today, obedience seems to be a word that is less than palatable to us. But Hildegard managed to cultivate obedience and humility as virtues, which still allowed for flexibility. For example, she called into question the conduct of the clergy and the rulers of her time as being unsuited to their office and contrary to the will of God. Obedience did not require one to be blind to the failings of those who did not grace their office with suitable obedience to *their* higher authority, whether to immediate superiors or, more than likely, to God.

Hildegard believed that there was an appropriate function for the Church and for the state and that for governance of people's spiritual and temporal lives both were necessary. She disapproved of the idea that there should be a radical papal supremacy, and she also disapproved of church leaders taking part in secular enterprises.[39] Clerics should not be preoccupied with worldly concerns, and secular rulers should not try to manipulate the clergy for their own political ends. Hildegard was even critical of the involvement of many religious in the Second Crusade, which is particularly noteworthy, since her spiritual mentor, Bernard of Clairvaux, took such an active role in promoting and launching it. She took her own role as a religious superior seriously and expected others to do the same.

Shaping Forces and Hildegard's Personality

As we have seen throughout this chapter, Hildegard was formed in many different ways by outside forces and by her own gifts and experiences. We presented with a picture of a life with a complex texture, of a woman whose view of herself and the world often resulted in the realization of tensions and polarities and yet saw beyond them to glimpses of resolution. She was ignorant yet learned, visionary and practical, cloistered yet worldly wise, a seeker of God's light and invisible heaven and a firm believer in the goodness of God's visible creation, vital and sickly, one who composed and sang songs of praise yet was fully capable of rebuking others in God's name. Hildegard lived out many threads in her life, or many melodies, if we are to keep in touch with the metaphor of mystical polyphony. Why is the metaphor of mystical polyphony a compelling one when we consider the sources and shaping forces of Hildegard's life?

The answer is, as she is, simple and complex at the same time. One of Hildegard's characteristics is the stability she gained from her sense of divine order, of the mandate of the Scriptures and the teaching of the Church, of her conviction of the centrality of the Incarnation. But because of the revelations she received, the gifts she possessed, and her desire to know, serve, and praise God she was never totally dominated by this awareness of stability and structure, nor was she ever really derailed by the turbulence around her. She is a mystic because of her commitment to a life lived both with and for God: this included contemplating God's goodness and the Living Light in itself but also living out and cultivating a life of virtue and charity in accordance with God's will, even against her own inclinations and temperament. She is polyphonic because of the simultaneity of melodies in her life, which she brought together in the harmony of one personality. She never abandoned one gift for another but instead added it to the whole. This is the fruit of the gift of her "double-vision," a vision of the visible and invisible, which she firmly believed God commanded her to share with the world. She simultaneously managed to emerge as a societal force while remaining an active member of a religious order, a leader of her community, a composer and singer, a correspondent with those important in the Church and the world around her, a spokeswoman for the need for reform in "an effeminate age," a woman constantly plagued by illness but never stopped by it, whose vitality challenges us today.

These interlacing melodies made up a polyphonic hymn to the praise of God in the characteristic voice of Hildegard von Bingen. How this woman, as she emerges for us in this chapter, specifically lived out the individual lines of her mystical polyphony will be the subject of the next four chapters of this book. The significance of considering all of these forces that shaped her life apart from specific works and subjects in this chapter is to underline the many facets of Hildegard that are *simultaneously present.* It is easy even for one familiar with her to lose track of everything else she is and does when paying attention to any single type of her activities. As we move into Chapter 2 we need to remember that the author of the visionary trilogy was at the same time composing music, leading and tending to her community as *magistra,* or abbess, corresponding with many people of all different social ranks giving advice and counsel, suffering off and on with a series of debilitating illnesses, preaching and prophesying, investigating nature and healing with herbs, and through it all leading the structured religious life of any Benedictine nun with its observance of the Rule and the Liturgy of the Hours. Her life-song is certainly multifaceted, a polyphony resolving into the celestial harmony for which she always hungered.

II

Mystical Polyphony
in the Visionary Works

One of the difficulties we encounter when we consider Hildegard's vast array of talents is the tendency to separate them from one another in order to gain a better understanding of what each of these talents means, both in itself and for Hildegard as a person. Therefore, although in this chapter we begin to consider Hildegard's many gifts and talents grouped under a particular heading, we will always want to bear in mind what else she is doing and experiencing around the same time. For example, it has been customary to combine her three theological-visionary treatises into one chapter, facilitating analysis of the three of them in combination. Although we will be considering all three here, we want to make note of the evolution in her thought, the differences between the treatises, and the fact that many of her other writings are visionary in content as well. Moreover, it is hard to comprehend the density of the theological works without consulting her correspondence and her *Life*. For the reader just being introduced to Hildegard, however, it still is helpful to group these treatises because of their style and their theological survey of her thought. We will see in the following chapters how vital these themes are to the other writings of approximately the same time frame.

There are several central questions that need to be addressed while discussing Hildegard's visionary treatises. We will integrate these into the narrative and then consider them more fully at the end of the chapter. The first is that of the authority of the visionary: in other words, what proportion of these treatises is based on divine vision and how much on Hildegard's own contribution? Although it will be impossible to answer this question fully and to anyone's satisfaction, it nevertheless is a central concern. The second is that of the priority of image or text when interpreting this literature. This has a great deal to do with how we interpret Hildegard's experience of the visions and, as a consequence, how we interpret both their intent and her own sense of calling. Third, the opacity of the text and the depicted visions are of interest and worthy of close consideration. Unfortunately, examples of the plates in color, which would be the optimum way to explain their intricate symbolic value, cannot be used in this book. However, by using several examples of color commentary along with the black and white equivalents, it is possible to evoke their significance through use of the imagination.

The Calling of God: The Preface to the *Scivias*

> It happened that, in the eleven hundred and forty-first year of the Incarnation of Jesus Christ the Son of God, when I was forty-two years and seven months old, Heaven was opened and a fiery light of exceeding brilliance came and permeated my entire brain, inflaming my whole heart and my whole breast; not as in a burning flame but like a flame which warms, like the sun warms anything its rays touch. And immediately I knew the meaning of the exposition of the Scriptures, namely the Psalter, the Gospel and the other catholic volumes of both the Old and New Testaments; but I did not have the interpretation of the words of the texts, or the division of the syllables, or the knowledge of cases or tenses. But I had sensed in myself since childhood—from the age of five up to the present—in a wonderful way the power and the mystery of secret and marvelous visions. This, however, I showed to no one except a few religious persons who were living as did I; until the time when God in His grace wished it to be shown, I concealed it in quiet silence. The visions which I saw I did not perceive in dreams, or sleep, or delirium, or by the eyes of the body, or by the ears of the outer self, or in hidden places; but I received them while awake and seeing with a pure mind and the eyes and ears of the inner self, in open places, as God willed it. How this might be is hard for us mortals to understand.[40]

Hildegard's version of her experience in the preface gives us information about her divine revelations and her affective response to these experiences and describes for us in great detail the way in which these visions were received by her. While there is great interest in the revelations and the way in which they were received, what can be overlooked is the tone of the passage and the affective response with which Hildegard responds to these visions.

While the passage recorded in the *Scivias* is meant as a prologue to the visions contained in the book, Hildegard's tone is both passionate and affectionate. These revelations or moments of insight had been familiar to her since an early age, a comforting if occasionally disquieting or embarrassing experience. For her, God is "the Living Light, Who illuminates the darkness." We can see here that such revelations were a normal part of her prayer life. Even so, we sense an urgency and a passionate excitement here in the preface, for while it had appeared beforehand that these visions were part of Hildegard's life, she did not explicitly have a call before this time to speak out widely about their content to others. It is likely that she received a powerful new set of visions or a renewal of partial glimpses she had been having throughout her lifetime. The flame is still "warming" rather than "burning," but the effect is to "inflame" and inform her whole mind with God's visions and God's command:

> O fragile human, ashes of ashes, and filth of filth! Say and write what you see and hear. But since you are timid in speaking, and simple in expounding, and untaught in writing, speak and write these things not by a human mouth, and not by the understanding of human invention, and not by the requirements of human composition, but as you see and hear them on high in the heavenly places in the wonders of God. Explain these things in such a way that the hearer, receiving the words of the instructor, may expound them in those words, according to that will, vision and instruction. Thus therefore, O human, speak these things that you see and hear. And write them not by yourself or any other human being, but by the will of Him Who knows, sees, and disposes all things in the secret of His mysteries.

It is clear from this passage in God's voice that Hildegard is privileged to utter what God commands and to explain the things she sees and hears to others. It is equally clear in both passages that the knowledge comes directly from God without the interference of human constraints. Thus, Hildegard in her own voice explains the miraculous way in which she comes to understand the Scriptures and has a grasp of grammar and syntax that could never be her own. It is clear to her from God's command and from her own interpretation of her reception of that command that it is God's words that are to be spoken, and it is at the peril of the seer and any other to alter or change the revelation in the words given to her by divine command.[41] What we apparently have here are the confident words of a prophetess sent forth by the explicit command of God. But it did not evolve exactly in that way, for Hildegard was not at all confident about her visions from the start. In the preface, God has to repeat several times to her what her task is:

> And again I heard the voice from Heaven saying to me, Speak therefore of these wonders, and, being so taught, write them and speak. . . . Again I heard a voice from Heaven saying to me, Cry out and write!

Hildegard explains in her preface that she doubted her authority and her calling to publicly declare God's words and her own visions. She tells us of her refusal to write, "out of humility," or more aptly, out of fear. It is not until she is afflicted with serious illnesses that she endeavors to take on the task laid upon her. It is an interesting passage with its use of the virtue of humility: Hildegard explains to us that because she has had this exceptional gift all her life, she has also suffered "in the flesh" so that she might be humble with God's favors. Ironically, it is that sense of humility that initially prevents her from having the courage to take up what she hears as the divine command, and the result is the very suffering that made her humble in the first place! Hildegard's bodily frailty and susceptibility to illness are a constant in her life, yet it has many interpretations, even by the seer herself. We see this in her struggle to accept the calling of a visionary, one sent to speak out to the People of God in her time. She has to reverse her previous ideas about being silent concerning the visions, and that illness is a way of keeping her from taking secret pride in them. Now in her maturity she is being called to do the opposite: speak boldly of the visions to all and suffer the consequences of illness should she refuse to obey God's will in this matter.

Lest this seem too facile an explanation of the tone of the preface and her struggle with her calling, it should be remembered that before the visions ever began to be repeated and recorded for public use she had confided in both Jutta and Volmar about them. The ones that came upon her in the *Scivias,* with their sense of urgency, must have frightened her; she began to write them down only at Volmar's insistence and because he believed them to be of supernatural origin. Public preaching was another matter, however, and she postponed this as long as possible. As a result, in 1146 she wrote to the great Cistercian reformer and spiritual leader Bernard of Clairvaux, confiding to him about her visions and her concern about what to do about them. Bernard supportively but somewhat abruptly assured her they *were* from God, and who was he to tell her what to do about them when God has made that abundantly clear?[42] She was much reassured by this, but the interval between the first reception of the visions and her letter to Bernard shows us five years of interior struggle as to what exactly these visions meant for her. They seem to have transformed her personally, enhancing her creativity as evidenced by her increased composition of liturgical music as well as by the dictation of the visions themselves and the authority she wielded as superior of the convent.

From the Preface to the Content of the *Scivias*

As it turned out, the Synod of Trier, held in 1147–48 for other reasons, gave Hildegard's visions a place of prominence and the seal of approval of the Church in the form of Pope Eugenius III, a Cistercian influenced by Bernard before he became pope. A delegation from Disibodenberg took a copy of the writings she had been making for Volmar, and these were read aloud at the synod. The Pope was sufficiently impressed to grant papal approval and authorization for Hildegard to publish all she received in her visions as commanded by the Holy Spirit.

Considering Hildegard's respect for the divine order present in the world, including the hierarchies of Church and of society, the insistence of the divine voice, the support of her community and of the Benedictine reformer of Clairvaux, she hardly had a choice about speaking forth. By this time, however, it is quite likely she was ready to do so in her own right, having struggled with the question for a period of years, recording the visions for Volmar all the while.

There is some doubt about whether or not the miniatures of the visions drawn to illustrate each of her revelations were actually seen at Trier. Since they are indispensable to the understanding of the *Scivias,* there is a tendency to assume that they accompanied the text of what she had heard from God. Despite their importance, there are several reasons they might not have been included. From a practical point of view, carrying drawings elaborately embellished with expensive gold and silver leaf might have been something the delegation from Disibodenberg would have felt was unsafe. From a historical point of view, since Hildegard was struggling with what to do about the visions, the drawings may have been made but not yet completed or illustrated fully. From an analytical perspective, some have suggested the illustrations themselves were so powerful and infinitely more subversive than the text that they were deliberately not presented to the synod.[43] This brings us to the issue of the priority of text over image or image over text.

It would appear that in considering this issue the theological-visionary treatises are treated as a whole, a set in which the same approach is always the case. Taking each of the treatises in its own right, the answers are much less certain. The majority of those analyzing the treatises from the literary point of view take the position that the illustrations are secondary to the text itself. First, we have the words and lessons of God, and then we have a visual image that corresponds to the inner vision of the seer to accompany the text.[44] Others have suggested that in a feminine mode of writing and seeing, the imagery itself would be primary and the analysis would be secondary.[45] Thus the visions as depicted in the illustrations take on much more authority than they have in the former case. All of this is complicated by the fact that there are passages written to accompany each vision that do not appear in the illuminated pictures, and sometimes there are details in the illuminations that are not really reflected in the text. The *Scivias* is the clearest example of how important this issue might be in considering Hildegard's revelations, since of the three works it is the most lavishly illustrated (thirty-five miniatures in all) and the writing is the most clearly interactive when it comes to considering the text and the illustrations as representative of her visions. Her second visionary work does not have illustrations, and her final work contains fewer illustrations than we find in the *Scivias,* although they are important in their scope.

In the case of her first visionary work I tend to agree that the actual illustrations take some priority over the text; furthermore, they add to the singular quality of Hildegard's telling of the Christian story by giving it a different cast than one would get from the text alone. The text, however, is no mere addendum to the illustrations: both are part of the knowledge received by the visionary. That is why we cannot refer to either the illustrations or the textual commentary as being the "visions" on their own. It is the way in which they are interwoven that is important. There is some evidence that the visions were taken down in dictated form both as spoken and as visualized simultaneously, although it is certain the drawings were carefully made to the seer's satisfaction some time after the initial experience of a particular vision. It has been suggested that Volmar wrote the words as Hildegard imprinted the essential visual parts of the revelation into the wax tablets, an idea taken from one of the illustrations of Hildegard receiving the visions.[46] It may be more realistic to assume that although both underwent some form of scribal record, they did not undergo a scribal editing or transformation. The visions remained essentially as Hildegard vividly remembered them, whenever they were set down. I agree strongly with the opinion of the art historian Madeline Caviness about the pictorial visions being inherently Hildegard's and essential to her identity precisely as an artist who was a visionary:

> Hildegard's unique talents would have been viewed as part of her prophetic gift, and even artists of the highest reputation were not honored as "geniuses," in the sense of being regarded as having their own private source of inspiration. Nonetheless, I believe that Hildegard can be credited with the quintessential part of creativity that Renaissance theorists regarded as the highest level of artistic creativity, that is, *idea* or concept. To claim such a role for her is compatible with the fact that none of her original works survive.[47]

Thus Hildegard is shown again to have an authentic "double-vision," a layered and polyphonic ability in life to create at more than one level at the same time and excel at each.

The title *Scivias* is a contraction of the longer Latin phrase *Scito vias Domini,* "Know the Ways of the Lord." This visionary text takes as its theological core the retelling of the essentials of the Christian view of the world, a type of treatise on the structure of salvation in which the hearer

30

(let us not forget oral tradition) or reader is reminded of the Lord's ways and the urgency of remembering their meaning. It is composed of three separate parts, each with its story to tell. The first and second parts are roughly equivalent in length, whereas the third part is as long as the first two combined. The tripartite structure is a reflection of the triune God. After the preface with which we began, the first part introduces the themes of creation both in its original beauty and considering the results of the Fall in six visions; the second part then proceeds to the concrete salvation of Christians through the incarnation in Jesus Christ and present to the believer through Church and sacraments in seven visions; the third part pulls the reader toward the coming kingdom of God through the recounting of the process of coming to holiness (sanctification), in which recounting the mounting tension between evil and good takes priority, in thirteen visions. The visions in the third part do not approach salvation in a way that is historical alone but also in a way that is highly allegorical, as befits the future. The book finishes with an appendix of several songs plus a partial copy of what later would be a separate work: a sung morality play called the *Ordo virtutum*. It took Hildegard ten years to complete the *Scivias,* and she did so under a bewildering array of circumstances. It is all the more impressive in its general stylistic symmetry because of this. When the *Scivias* was begun, as we have noted above, it was with trepidation and with an uncertain direction; Hildegard had been the leader of her community for approximately five years when the command to speak came to her. Shortly after her fame spread as a result of these writings and their hearing at the Synod of Trier, she began to correspond with many people on spiritual matters. In 1148 she received a divine vision calling her to lead the sisters to another location and to move her convent to Mount St. Rupert. Because of this she had to deal with the necessities of acquiring the property, with the displeasure of the monks of Disibodenberg at the thought of losing her (and her power to draw people to the monastery), and with the actual practical headaches involved in starting a new foundation. They were only permitted to move in 1150. The *Scivias* was finished in 1151 or 1152, only a short time after her move to Rupertsberg was completed. She could never have completed it without the support of her teacher, Volmar, and the assistance of one of her nuns, Richardis von Stade. Richardis will appear in the drama of Hildegard's life as the center of controversy about a year after the completion of this visionary work.

Scivias is both an impressive work and one difficult for the contemporary reader to read with any ease. Its wording is difficult, made more so by Hildegard's interesting use of grammatical constructions. It is full of allusions, especially to biblical sources, which are at times commented on explicitly and at other times are references the reader or hearer was expected to know. Its syntax is occasionally tangled, its tone at times ponderous, and the explanations, more elliptical than direct, often leave one more confused afterward than at the start. While it is overall an inspirational work of great individuality, a lofty retelling of the salvific structure of the cosmos and a work of poetic insight, it cannot be called an easy introduction to Hildegard herself for the twentieth-century reader. In addition to all these considerations, we have to add that the historical time in which the work was written is essential to an understanding of both its style and its content. Hildegard believed that God had chosen her, a woman, to speak forth strongly to "a womanish time" when Christians were not heeding or hearing the words of God.[48] We have mentioned previously that the Middle Ages was a time saturated with a Christian view of the world, a religious outlook that was fundamental to the way people viewed themselves and the universe. To us it may seem an alien world, even more so when we add to it that since God was the initiator of all things believers of the time saw no contradiction between astrology, numerology and other systems of observing and predicting the circumstances around them and a solid Christian faith. At the time there was also a firm belief in apocalyptic prophecies, and Hildegard's is the most powerful of these. Apocalyptic is a curious but particular genre that focuses its attention on the imminence of divine judgment and the coming kingdom of God, which would abolish all error, sin, and darkness, though not without a period of struggle on the part of humanity. It was not that there was an expected time for the ending of the world but rather an expectation that its destiny was fully in God's hands. In times of turmoil God was wont to remind the people that their destiny was not their own, whether it was through the prophets of the Old Testament—Hildegard identified in particular with Jeremiah, a very interesting choice, since he preached to a people unwilling to listen to God—or the preaching of the gospel of the New Testament by the apostles and followers of Christ. Christian history also attested to the value of witness brought to the people through the actions of the martyrs, both "red" (those put to death) and "white" (those who lived yet stood as examples). Hildegard is unique as a prophetic figure for the twelfth century, deliberately speaking with the voice of a prophet claiming to utter the words of God to the people. The *Scivias* is a proclamation to an age drifting away from the knowledge and truth of God to the peril of individuals and collectively to the Church itself.[49] It stands both as a reminder and as a call to repentance so that people might hear in a new way the gospel that had always been true but had not recently been zealously followed or put into practice.

Part of the originality of Hildegard's work lies in her unique claim to prophetic insight, and part of it lies in the use of allegorical figures to push her points home in the miniatures and in the text. These figures are all the more striking because of their femininity: *Ecclesia, Synogoga, Caritas, Sapientia.* If it were not for the visual images accompanying the text we might be tempted to explain the feminine imagery away on the strength of the argument that these nouns *are* feminine in Latin. Some, like the Church, were traditionally perceived as feminine, for the Church is the bride of Christ, the *sposa Christi.* Others are individual to Hildegard's visionary work. Whatever their origin, these figures become powerful forces in the narrative and the pictures, since they are central to the visions Hildegard received. It is possible to construct a theology of the feminine divine using some of these images and combining them with other information from Hildegard. We will consider this in due course. However, before continuing to discuss the *Scivias* as a whole, we ought to look at some specific representative examples from Hildegard's first visionary treatise that will give us the spirit of this particular piece of her writing. However, one of the most difficult things about the *Scivias* is deciding which of Hildegard's wonderful images to use. While the others will be described and summarized, in general the visions used are not the ones most attractive to the author or reader but those that most characteristically portray the theme of the work and the particular part we are concentrating on at the moment.

Part One: Creation and Fall

Part 1 consists of six visions and the commentary upon these visions. We will be concentrating on Vision 2 but will place it within the surrounding context of the rest of the visions in shorter summary form. The commentary is the *precise words of God explaining the vision.*

The first vision shows God as the one who gives light to humanity: God sits on an *iron mountain,* expressing the stability of God's enthronement and reign, and embraces both the good and evil activities of all under outspread wings. Those at the foot of the mountain show what disposition the believer is to have toward God: a figure consisting of eyes all over, formless, which signifies *fear of the Lord,* and a figure whose head is unclear because of the light streaming on it from above, which indicates *poverty of spirit.*

VISION 2

We will consider the second vision in detail, for it represents most clearly the major theme of this part of the book: creation and fall, and the relationship humanity has with God in past, present, and future. Please consult the reproduction of the miniature when reading the descriptions below, not only for the pictorial representation but also for the way it is

33

FIGURE 3

34

presented in manuscript form. Hildegard often makes separate comments on each of her visions. If you look at the Latin text accompanying this vision, you will see that she has numbered them. In the color facsimile the numbering is in red and the text is in black lettering. During the following commentary, after hearing her description, the actual colors of the miniatures will appear in brackets. She describes the vision (remember, picture and text are reflecting the experience described) in the following way:

> Then I saw a great multitude of bright living lamps, which received fiery brilliance and a serene splendor. And behold: A pit of great breadth and depth appeared, with a mouth like the mouth of a well, emitting fiery smoke with a great stench, from which a loathsome cloud spread out and touched a deceitful, vein-shaped form. And, in a region of brightness, it blew upon a white cloud that had come forth from a beautiful human form and contained within itself many and many stars, and so doing cast out both the white cloud and the human form from that region. When this was done, a luminous splendor surrounded that region, and all the elements of the world, which before had been in calm and great quiet, were turned to the greatest agitation and displayed horrible terrors. And again I heard Him Who had spoken to me before.

After this, she describes what God revealed the vision to mean in thirty-three different sections of textual commentary! To summarize, the *living lamps* are the stars we see in the upper part of the picture (in color these are golden outlined in red, and the smaller ones are silver against a dark blue background), representing the angels who are steadfast in their love for God, even to praising the expulsion of Lucifer in his pride at those who accompanied him. The trees in the lower right represent Paradise (in color they are light greenish-brown), and the human figure is Adam (natural coloration of flesh), the cloud with stars is Eve (cloud the coloration of flesh, the stars within a bright whitish-yellow), who is formed from Adam's rib. The cloud with its shining stars represents not just the figure of Eve but her meaning: she will bring forth all human beings from her womb, and the stars within the cloud represent this. However, the dark tower-like figure (black) with the outstretched tongues of fire in the trunk is an evocation of the tree of the knowledge of good and evil, which is forbidden to humanity by God, and the outstretched limbs and darts of fire represent the insatiable hunger of hell for souls, the *pit of great breadth and depth* (the flames and the pit are dark red). The *loathsome cloud* that spreads out into the *vein-shaped form* represents the reaching out of the devil in the form of the serpent to cause the fall of humanity as well as of the angels (black with red eye and outline around the serpent's mouth; outstretched tongues of the serpent are black). When it blows upon the form of man

35

and the cloud, causing their entry into the pit, there is *great agitation* and *terrors* as the heavenly host watches humanity, in God's image and likeness, fall from paradise into sin. Along with the explanation of the illustration, many parts are the voice of God speaking about matters related to the fallen condition of humanity. These are themes such as the nature of marriage and sex (11, 13, 16-22); the fact that God is just but the human race acted unjustly, deserving their fall because of presumption in claiming to be wiser than God (27, 29, 30); that the incarnation of the Son of God was the only means of saving the human race from the consequences of the Fall, and because of this humanity arises brighter than before because of the grace of God and the virtues brought about through Christ and the Holy Spirit (14, 31, 32); and commendations of chastity, and of humility and charity as the greatest of the virtues (24, 33). Throughout the narrative there are biblical references and commentary too: from the books of Wisdom, Job, John, and others. In number 32 there is an allegory likening the condition of the human race to a garden, a sheep, and a pearl, giving us still more pictorial imagery, which does not appear in the miniature itself. Also of interest for her use of words characteristic of her thought is the description of paradise (28), which is a place of delight filled with "the greenness *(viriditas)* of flowers and herbs" and the beautiful odor they produce, a place where the dry earth is filled with moisture and life. This brief paradisial account contains several of Hildegard's unique constructions in word and image: that of *viriditas,* of moisture and moistening power, and the use of flowers and herbs to accompany both. She also uses fragrance or odor for her idiosyncratic way of referring to the clergy: *pigmentarius* (perfumer) for a priest and *odor vivens* (living fragrance) for a monk.[50]

Note the complexity of the wording and the imagery, the number of references to the human condition made as a result of this single vision, and the emphatic negative and positive elements juxtaposed in Hildegard's narrative, which is typical of her theological approach as she interprets it directly as God's actual spoken words.

• The third vision is that of a cosmic egg, which represents the universe. The outermost area is a symbol of almighty God, represented in bright fire. There are complex images symbolizing Christ, the Church (seen here as the moon that is the feminine reflecting the fire of God as Son and Sun), baptism, innocence of those united to Christ, humanity as supported by the four elements traditional to medieval understanding (earth, air, fire, and water). This vision points to the endowment of humanity with God's image and its responsibility to bring the universe into the closeness of a relationship with God.

• The fourth vision is shown in three separate miniatures that portray the life of man from conception until death. Pictorially and textually

36

we see the uniting of the soul to the body, the dangers of temptation and sorrow, and the joy of life waiting for the soul at its final destination participating in eternal life.

• The fifth vision is of the synagogue, personified as a tall woman whose eyes are closed and arms are crossed; in her arms are the patriarchs and prophets who foretold the coming of the Savior, the most prominent of whom is Moses higher up on her breast. The lower part of her gown is dark because of the Law being broken, and her feet bear the blood of Christ. Surrounding her head, however, is a redeeming circle of light, which represents the Virgin Mary, who brought the Savior into the world, and her feet are supported by a light cloud, which represents the salvation of Israel that will come at the end of time.

• The sixth vision is of the nine choirs of angels, each with their definite characteristics, shown in the form of a celestial chorus encircling the light. Music is predominant here; and on this positive note we move on to the second part, where fallen creation awaits its Savior.

Part Two: Incarnation and Salvation

Part 2 consists of seven visions. We will look in detail at Vision 6, again because it closely reflects the major themes of this part of the work.

• Vision 1 concentrates on the role of the Redeemer. The triune God is symbolized by a gold disk at the top of the miniature; the six days of creation are shown beneath it, and the offer of everlasting life is represented in a white flower presented to Adam, who smells it. In his rejection of obedience, darkness appears and covers the center. There are lights in the darkness representative of the prophets who predict the coming of the Savior; there is a greater light on the edge that represents Mary, who is the dawn. From her proceeds the Christ, portrayed in gold with immense brightness, reaching into the dark for Adam and raising him to new life.

• Vision 2 is a stunning evocation of the Trinity. The outer circling light, appearing to be white or silver light, represents the Father, the uncreated Creator. Flooded in light and appearing at the center of the circles is the figure of a person who is bright sapphire blue, the symbol of the Son as the eternal spoken Word. The reddish-gold flaming circle in the center represents the Holy Spirit, which penetrates all things. The three are one Light, One God.

• Vision 3 concerns baptism and introduces the idea of the Church (*Ecclesia*) as the mother of all believers. The miniature is in four parts, representing the salvific function of the Church: her embracing of the altar of Christ; her declaration of the need to conceive and give life; the regeneration of her children in her lap, seen as a net, and transformed by breathing them forth in baptism in the presence of the Trinity; and pointing toward the two possible paths for baptized believers—toward the light or toward the darkness.

• Vision 4 concerns confirmation, showing how the Church is fortified by the Holy Spirit, who appears as a powerful tower; people live in the Church's embrace, but some break loose and go their own way, refusing the grace given them.

• Vision 5 is a pictorial and textual discussion of the hierarchy within the Church. Its three levels or states are the apostles, seen in a white light; Virginity and her children, representing bishops, priests, and monks; and a cloud of white light, representing the laity. All of them honor the Church and are surrounded by the glory of their heavenly hopes.

VISION 6

Vision 6 manages to use two miniatures to convey its theme to the reader, along with one hundred and two sections of commentary! Its basic theme is that of the sacrifice made both by Christ and by the Church, both of which are central to salvation. Hildegard says in this long account:

> And after these things I saw the Son of God hanging on the cross, and the aforementioned image of a woman coming forth like a bright radiance from the ancient counsel. By divine power she was led to Him, and raised herself upward so that she was sprinkled by the blood from His side; and thus, by the will of the Heavenly Father, she was joined with Him in happy betrothal and nobly dowered with His body and blood.
>
> And I heard a voice from Heaven saying to Him: "May she, O Son, be your Bride for the restoration of My people; may she be a mother to them, regenerating souls through the salvation of spirit and water."
>
> And as that image grew in strength, I saw an altar, which she frequently approached, and there each time looked devotedly at her dowry and modestly showed it to the Heavenly Father and His angels. Hence when a priest clad in sacred vestments approached that altar to celebrate the divine mysteries, I saw that a great calm light was brought to it from Heaven by angels and shone around the altar until the sacred rite was ended and the priest had withdrawn from it. And when the Gospel of peace had been recited and the offering to be consecrated had been placed upon the altar, and the priest sang the praise of Almighty God, "Holy, holy, holy Lord God of Hosts," which began the mystery of the sacred rites, Heaven was suddenly opened and a fiery and inestimable brilliance descended over that offering and irradiated it completely with light, as the sun illumines anything its rays shine through. And, thus illuminating it, the brilliance bore it on high into the secret places of Heaven and then replaced it on the altar, as a person draws in a breath and lets it out again; and thus the offering was made true flesh and true blood, although in human sight it looked like bread and wine.

FIGURE 4

And while I looked at these things, suddenly there appeared before my eyes as if in a mirror the symbols of the Nativity, passion and burial, Resurrection and Ascension of the Savior, God's Only-Begotten, as they had happened to the Son of God while He was on earth. But when the priest sang the song of the innocent Lamb, "O Lamb of God, Who takest away the sins of the world," and prepared to take the Holy Communion himself, the fiery brilliance withdrew into Heaven; and as it closed I heard the voice from thence saying "Eat and drink the body and blood of My Son to wipe out Eve's transgression, so that you may be restored to the noble inheritance." And as other people approached the priest to receive the sacrament, I noticed five modes of being in them. For some were bright of body and fiery of soul, and others seemed pale of body and shadowed of soul; some were hairy of body and seemed dirty in soul, because it was pervaded with unclean human pollution; others were surrounded in body by sharp thorns and leprous of soul; and others appeared bloody of body and foul as a decayed corpse in soul. And all these received the same sacraments; and as they did, some were bathed in fiery brilliance, but others were overshadowed by a dark cloud.

Although the passage is of great length, it is interesting in several ways. Note by looking at the images that the vision moves from one miniature to the other; it is not descriptive solely in order, or of one picture alone. Note also that this vision is depicted in the images more precisely as the visionary narrative is presented; thus, despite the great number of explanatory comments on these pictures and the vision, much of what Hildegard sees and intends us to see is evident in the combination of text and illustration. Some things that might be obscure, such as the Church's *dowry* (or marriage-portion), is explained as the gift of the sacraments (4). At this time the number of the sacraments was not yet fixed; with God's presence everywhere, people spoke of meeting God sacramentally more rather than less.[51] Hildegard herself shows the importance of the sacramental throughout this entire section, if we take "sacrament" to mean the meeting of the human and the divine in the tangible things of this world. Although she is concentrating primarily on the Eucharist as Christ's real and enduring presence, even the figure of *Ecclesia* is an embodiment of the Holy Spirit in the world. She normally appears clothed in gold from head to toe, coloring usually reserved in the pictures for illuminations of the divine presence. In the reproductions you see here, the colors are as follows: in the first illumination, the figure of *Ecclesia* appears entirely in gold. The background at the top left where she stands is dark blue with a dot pattern of gold behind it reminiscent of the stars of heaven in the illustration we discussed above, and it descends to be the backdrop of the lower portion of the picture; the rest of the upper background is pure gold, signifying the divinity of Christ and the moment of salvation on the cross. The cross of Christ appears silver-gray; the nimbus is again gold, and the parchment hanging from the cross, brown. The figure of Christ is at its most human in the many pictures Hildegard represents him in: he appears in his full humanity, with dark brown hair and clothed in red, the same red as that of his blood. The garment is edged very subtly in gold. In the lower part of the picture, the altar cloth is brown, but the altar underneath and streams from the cross above are pure gold. The chalice of wine and the bread are the color of the altar cloth. In each of the visions in circles, the background is gold and the predominant color is red, all prefiguring the sacrificial death of Christ and the sacrifice of his body and blood now offered in the Eucharist. In Hildegard's commentary it is abundantly clear that she regards this portrayal as the pivot of all of divine and human history: Christ's passion, death, and resurrection, which enables us to partake of heavenly food, like the manna God gave the Israelites in the desert (42). Again, her framework is trinitarian: three things must be present in the sacrament in honor of the Trinity: bread, wine and water (44). She also stresses that when *heaven is opened and a fiery and inestimable brilliance descends over that offering,* this means "the fresh and living *(viriditas)* breath of the royal kiss has been given," the fruit comes forth, and sweet sounds are heard and brightness covers all (10).

In the second miniature gold and red again predominate; when she speaks of figures who are light in soul and body, they are golden; others have the background coloring of blue with gold markings; those below are red, brown, muddy red-brown, and mixed, respectively. The priest is wearing a chasuble of red decorated with gold and a stole of blue and gold. His alb and the altar covering are gray or silver, as is the angelic wing and the attire of the heavenly host, except for one in red. The background, both upper and lower, are pure gold, and the chalice in the upper area is gold. Although the events it depicts come in the middle of the vision, we find that Hildegard has separated them visually, dividing them into the pure theological statement about Christ's salvific death and a commentary on how the Mass should be celebrated and how it affects people differently according to their disposition toward God. So the upper portion of this illumination is a representation of how the Mass should be conducted and said, as it is in the vision, the lower portion attends to the state of body and soul in which various persons find themselves in coming to the sacrament. The coloring is significant in this regard: the sacrament as represented by the gold leaf is always divine and pure. The people—even priests and religious, as she speaks of in the commentary—vary, and few have achieved a state of blessedness. She explains the five states as follows: those who are *bright of body and fiery of soul* are "clear about the sacrament and not in doubt that it is the true body and the true blood of my Son [God's voice]" (52); those who are *pale of body and shadowed of soul* are weak in faith, filled with apathy, doubt, and incomprehension about the sacrament but are passive recipients (53); those who seem *hairy in body and dirty in soul* (an evocative phrase!) are those who are polluted with uncleanliness and need God's mercy to be cleansed (54); those who are *surrounded in body by sharp thorns and are leprous of soul* are those who have anger, hate and envy, thorns that drive out the opposite virtues, and they desire evil, not good, and must have a bitter repentance (55); and finally, those *bloody in body and foul as a decayed corpse in soul* are cruel, divisive, and wickedly destroy others—by receiving the sacrament in this state they actually harm themselves, though if cleansed of wickedness even they can be forgiven. The stress is on the mercy of God in giving the Son up to death for humanity's sake, a sacrifice that makes it possible for even those sunk low in vice to rise up again if they will accept the sacrifice God has made for their salvation, repent, and practice virtue.

This vision, in the commentary, adds a great deal more than we see visually by making explicit the conditions for celebrating the sacrament and by whom. We should emphasize here that in the *Scivias* the commentary is written as an exact transcription of God's words; the subjective element of Hildegard rarely appears except in the description of the revelation she receives and in the quotation of biblical or church authorities. There are many long sections on the attitude and conduct of priests, which, if inferior to their office, makes them like servants of Baal or the devil and crucifiers (61, 65). There are exhortations to confession and to believe in the power of repentance, and that in emergencies someone other than a priest may hear a final confession. There is an interesting section on purgation (83), which shows the emerging doctrine of the time.

Additionally, we see in this example the complicated interweaving of images and text, commentary and vision, revelation and received wisdom. It is the pivot of salvation history, so theologically it is the center of the visionary-theological treatise.

• Vision 7 shows the chaining of the devil in the form of a huge and strong serpent with its jaws outstretched to breathe on and contaminate all who come near of their free will. The devil is chained to hell and cannot harm any who avoid his temptations. Indeed, the saints tread upon the snake inspired by the fire of Divine Justice.

Part Three: Tribulations and the Coming Kingdom of God

Because of the length of Part 3, some explanations of the visions may be shortened. This normally does little harm to the text, since many of the visions are about the building up of the Church in preparation for the kingdom of God and repeat themselves in content somewhat. We will be looking closely at Vision 11.

• The first vision is that of the Almighty seated in a throne representing Faith. It rests upon a cloud symbolizing Human Wisdom, which in turn floats above a sapphire rock indicating the fundamental attitude of humanity toward God, which is the Fear of God. A second miniature shows the fate of the stars that have been hurled from the heavens, Lucifer and the fallen angels; as they fall into the abyss their light goes out and they become blackened.

• The second vision is the first of a series depicting the construction of the house of salvation by the Divine Virtues. On the rock of the Fear of God walls and towers grow greater and higher over time.

• The third vision shows the Tower of the Decree, in which a crenellated, circular tower contains the figures of the Divine Virtues, all personified as female except Victory, who is covered in armor head to foot. The Virtues are Divine Love, Discipline, Modesty, Mercy, Patience, and Heavenly Desire. The last two look toward the crucified Christ. In a separate miniature the Divine Virtues display their characteristic attitudes and stances as we saw them previously in the first miniature accompanying this vision, but now they appear at full height and in detail.

• The fourth vision depicts the column of God's Word, which shows those on whom the building must be built. The first branch shows Moses and the other patriarchs ascending, looking with wonder at the second branch, containing those who witnessed the New Covenant: the apostles, martyrs, and saints. The third side is taken up by the Doctors of the Church (not shown in the miniature), and above the whole column is the bright golden light of the Holy Spirit, making it known that all these witnesses (especially from the Scriptures) have been inspired by God. Also included is another miniature with the figure of the Knowledge of God, which people can accept or reject but which calls to all of them constantly.

• The fifth vision shows a frightening winged head that is on the corner of the building and that chases away darkness and attacks on redemption.

• The sixth vision is of a triple wall in the house, which is Old Testament Law: at its beginning stand the virtues of Abstinence, Generosity, and Piety; at the end the Virtues of Truth, Peace, and Beatitude. At the end of the wall Discretion and the Salvation of Souls, two more Virtues, are leaning to lead over into the New Covenant.

• The seventh vision is of a very strong west wall, purple in color, symbolizing the Trinity; believers in the triune God will be built into the wall of the New Covenant, and unbelievers will be cut off from divine life like feathers, rotting wood, and straw.

• The eighth vision depicts the column of the manhood of the Redeemer, which, with strong supports in faith and the eternal predestination of God, is not yet complete. The Virtues, among them Humility, Charity, Fear of God, Obedience, Faith, Hope, and Chastity are busy climbing up and down with building stones. They are all shone upon by the light of the Incarnation, and at the top of the pillar is the Grace of God personified.

• The ninth vision is that of the Tower of the Church, showing her besieged and incomplete, worked on by the apostles and others. But she is protected: in front of her is Holy Wisdom, standing on the seven pillars of the Holy Spirit while three Virtues support her: Holiness, Justice, and Fortitude.

• The tenth vision shows Christ as the cornerstone, uniting the house; the end is not yet, so in the illustration we cannot see his feet, but we see the Mystical Body depicted by five Divine Virtues: Perseverance, the Desire for God, Contrition of Heart, Perfection, and Concord. In this vision we also have an evocative reference to the contrast between a dry field and a green one, echoing both the parable of the sower and the seed and Hildegard's consistent use of greenness and moisture as life-giving *viriditas,* as opposed to that which is dry and dark.

VISION I I

Vision 11 shows the culmination of the conflict between good and evil during the Last Days, presided over by the Antichrist. It might seem a particularly ugly vision to choose, but it has all the elements of this section and its commentary in it: the forces of good and evil personified; the invincibility of the outcome shown by the coming of Christ and the persistence of his Church; scriptural references to the Last Days from the book of Revelation, and the reappearance of the awaited figures from the Old Testament, Elijah and Elisha. Hildegard recounts the struggle:

> Then I looked to the North, and behold! five beasts stood there. One was like a dog, fiery but not burning; another was like a yellow lion; another was like a pale horse; another like a black pig; and the last like a gray wolf, and they were facing the west. In the West, before them, a hill with five peaks appeared; and from the mouth of each beast one rope stretched to one of the peaks of the hill and all the ropes were black, except for the one from the mouth of the wolf which was partly black and partly white. And behold! in the East I saw again that youth whom I had first seen on the corner of the wall of the building where the shining and stone parts come together wearing a tunic of purple. I now saw him on the same corner, but now I could see him from the waist down. And from the waist down to the place where a man is discerned he shone like the dawn, and there was

FIGURE 5

a lyre in his lap lying with its strings across his body; and from there to the width of two fingers above his heel he was in shadow, but from there down to his feet he was whiter than milk. And I saw again the figure of the woman whom I had previously seen in front of the altar, which stands before the eyes of God; she stood in the same place, but now I saw her from the waist down. And from her waist to the place where a woman is discerned, she had various scaly blemishes; and in that latter place was a black and monstrous head. It had fiery eyes, and ears like to an ass, nostrils and a mouth like a lion's; it opened wide its jowls and terribly clashed its horrible iron-colored teeth. And from this head down to her knees, the figure was white and red as if bruised by beatings repeatedly. From her knees to her tendons where they joined her heels, which seemed white, she was covered in blood. And lo! That monstrous head moved from its place with such a great shock that the figure of the woman was shaken through all her limbs. And a great mass of excrement adhered to the head; and it raised itself up upon a mountain, trying to climb the height of Heaven. And behold, there came a thunderbolt striking this head with such force that it fell from the mountain and sent its spirit into death. And a reeking fog enveloped the whole mountain, which wrapped the head in such filth that the people who stood by were terrified. And that fog remained around the mountain for a while longer. The people who stood there, seeing this, were shaken with great fright, and said to one another: "Alas, alas! what is this? what do you think that was? wretches that we are, who will help us and deliver us? For we do not know how we were deceived. O Almighty God, have mercy on us! Let us return, turn back; let us hasten to the Gospel of Christ. For ah, ah, ah, we have been bitterly deceived!" and lo, the feet of the figure of the woman glowed white, shining with a splendor greater than the sun's. And again I heard a voice from Heaven speak to me.

When we compare the illustration of the miniature with this account we are immediately struck by what we have easily understood in one and not in the other. At first glance it is obvious that the afflicted woman is the Church, *Ecclesia*, since she appears as is customary above the waist entirely in gold and crowned as usual. It is also clear that the young man is in fact Christ appearing in the last days of the old times. The description of the animals is about even, corresponding well between text and illustration. One needs the text—and the commentary—to have a grasp both of the nature of the Antichrist figure and the succeeding movements, which all appear to be static rather than sequential in the picture. What do we have in this vision, then?

We have an interesting combination of the traditional Last Days and a Hildegardian way of depicting them. The animals all have allegorical meanings: the dog produces people of a "biting temperament"; the lion represents warlike persons; the pig represents the impure; the wolves are robbers and cunning deceivers; and the pale horse stands for those who

46

sink themselves in sin (this last is also an echo of the book of Revelation, where death comes on a pale horse). They are there to show dissension in the final days of the world. They face the West because they will vanish as the sun sets (1–6). The Christ, appearing in the upper right corner, is seated on the building that has been under construction until now and is nearing completion. The most gruesome part of the whole picture is the image of the Church, scarred and bleeding, with the head of the Antichrist where the genitals would be. In the commentary the placement seems to have multiple meanings: the figure of Christ has harmony where the genitals should be (the lyre); when he joins his true spouse the monstrous aberration will leave her, torn away by the power of God embracing the bride. Hildegard also warns about the mother of the Antichrist as steeped in sin (25, 26) and who will teach the Antichrist the false ways of magic and power (27). The placement here could also mean that the human failings of those inside the Church help to give birth to the Antichrist, leaving the true Church maimed, beaten, and bleeding. At the bottom right we see the golden thunderbolt striking the *monstrous head* and its subsequent descent into the pit (which is all so black that it can only be discerned by its terrible teeth, since its cruel red eyes have, at that point, been snuffed out). The commentary stands as a warning also to Christians to beware the Day of Judgment because one does not know when it will come. Like the people in the vision, many will cry out about how they have been deceived, fooled until the end. It is a dire and apocalyptic warning, personified in a particularly gruesome way. However, there are as always the hints of hope that end the commentary. Once the Church is freed, she shines forth in all her golden glory, and the people sing the praises of the conquering Savior.

• The twelfth vision has two miniatures, one vision—the Divine Judgment and the creation of a New Heaven and New Earth. In the Divine Judgment Christ appears on the clouds of heaven with the angels, bringing the cleansing tempests and hurricanes, tossing about the four elements, and summoning the dead. Some bones rise to glory, others fall to perdition. When the tempest of judgment is complete, then the real everlasting reign of God can begin. The depiction is one of great harmony, and the miniature uses circles to represent this serenity. No longer is there day or night: in their place is everlasting light; at the bottom, a circle symbolizing the "ways of the Lord," which find themselves in the embrace of the trinitarian God.

• The final, thirteenth vision is a collection of hymns and songs praising God; Hildegard hears the songs of praise for the great deeds of God in the saints. This includes parts of the *Ordo virtutum* that speak of the harmony of the Divine Virtues and that in its final version as a play will depict the Devil's attempt to assault the unassailable Virtues.

47

Scivias: *Observations and Remarks*

Although close textual readings help to get the impact of the book as it was written in the density, passion, and prophetic voice of God that echoes throughout, it is also easy to overlook the themes that tie these intricacies together. We have mentioned many of them before. Although it is not as explicitly used as it is in her last visionary treatise, we get the continual sense that the life-giving power of God permeates everything that is good: *viriditas* is the animating source of all life.[52] There are also characteristic juxtapositions of word and image: light/dark, moist/dry, fragrant/stench, virtue/vice, healing/pain. It is significant that the root word for salvation, *salus* in Latin, conveys the meaning of healing, which will so dominate Hildegard's works, especially this first treatise on the meaning and importance of salvation. It is a cautionary but positive treatment of the healing (*salus, viriditas*) brought to the world in and through Christ.

We are still confronted with some contemporary questions requiring an answer, although some are best left to the summation of all the theological-visionary works. However, on the strength of the miniature illuminations that accompany the *Scivias,* it has been suggested by some that the images of light and brilliance coupled with the details of the pictures indicates that Hildegard's visionary work was the result of a medical condition. This medical condition is most usually referred to as a variant of migraine called "scintillating scotoma," although one author has tried to trace her visions to the hallucinatory components present in the local fungi at certain times of the year.[53] Because it is the more influential, we will briefly discuss the migraine theory here. The argument has been a heated one, probably because some authors, such as Charles Singer, are obviously searching for a "rational" explanation of who Hildegard is and what she sees. There is no denying that Hildegard had a history of ill health from childhood and that the image of blinding light could intimate that she suffered intermittently from migraine. There are two quite different issues at stake here. One, did Hildegard possibly suffer from migraine, especially of a particular type? Two, if she did, does that explain her visions, revelations, and works and dispose of their divine authority in a rational, scientific way? Often the argument mixes these two points together to the detriment of the validity of both.

Hildegard's visions contain certain elements common to the scintillating scotoma version of migraine, some of them strikingly similar. In this type of migraine things often appear in the form of bright lights (stars, dots) on a darker background—the vision of the fallen angels as stars in part 2 is offered as a good, clear example of this. There is also a perception of auras. In this disorder there also appear to be many edges and crenellated structures: all of the building imagery in part 3 would support this contention, especially those illustrations that are angular and have many edging details that are geometric in shape and kind.[54] Hildegard's descriptions of the overwhelming brilliance of God's presence and the use of the Living Light and its reflection to describe her revelatory experiences all provide us with decent evidence that a symptomatology for migraine is present, and the diagnosis could well be correct.

Most of those opposing the idea of Hildegard and migraine are worried about the second issue: does this then explain away the divine inspiration and origin of Hildegard's works? Can we state that a condition diagnosed as a recurring illness today simply explains away a great prophetic voice of the twelfth century?

It seems we need to look at both of these questions together in the light of the incarnation, the main theme of *Scivias*. For is it not the case that Christianity presents the human person as a whole, a combination of physical, psychological, and spiritual in a unity? This is certainly the Hebraic sense. Thus while the issues raised by many are different because their agendas are different—the former with investigating symptomatology, the latter with the initial cause and truth value of the visions—they essentially can form a whole if we look at it from another angle. If we postulate that Hildegard's visions are symptomatic of migraine, we need not at the same instantly rule out that they are gifts from God. God brings the good and the revelatory out of what is at hand in the human person; who is to say that the union of the somatic, psychic, and spiritual cannot express God's will even when not considered "normal" by contemporary standards? No one person is the same combination of these factors in any case. The most authoritative voice speaking for this point of view comes from the medical rather than the theological community. In his book on migraine the prominent neurologist Oliver Sacks does conclude that it is likely that Hildegard had migraine, yet he also concludes that it essentially does not matter. Why? Because he states that it is not what our malady or symptomatology is in itself that matters nearly as much as what we choose to do with it that counts.[55] This medical view is in full harmony with the theological view that the Spirit of God expresses itself as it wills in whatever incarnate being and under whatever conditions are present. If Hildegard had migraine, she did not so much "suffer" from it as receive great joy from its symptoms. If she did not, then the likenesses are coincidental. Neither hypothesis confirms or denies the divine origin of her visions or the authenticity of her call to prophesy. Indeed, if migraine did not cause her to suffer but gave meaning and shape to her life, then perhaps the pain associated with the symptoms was spiritually lifted from her through the working of God's grace. It is an interesting hypothesis, but it does not definitively answer what for the

49

modern consciousness is the most pressing question: did she really receive the actual words of God and true revelations through visions, as she claimed? This is a question we will return to again after looking at all the visionary treatises, even if the emphatic insistence on the words of God is strongest in the first work.

When Hildegard finished the *Scivias,* she was beset by crises. There was her need to solidify the foundation she had made at Mount St. Rupert and transform it into a viable community; she experienced the bitterness and loss of some of her sisters because of the move, and her attempt to impose the Rule of Benedict either more strictly or for the first time met with resistance as well.[56] She was still settling the relationship between the Rupertsberg and Disibodenberg, dealing with the disenchantment of the monks. Most traumatic of all, she was to lose one of the two constant companions who gave her support and assistance throughout the writing of the *Scivias:* Richardis von Stade. Richardis held a special place in Hildegard's heart, as we shall see more poignantly in the *Letters;* by all accounts, she was talented musically, lettered and educated in some fashion, and of a supportive and affirming temperament. Richardis had supported Hildegard in her writing of the *Scivias,* and the two women had a mutually supportive mother-daughter relationship in other ways as well. Richardis von Stade was the only other affectionate confidante we find Hildegard mentioning in her life besides Jutta and Volmar. She left the Rupertsberg in 1151 after the completion of *Scivias* to assume leadership of the community at Bassum, a position probably procured for her through family influence. Since she came from the highest ranks of the nobility, it was natural for them to wish her to head her own religious community. We know very little about Richardis' mind on the subject. However, after bitterly struggling against the move and attempting to win her back, Hildegard had to face the death of Richardis in 1152. During Hildegard's long life we know of only several companions by name and by a significant role they played in her life; although she was in contact with many people her intimates were few. The death of Richardis must have been a severe blow to her.

Hildegard did not begin her second visionary treatise, the *Liber vitae meritorum,* until 1158. Instead, she worked on her scientific and medical works (which we will look at in the next chapter) and her duties as the leader of her community in its new foundation. Her activities during this time seem to have focused on the needs of the Rupertsberg, whether dealing with property, healing, biology, or music. Leaving aside the biographical notes, we will continue past this period to 1158 and turn to the content of the second theological-visionary treatise. In this treatise we will find both contrasts and similarities to the first.

The *Liber Vitae Meritorum*

The most striking thing about this work after examining and discussing the *Scivias* is the complete absence of miniatures and illustrations to accompany the text of the work. Instead of pictorial representations, here the visions are evoked by the use of language and imagination; she uses powerful imagery as the underlying structural integrity of the book. Because of the lack of pictorial imagery and because of the themes covered in this visionary treatise, it is often the most neglected of the three of Hildegard's theological-mystical works despite its intensity and applicability to immediate situations.

The single, striking, unitive image is that of a man who is so tall that he extends from the depths of the oceans up into the heavens. In each of six sections, the man turns his eye toward a different direction: he then speaks of what he sees and hears, interpreting its meaning. In section 1 he looks to the east and the south; in section 2, to the west and the north; in section 3 to the north and the east; in section 4, to the south and the west; in section 5 he looks out over the whole world; in section 6 he moves himself within the four zones of the earth. It is possible that the construction is a consciously numerological one: sections plus directions give quantities divisible by three (the Trinity) into four (Old Testament justice) and two (signifying movement, the multiplicity of things, the many).[57] The book seems to be organized in such a way that it could be read aloud in the refectory at the Rupertsberg and elsewhere. Unlike the *Scivias,* its purpose is on a less grand scale; its intent is to be edifying as well as enlightening and has a repetitive quality that conveys greater power when read aloud in sections rather than reading it straight through.[58] In sum, it is the meeting of the Word and the Flesh, concentrating not on the overall structure of the divine plan but instead on the challenges of daily Christian life. In this way, it speaks of the microcosm of humanity and what temptations it comes across and can resist with the help of God. The immanence of the divine is implicit rather than explicit in Hildegard's last visionary work: if the man-figure is Christ, then it is in the splendor of Eternity from whence he views the situations met with in the world of human dramas.

This work concentrates not on the overall drama of salvation but on one of its themes in particular: the relationship of the virtues and vices. It is this linked duality that is the most significant use of numbers in the book. In this way, the *Liber vitae meritorum* is exactly what it calls itself, a book about life's merits. It lacks the grandeur of *Scivias,* but it also lacks its opacity. The overall purpose is to demonstrate the advantage of living a virtuous life, one that will glorify God. We are not introduced to the stereotypical seven deadly sins and the virtues that defeat them but rather to a host of possible vices and virtues that might be encountered in endless variation in human experience. To this end we are shown thirty-five examples of paired vices and virtues spread throughout the work. As in *Scivias,* the book begins with a preface, although this one is shorter and more confident in manner than in her first treatise:

> When I was sixty-one years old, which was the year eleven hundred and fifty-eight of the Incarnation of Our Lord, while I was still under pressure from the Apostolic See and while Frederick was the reigning emperor of the Romans, I heard a voice from Heaven saying to me:
>
> From infancy you have been taught, not bodily but spiritually, by true vision through the Spirit of the Lord. Speak these things that you now see and hear. For from the first of your visions certain visions were shown to you, just like liquid milk. Others, however, were uncovered for you like sweet and soft food. Still others, however, were manifest to you like solid and perfect food. Speak and write, therefore, now according to Me and not according to yourself.
>
> And I set my hand to writing down the testimony of that person whom, as I have said in earlier visions, I had privately sought and found. I also had a young maiden assisting me in writing down this testimony. And again I heard a voice from heaven speaking to me and teaching me in this way.

She is once again careful to place the visions within a historical time frame, which is the purpose of the first paragraph; it is also much more matter-of-fact in tone, as in the third paragraph, which describes the authority and conditions under which the book was written. God's voice, in the second paragraph, seems to be evoking the imagery in Paul's letters, where there is a progressive ability to "digest" the Word of God and God's ways. There is the insistence that these are to be written according to God's dictation and not Hildegard's imagination, although the phrasing is considerably less emphatic. Perhaps this is because she already has one visionary treatise behind her; more probably it is because she is now an acknowledged and endorsed visionary and feels less pressure to prove her case about prophetic and mystical insight. At the beginning of the first section and the end of the sixth she places a large heading that reads: "This Book of the Rewards of Life [Begins/Has Been Explained] Through a Simple Person From the Living Light of Revelations."

Once again it is the "Living Light" who authors these words, is the authority behind them. Hildegard is a vessel or a vehicle for the Divine Spirit to reveal things of importance to her contemporaries. How much of this work was influenced by Hildegard's obvious concern with and wide observation of human behavior is conjectural, as usual, although during this part of her life she was very much involved in dealing with others both inside and outside the convent.

In each section of this visionary work there are a variety of parts, similar to the organization of the commentaries in the *Scivias*. In the first section there are 124 parts or headings; in the second, 85; in the third, 84; in the fourth, 70; in the fifth, 86; in the sixth, 45. As with the commentaries of the *Scivias,* these are all part of God's revelation, although for them to be taken in detail is too much for us to consider here. Instead we will look at and summarize each major section, using examples of passages that typify the work so the reader is able to get the feeling of this theological-visionary treatise. Since the schema here is not as concerned with forward movement as the *Scivias,* we will first summarize each section and the topics each covers.

Contents of the Liber Vitae Meritorum

The grouping of sins and the opposing virtues are present in every section except the final one, which comments on the virtues in true believers. In every section the sin portrayed is described in earthy and evocative language; in contrast, the virtues sometimes pale by comparison because they are presented in a more stylized fashion. This has the rhetorical effect of bestowing a certain human immediacy on the vices/sins instead of dismissing them as purely paradigms of evil. This is perhaps the most impressive facet of the work and the one from which we will take our examples. In a way, the *Liber vitae meritorum* is a purgatorial work: it will describe purgatory in the last section as a sort of upper level of hell; before this description, every section offers suggestions about how to atone for sins by penitence now, thereby avoiding the even more painful remedies that may be the only recourse in the future.

Concerning the three issues we raised at the beginning of the chapter, we have already spoken of the third, opacity. The issue of the relationship between image and text takes a different turn here, for it is the narrative that constructs the visual image in the mind, quite deliberately. So in the *Liber vitae meritorum,* the image and the text are interlaced to appeal to the imagination and provide the reader with a glimpse of what the visionary sees: it is a cooperative effort and mutually self-dependent. In some sense the image is still prior here, except that the image is an imaginative one awakened by the lyrical use of textual expressions. The tone of the commentary is different in its use of description and choice of wording. The issue of gender proves an interesting issue. Most abstract nouns in Latin are feminine, and so—with some exceptions—most of the vices are feminine, as are the virtues. This could merely be a linguistic accident, but Hildegard uses it deliberately to "enflesh" the vices, even though they are not equated in any way with the eternal feminine. The fallen, fleshly humanity she often associates with Eve shows through in the depiction of some of the vices.

The first section begins with a detailed description of the man *(vir)* whom the seer encounters in the vision. His head above the shoulders is in the pure ether; from his shoulders to his thighs he is in the clouds; from the thighs to the knees he is in the air of the earth; from the knees to the calves he is immersed in the earth; from the calves to the soles of his feet he stands in the waters of the abyss, actually standing on the abyss itself *(quod etiam supra abyssum stabat)*. From his breath into the clouds come forth three clouds: a fiery cloud, a stormy cloud, and a luminous cloud. He surveys the clouds, listening to the voices that speak to him out of their midst. He is the embodiment of eternity, surveying what he finds in each direction and moving into action only in the final section of the work. When the figure looks in this direction, he uncovers seven pairs of vices and virtues: love of the world versus love of heaven; impudence against discipline; jesting opposed to shyness; hard-heartedness antithetical to mercy; sloth contrasted with (divine) victory; anger set apart from patience; and foolish joy compared to sighing for the Lord.

The second section mentions that the man has winged shoulders and wings on his chest and back, each inscribed with a message. The winged shoulders have open books upon them, telling the story of the Flood and the coming of the Word. The wing on back is written on by the finger of God; the wing in front contains the writings of those with wisdom. This section pairs the eight following vices with their pursuant virtues: gluttony with abstinence; bitterness with generosity of spirit; impiety with piety; falsity with truth; strife with peace; unhappiness with blessedness; excess with discretion; the destruction of souls with the salvation of souls.

The third section sees the man turning to the north, where the green earth covers him from thighs to knees. The man is shown to be God, threatening to purge the raucous elements with branches, tormenting all until they return to him. Seven more pairs of sins and graces appear: pride versus humility; envy opposing charity; empty glory confronting fear of the Lord; disobedience against obedience; lack of faith challenging faith; despair as the opposite of hope; and luxury in combat with chastity.

The fourth section shows that the earth in which he stands is moist, green and sprouting: his virtues grow beautifully, and it is the matter out of which the humanity of the Son of God is made. Eight more pairs of vices and virtues appear: injustice and justice; numbness and strength; forgetfulness and holiness; flightiness and steadiness; earthly cares and heavenly desires; obstinacy and contrition; desire and contempt of the world; discord and concord.

The fifth section shows the man looking over the whole earth, which is being purified by the waters of the abyss that supports and strengthens his power and his institutions. He speaks, calling for repentance, lest people be whipped by the rod of justice. The final five pairs come forth: scurrility attacks reverence; aimlessness is the opposite of quiet stability; wrongdoing is opposed to the true care of God; avarice threatens contentment; and worldly sadness is set against the joy of heaven.

The sixth and final section does not introduce any more of the virtues and vices; its thesis revolves around the strength of God at the end of the world as the man moves throughout the four zones of the earth, signifying the coming Judgment. The elements are shown to be in people generally; similarly, the virtues are to be found in the faithful ones. Each element relates to the virtues. The element of fire inflames the body, and the virtues set the soul on fire; as air is exhaled from the lungs, the virtues "inhale" heavenly things into the soul; as water moistens the body, the virtues bring water to the soul; as earth brings forth life, the virtues make people bear good fruit. The elements and the virtues are joined, as the body and soul are inseparable. After the Judgment the devil will no longer have sway or influence, and those in hell will suffer torments. The rewards of the virtuous will be fulfilled in the establishment of heaven. The book ends by describing the indescribable joy and beauty of heaven: when people gaze on the wonder of God they will forget all the earthly things that have gone before.

Specific Examples from the Liber Vitae Meritorum

To get the essence of the type of work the *Liber vitae meritorum* is we need to look at several pairs of virtues and vices. However, we would not have a complete feel for the work if these are presented without some of the later commentary upon the vices, and how they might be remedied. We will use two examples. The former is particularly apt in showing how Hildegard uses her visual talents to conjure up the image of the vice and the reply of the virtue; the latter shows the completeness of her thought if we examine the commentaries alongside another pairing of vice and virtue. We begin with a set selected from section 3, parts 14–16:

> The seventh appearance had the form of a woman who was lying on her right side. She had bent her legs and drawn them up to herself, just as one who is comfortable and leisurely upon her bed. Her hair, however, was as flames of fire, and her eyes were white like chalk. She had white shoes on her feet that were so slippery that she could neither stand nor walk. From her mouth she panted forth a poisonous froth. At her right breast she nursed a young dog; at her left breast she nursed a serpent. She plucked some flowers among the trees and some herbs from the grass, taking in their smell with her nose. She was not specially dressed, but was naked except for a cloak of fire, and because of her burning everything dried out near her, just like an open window. And Luxury said:

I will surround God's image with filth, even if it bothers God; in this way, I can ruin all things. For I am a glorious and high one and I draw all things to myself, which is the nature I was born with. Why should I restrain myself and why should I tear myself away from the favors of a luxurious life and a saving mind? If I accomplish only a small part of what I want to do, this is blameworthy? If, however, I don't do what my flesh demands, I will wind up angry, sad, deceitful, tormented and restless. Heaven has its desire for justice and earth has its ways too. If the nature of the flesh were really so troublesome to God, he would make it something we could possess less easily.

I again heard a voice from out of the storm cloud, the same one from the diadem of the king, giving an answer to this form, the voice of Charity:

I am not indifferent as you are, filthy one, with nothing to do here in the middle of your outrageous flaunting of yourself! I won't lie on that bed where you lie, where you play with wantonness. I do not speak poisonous words that teach slippery ideas, but instead I draw a drink of the sweetest water from the well of blessing since all my works have the coolness of God. For I sit in the sun and look at the King of Kings when I do all my good works freely. I do not want to be wounded with the uncleanness of that scorpion. I have joy in a pleasant life of honesty and modesty for the life I possess does not keep me back with blasphemy, lewdness and baseness. You, O most sordid creature, are yourself the ravening belly of the serpent, you who sprang from the ears of Adam and Eve as they listened to the serpent and let obedience vanish. But I come from the high Word of the Father. Heaven and earth will confound you when they see you naked and in confusion.[59]

We notice familiar imagery here, with the centrality of the serpent-scorpion figure that characterizes evil inclinations and the fetid breath that signals, in Hildegard's writing, the voice of hell. Notice the appeal to a wide array of the senses in the description of the vice, Luxury. There is a deliberate appeal to comfort of the flesh, sensual in regard to the body and its surroundings. Luxury misuses and does not appreciate these things, but the imagery is highly tactile. Throughout, we are pulled into the narrative itself, forced to imagine visually what is being described here, so that the eyes of the mind are involved. There is the smell of the breath, repulsing us from the figure of Luxury, as the sight of the nursing beasts means to do. Charity tastes cool and sweet water that comes directly from God. Moreover, we hear both speak. Charity points out that the words Luxury utters are those heard at the Fall with the cruel and evil deceptions of the serpent. Hearkening to these words will ultimately lead to Luxury's confusion and undoing when the real order of the world, heard in the Word of God, is made clear. All of the five human senses are of use in this debate between the vice and its rebuking virtue.

Using this example can place undue weight on a negative image of the feminine in Hildegard's work. The vices are by no means predominately human, let alone female. However, she personifies luxury in this way because of the connection woman has to the body and the flesh. In the commentary (42) she makes it clear that the intent of woman is childbearing, but the flesh can demand whatever desire and sin it can conjure up to obscure the natural intent. She virtually drags men into the flames of desire and concupiscence; she cannot stand because she rejects righteousness and stability. Parts 67–84 also discuss in detail the sins of the flesh, which people fall into because of Luxury. The conditions for repentance and for the cleansing of Luxury form the crux of the commentary. The attention to detail is also evident in our next example, from section 5, parts 9–11:

I saw the fifth image in the form of a woman at whose back there was a tree standing whose leaves had completely dried up. This image was entangled in the branches, for one branch went around her throat, and one over the top of her head, and another held her right arm and another her left. The branches were not outstretched but were tight around her, and the hands hung down from them with fingers like a raven's claws. Also, one branch from the right side of the tree and one from the left side were wrapped around her stomach and legs, surrounding them completely. Her feet were made out of the wood of this tree, however. This image did not wear any clothing except for the branches that surrounded it. Finally, wicked spirits had filled this tree with a black cloud and a horrible stench so that the tree itself bent and lamented. The Worldly Sadness said:

Alas, that I was ever created! Alas that I am alive! Who will help me? Who will free me? If God knew me, I would not be in such peril. Although I trust in God, he gives me nothing good; although I rejoice in him, he does not take away evil from me. I listen to a lot of things from philosophers who teach that there is much good in God, but God does not do any good for me. If he is my God, why does he hide all his grace from me? If he were to confer any good on me I might know him. I, however, do not know what I am. I was created for unhappiness, I was born into unhappiness, and I live without any consolation. Ah! what good is life without joy? Why was I created since there is no good for me?

I again heard a voice from the storm cloud respond to this image, and Heavenly Joy responded:

You do not know what you have said, O blind and deaf one. God created man bright, but through a transgression the serpent seduced man into this lake of misery. Look at the sun, moon and stars, at all the embellishments of the earth's greenness and consider how much prosperity God gives man with all these things, even when man sins against God with great temerity. You do not realize that salvation is from God. Who gives you these bright and good things unless it is God? When the day

57

rushes up to you, you call it night, when salvation is present to you, you name it a curse, and when good things come to you, you say they are evil. You are therefore from Hell! I, on the other hand, have heaven when I observe all the things God has created and you call noxious. I also gently gather into my lap roses and lilies and all greenness when I praise all God's works, while you only gather sorrow to yourself in yours. . . . The soul bears witness to heaven and the flesh bears witness to the earth; the flesh afflicts the soul; the soul, however, restrains the flesh. Therefore, foolish and blind one, think about what you have said.

Although a tree and its branches are being described in the case of the vice, it is only in the reply of the virtue that we get to Hildegard's characteristic affirmation of the life-giving principle, the greenness and moistness that enlivens the world by grace. Heavenly Joy describes how she collects flowers and *omnem viriditatem* in her lap; in the previous part she has spoken of the "embellishments of the earth's greenness" *(omnem ornatum viriditatis terrae)*. In contrast to the previous example, it would seem as though in this example the vividness of the senses comes with the language of the virtue as she speaks; Worldly Sadness seems paralyzed in body and speaks as though her mind were separated from it– she listens to philosophers, for example, but does not see the world of creation that surrounds her and of which she is a part. Hildegard often associates the life force of *viriditas* with images of flowers and flowering, growth and blooming. Here we see these themes strongly drawn to our attention, for the vice consists in blindness to the creation. What does the commentary have to say that would enlighten us further?

Parts 62 and 63 constitute the commentary on this vice, first speaking of cleansing punishments, then of repentance.

Concerning the Cleansing Punishments of Worldly Sorrow

I saw a dry and arid place, surrounded by darkness and full of vermin, and the souls of those who had drawn worldly sorrow to themselves while they had been alive were punished in this place. Wicked spirits drove them hither and yon holding fiery whips, shouting after them, "Why did you not put your trust in God?" Because their joy of heavenly things had not been strong, they were here; because they had lived with bitterness in their hearts, they were tortured by vermin; because they had neglected true and full blessedness, they suffered the contrariness of the darkness; and because they had been ensnared by these evils and lacked faith in God, they were pursued by these wicked spirits.

Concerning the Repentance of Worldly Sorrow

I saw and understood these things through the voice of the Living Light that said to me: These things that you see are true and are as you see them, and there are more things. Therefore, if those who have gathered worldly sorrow to themselves are eager to escape its punishments, let them turn to the spiritual life while they are alive. If they are already on a spiritual journey, let them follow the ordinary common strictness, let them submit themselves to humble obedience, and let them contemplate those Scriptures that bring them heavenly joy. However, let them not do all these things boldly, but only under the direction of a spiritual advisor.

The statements here are straightforward: first, there is a word picture of the destiny of those who have worldly sorrow and cling to it, again appealing to the eyes of the mind and the senses. The section on repentance brings forth the potential for hope, however, and gives common-sense spiritual guidance to those who may recognize something of themselves in the description and laments of Worldly Sorrow. There is one final section, which is a further expounding on Hildegard's understanding of God as the source of all life and meaning:

Concerning Fearful Worldly Sorrow

Worldly sorrow does not have the joy of heavenly things. It is like a wind that does not have the usefulness of greenness or dryness, but simply scatters everything it touches. Without a righteous stand anywhere, worldly sorrow says: "I do not know who or what is said to be God." As a result of not having spiritual breath, worldly sorrow dries up all living things. It is also divided into many parts so that it gathers many things to itself with sorrow and finds no joy in them, so that it does not call out to a friend with gladness, and so that it does not try to appease an enemy. After it has done all of this with sorrow, it hides itself in a hole like a snake because of its fear of all that passes by. It is similar to death, because it does not seek heavenly things, but it does not trust the world. Therefore, my zeal will fall upon it.

Here we find the explanation for the imagery surrounding the figure of Worldly Sorrow in part 9. Even when she draws the green, living tree to herself it dries up and surrounds and constrains her very being because she lacks the "breath of the Spirit," which is the presence of the living God. Again we see Hildegard's use of the natural world, its environs, and its elements as a crucial part of the point she is attempting to make, including the use of *viriditate*. We will see this microcosm of the world and the dense and moving imagery, used here to inspire repentance, and a good, upstanding moral life used in a more cosmic way in her final visionary-theological treatise, the *De operatione Dei*, to which we turn next. Before turning to this treatise, what can we say in brief summary about the *Liber vitae meritorum?*

Those who wish to place the three theological treatises in isolation from Hildegard's life will fail to see the importance of the setting

surrounding each of her works. Because of its moral tone and its purgatorial warnings, the second visionary treatise can be overlooked or un-
derappreciated in Hildegard's development as a writer, whereas it is a
vital link between the grander schemes of the macrocosm typical of the
first and third treatises. While Hildegard wrote the *Liber vitae meritorum*
she was beginning to undertake several of her traveling preaching tours,
which may also account for the subject of the work and the fact that it
was used in places other than the Rupertsberg. Interestingly, this work
mentions the matter of schismatics; although Hildegard was officially
taking a neutral stance toward Frederick Barbarossa at this time, the evidence here shows that instead of peace and concord, a divisiveness in the
attitudes of people promoted vice in its many forms. She may be speaking about the schism within the papacy as well as about situations of individuals. Considering her focus on the Rupertsberg and its flowering
into an independent convent at this time, plus her travels, the use of the
imagery around her in the world is a natural occurrence. The visionary
transformation of this imagery gives it a greater significance, but it is the
vision as expressed through Hildegard's sight, her "double vision," of
which we spoke previously.

In sum, the *Liber vitae meritorum* may enable us to better answer the
question of where the visions originate, even if the answer is not a complete one. The visions are part of Hildegard herself: as an incarnate woman
of the twelfth century with the life she led and the personality she possessed, she contributes her eyes and observations to the expression of
the visions. Yet she sees double: the words and insights are those that
God commands, perhaps using the very images that she and others would
best understand to communicate their meaning to the Christian world.
Hildegard may then be as inspired as she considered herself to be, but
we may not take it quite as literally. For, as with the study of Scripture,
we can see that inspiration requires the Spirit of God guiding the chosen,
incarnate human person in the task of writing what is revealed. And it is
this perfect blend of the two in Hildegard, which begins to fully emerge
in this treatise, that makes her able to be the first of the prophets of the
medieval world.

The De Operatione Dei

As we begin to look at her third and final theological-visionary treatise, the *De operatione Dei*,[60] we do well to bear in mind the significant part
the image of life-giving *viriditas* has played in the second treatise. For it is
in a combination of the macrocosm that is the first concern of the *Scivias*
and the microcosm that is the first concern of the *Liber vitae meritorum* that

this last and great treatise finds its center and its genius. Variously translated as "the activity of God" or "the works of God," the *De operatione Dei* is the visionary work belonging to Hildegard's mature years. It was composed and written between 1163 and 1173; its composition tends to be fixed closer to the latter date. During this time Hildegard continued all her former activities and added more as she was able. In addition to leading the community of the Rupertsberg she founded a daughter convent across the River Rhine at Eibingen in 1165; despite serious illnesses she completed two more preaching tours; aside from continuing her voluminous correspondence she took the emperor and the antipopes fiercely to task for dividing the Church of God. In her spare time she wrote several of her lesser works, including the *Life of St. Disibod* at the request of the abbot of Disibodenberg. Despite her age and the difficulties presented to her, we still find Hildegard in full command of her range of talents. She simultaneously uses them to one end: to proclaim the gospel and glorify God. Although her gifts were considered from the first to be prophetic in nature by others as well as by herself, it is during this last period of her life in which the prophetic gift is most supremely evident. We will look more carefully at her prophetic mission in chapter 6. Right now, we continue to look at her theological-visionary treatises, completing the trilogy by examining the scope and content of the *De operatione Dei*.

Despite the difficulties in getting an accessible critical translation of this work, it is often a favorite among twentieth-century authors and commentators with an interest in Hildegard as a figure relevant for us today. The reason behind this kindling of interest is the way in which Hildegard combines her previous themes and expresses them. The *De operatione Dei* is very much an analysis of the connection between the microcosm—the world of creation, especially of human beings—and the macrocosm—the universe as it is filled with and embraced by the Godhead. Some of the themes of the *Scivias* recur here, as we might expect; in one instance, Hildegard makes direct reference to her previous work in comparing the vision of the cosmic egg with the vision in the *De operatione Dei* of the universe in spherical form.[61] Another reason for its contemporary appeal is the use of female figures as personifications of not only the virtues, as in the *Liber vitae meritorum,* but also as figures that reflect the divine. Divine Love, or *Caritas,* and Wisdom, or *Sapientia,* are perhaps the most important of these figures. Moreover, this work has pictorial images of the visions, though less than in the *Scivias;* and while we are uncertain about whether they trace their ancestry back to the Rupertsberg scriptorium directly, they do indeed still complement the manuscript they accompany.[62] Finally, this visionary work seems to bring together the various threads of previous visions, combining them with lived experience and producing a final, great synthesis of Hildegard's perception of the world as God has revealed it to her, including the world to come when God will be "all in all."

The Structure and Contents of the De Operatione Dei

This final theological-visionary treatise has a decided structure which integrates the visionary's revelations and sheds light upon them. It is an occasionally repetitious work, as with Hildegard's other treatises; we need to be aware that for the visionary, God's repetition is divine command, and the spoken rather than the written version would seem less tedious if a point is stressed more than once. The *De operatione Dei*[53] is divided into three parts, again echoing the trinitarian nature of God: the first part concerns the world of humanity, the microcosm; the second part concerns the world of the hereafter, or human destiny; the third part concerns the history of salvation, or the macrocosm. Hildegard is presenting the Christian mystery in a cosmological context rather than a temporal one. The whole work comprises ten visions; the first part contains four visions that speak of the love God has for the created world, the second part consists of a single vision that shows the singular place of humanity in creation from the standpoint of morality and judgment; the third part has five visions that revolve principally around Hildegard's long meditation and exposition of the meaning of the prologue to the Gospel of John. The title itself has a multiple meaning. Humanity is the creation or "work" of God; the Incarnation is God's Word at "work" in the world, redeeming humanity and the whole cosmos; and human beings themselves cooperate in God's "work" through the Holy Spirit inspiring them to praise and to virtuous actions. As with her previous works, we will briefly summarize the visions themselves and the nature of the commentary, choosing several specific examples to give life to this summary by letting Hildegard's voice speak to us directly.

This treatise begins, as usual, with a prologue setting it in historical time and claiming the inspiration of the author. But perhaps we learn more about the inspiration behind the *De operatione Dei* through Hildegard's description of it in her *Vita* than we do from the prologue per se. This work was guided for her by an extraordinary vision in which she received insight into the meaning of the beginning of the Gospel of John:

> Some time later I had a marvelous vision so full of secrets that I was shaken in my inmost being, and I was out of my body and in a trance. For my consciousness was changed in such a way that I felt as if I did not know myself anymore. Just like gentle drops of rain, the Spirit of God entered my soul, just as the Holy Spirit imbued John the Evangelist when he received profound revelations which he sucked from the breast of Jesus where the hidden secrets were made known to him as he said: "In the beginning

was the Word" (John 1:1). For the Word, who was without beginning before creatures and who after them will be without end, ordered all creatures to be brought forth. And he did his work like the overseer who brings
his work to completion. What was decreed before the beginning of time in
his divine plan appeared now in a visible manner. Hence a human being
together with all creatures is the work of God. But a human being is also
the workman of God; he must be the shadow of the mysteries of God and
must reveal in every way the Blessed Trinity: he whom God made to his
image and likeness. Just as Lucifer by his evil could not destroy God, so
also he will not be able to destroy the nature of a person although he tried
to do that in the case of the first human beings.

This vision taught me every word of this Gospel which treats of the
work of God from the beginning and allowed me to expound it. And I
saw that this explanation would have to be the beginning of another writing which had not yet been revealed. In it, many questions of the divine
and mystery-laden creation will be examined.[64]

Several items worthy of note appear in this description. First, we
have the unusual statement that Hildegard was so profoundly moved
and shaken by this vision that she was taken out of herself. For one so
careful to speak about how her visions were all conscious, while she was
awake and aware, this sounds remarkably like ecstasy (the precise meaning of *ex stasis* is "to be taken out").

Apparently this vision, including the vital presence of the Divine
Word in eternity, so overwhelmed the normal state of human life that it
was distinctive. Second, the reason for this profound disturbance seems
to be the actual content of the visionary treatise. It attempts to link the
microcosmic universe of humanity and the rest of created being with the
eternal sphere of the Godhead in the macrocosmic sphere by means of
the indwelling of God in Word and Spirit. Third, the structure is quite
clear, and as we have described it above, in her own description of "man
as God's work" and also as "God's workman." This final visionary work
is both strongly inspired and carefully constructed, which Hildegard attributes to the unique quality of this overwhelming revelatory experience. Modern commentators, as we shall observe later, are more
comfortable in assigning this culminating vision to the congruence of
Hildegard's various sources of knowledge: the visions, certainly, but also
her encyclopedic knowledge of herbs and plants; her interest in biology
and its relationship to the sciences of the time, physical and metaphysi-
cal; and her possible acquaintance with theories of microcosm-macrocosm
from medieval and pagan sources.[65]

After situating the work in time and place, Hildegard goes on to the
first part of the treatise. There are four visions, each accompanied by a

pictorial representation. We notice that the link between the recounting of the visions and the commentary is much smoother and less separated from each other than we experience in her other works. All of the visions in this first part have to do with humanity and its place in the scheme of things; all of them represent humanity within a circular, mandala-like structure, which takes on different and more specific meanings in each of the subsequent visions. It is almost as if she is dissecting the layers of meaning found in the original revelation in spherical form, as we shall see.

• Vision 1 is about life: it revolves around a human figure with wings of splendor, which speaks of its power as the cause of all life, in which everything has its genesis. Themes of the seventeen parts of the vision are about the working of God in love for the sake of salvation, mentioning as reference points various crucial events in the history of the human race.

• Vision 2 is a vision of the world in which we get a glimpse of the re-lationship between microcosm and macrocosm. A circle emerges from the winged figure's center. At the center of the wheel is a human figure, point-ing to humanity as the center of creation with a special relationship to cre-ated things. The Godhead still surrounds the circle and encompasses it.

• Vision 3 is of the body and indicates its nature and its sources of en-ergy; the figure at the center of the wheel seems to be more anatomical.

• Vision 4 relates the human body to the rest of the universe, show-ing the connection between specific parts of the body and their moral functions, their relationship to the stars and to the rest of creation. It shows a close-up of the entire macrocosm in the visual image that accom-panies this vision. It is at the end of this section and this part of the book that Hildegard concludes the gloss on John's Gospel, mentioned above, and a section on the seasons and the calendar of human existence.

Part 2 consists of a single visionary section (vision 5) in which she sees the world beyond the body, commenting on Genesis specifically, and how creation is arranged. Each element has both a natural function and an allegorical meaning connecting the senses to morality as in the *Liber vitae meritorum* but showing an advance in her conceptualization of these relationships.

Part 3 consists of five visions that return to the familiar theme of salva-tion. However, their emphasis is not so much historical as it is spatial, linking the world of divine revelation to the world as human beings experience it.

• Vision 6 portrays a city with fortified walls, embodying allegorically the structure of God's predestined knowledge of the history of salvation.

• Vision 7 is the city at work, preparing for the incarnation and coming of Christ.

• Vision 8 is a vision of the work of Love, showing us a striking image of three female figures who, while reminiscent of the virtues as they are pictorially represented in the *Scivias,* have an even deeper and more profound meaning here. They stand in or on a fountain of living waters that irrigate the city, and they guard and defend the fountain.

• Vision 9 speaks of the interlocking operation of two of the allegorical feminine figures, Divine Wisdom and Power.

• Vision 10 is of the fulfillment that will come with the end of time, which will not end in the sense of closure but will be perfected by eternity. Here we find the third feminine personification, Divine Love.

Specific Examples from the De Operatione Dei

We will use three key passages for a closer look at the style, tone, and meaning of the *De operatione Dei.* The first passage will be from the opening in Vision 1; the second passage from the exposition on the Gospel of John in Vision 4; the third passage from Visions 8 and 10, pondering the meaning of the female personifications and the final, cosmic vision. We begin with the opening passage in Vision 1, where the voice of the figure you see in the accompanying illustration speaks out in this way:

I, the highest and fiery force, have kindled every spark of life and emit nothing that is of death. I decide on all reality. With my lofty wings I fly above the globe, and with wisdom I have rightly put the Universe in order. I, the fiery life of divine essence, blaze beyond the beauty of the fields, I gleam in the waters, and burn in the sun, moon, and stars. With every breeze, as with an all-sustaining invisible force, I awaken all things to life. The air lives by turning green and being in bloom. The waters flow as if alive. The sun lives in its light, and the moon is enkindled, after its disappearance, once again by the light of the sun so that the moon is again revived. The stars, too, give a clear light with their beaming. I have established pillars that bear the entire globe as well as the power of the winds that, once again, have subordinate wings—weaker winds, so to say—which by their gentle power resist the mighty winds in a way that they cannot become dangerous. In the same way, too, the body envelops the soul and maintains it so that the soul does not blow away. For just as the breath of the soul strengthens and fortifies the body so that it does not disappear, the more powerful winds, too, revive the surrounding winds so that they can provide their appropriate service.

And thus I remain hidden in every kind of reality as a fiery power. Everything burns because of Me in such a way as our breath constantly moves us, like the wind-tossed flame in a fire. All of this lives in this essence, and there is no death in it. For I am life. I am also Reason, which bears within itself the breath of the resounding Word, through which the whole of the creation is made. I breathe life into everything so that nothing is mortal in respect to its species. For I am Life . . . all life has its roots in me. Reason is the root, the resounding Word blooms out of it. . . . For this life is God, who is always in motion and constantly in action, and yet this life is manifest in a threefold power. For eternity is called the "Father," the Word is called the "Son," and the breath that binds them both together is called the "Holy Spirit." And God has likewise marked humanity; in human beings there are body, soul, and reason. . . . God created men and women in the divine image and likeness.

Hildegard explains to us that with its wings the figure embraces saints and sinners alike (although in different places), uniting the love of God and the love of neighbor in faith (5, 11). This figure wears a garment that glows brilliantly, representing the Son (12); the lower face shines "with starry light," representing persons who defend the faith (9); the celestial choir of angels is "dazzling" (8); and in 1.10 there is a reference to God creating the angels and then humanity by the command "Let there be light." The figure stands on and tramples all that is dark and without life (see figure 6).

In this first vision, two of Hildegard's favorite images prevail throughout, forming the axis of her theological insights. One we have just described is that of light, which is evident in the use of fire as a continual image in this passage. Light in all its forms speaks to us of God: whether it is in the brilliance of the Living Light; the reflection of that brilliance as we perceive it in the partial way that we can withstand, its presence in the created cosmos in sun, moon, and stars; its reflective shining, glowing presence in the waters. Light is life itself, and it illuminates us, quite literally, by enabling us to see that the light we see is the light of the truth, justice, and love of God. The second favorite image, is, of course, the principle of the life force. This is mainly expressed in *viriditas* and the images of flowering, blooming, greening, and growing. In the quotation, the very air turns "green" *(viriditas)* and blooms. From the fiery essence life emerges in the form of light and freshness. *Viriditas* is closely associated with water or moisture, and we see this in the sentence that follows, where the fiery essence "gleams in the waters." We are constantly and consistently reminded that the life-giving power lies in the combination of elements, all which are constituted in God: fiery brightness, the moistness of blooming greenness.

In addition to these motifs are added the feminine images of Wisdom and Reason, which will be depicted in the later personification of *Sapientia*. Many of the nouns in the above passage are feminine in Latin and may also indicate a greater willingness to use the feminine in connection with the divine, both in language and in personification.[66] While in the *Scivias* Hildegard preferred to speak more about divine revelation than about reason, here in the *De operatione Dei* reason is incorporated into the totality of the divine *and* into the image and likeness of the divine, which we discover in women and men. Reason blooms

FIGURE 6

forth from the root of the Word; reason is within that Eternal Word. The Word is the connection between the macrocosm and the microcosm. It is the living God entering the microcosm in the incarnation of the Word; through the resurrection of the Word, God will bring the faithful to full bloom in the macrocosm at the end of time. Reason is fundamentally connected to inspiration and life in and with God; conversely, inspiration is the root and foundation for hearing God's Word and thus having the ability to reason. Hildegard's theological argument and her imagery convey their sense in a few words with the help of a stunning set of visual pictures with their uncharacteristic (for the twelfth-century West) circular shape.[67] This intuitive, inductive presentation is breathtaking in its simplicity and its complexity and is extremely powerful in its impact on the hearer or reader.

The same terms, images, and lessons are drawn from the beginning of Hildegard's commentary on John 1:1 in Vision 4.105. It is interesting to contrast the approach and style of the two passages. She begins explicitly with the Scripture and theological intent in this selection. She begins for once with a *text and what she hears* instead of what she sees and then understands. Notice its complementarity with the first passage:

> I who without origin and from whom every beginning goes forth, I who am the Ancient of Days, do declare that I am the day by myself alone. I am the day that does not shine by the sun; rather by me the sun is ignited. I am the Reason that is not made perceptible by anyone else; rather, I am the One by whom every reasonable being draws breath. And so to gaze at my countenance I have created mirrors in which I consider all the wonders of my originality, which will never cease. I have prepared for myself these mirror forms so that they may resonate in a song of praise. . . . Afterward, I spoke within myself my small deed, which is humanity. I formed this deed according to my own image and likeness so that it would be realized with respect to myself as my Son intended to take on the garment of flesh as a man. I have established in a spiritual way this deed of mine through my Reason and indicated my possibility in it, just as the human spirit comprehends everything in its artistic ability through names and numbers. Only by names can humanity grasp the essence of a thing, and only by numbers can humanity know the multiplicity of things.

We hear the theme of light recurring, with an emphasis on the fact that it is the One, God, from whom light and reason come. Again, humanity is made in the image and likeness of the One as embodied in the Son. Interestingly, instead of using her imagery of blossoming in this passage, she replaces it with that of "mirroring," which is not only suitable in Hildegard's thinking for the reflection of the Light in all created things but is the place in which a meeting between microcosm and macrocosm may take place, however indirect. In this she echoes Paul as well as John and clearly links herself to the mystical tradition of using mirror imagery. Humanity grasps the essence of things in naming, the multiplicity of things in counting. At this point, Hildegard has already spent quite a bit of time with the microcosm, explicitly linking human attributes to macrocosmic structures. She will continue to do so in the next section, going through the parts of the body and connecting the senses to the divine purpose: the head shows our reasoning power and artistic abilities; our eyes allow us to clarify and distinguish things, reflecting how God foresees all; our hearing lets us know the sound of glory in hidden mysteries and the heavenly host; our sense of smell allows access to the fragrance of order and wisdom; and through our mouth, in speaking, we echo the reality of God's Word. Whereas we have spent time looking closely at the presence and figure who joins the microcosm and macrocosm, most of the detail in the first part is devoted to a discussion of how the seasons, the humors, the winds, and the stars all affect one another; the reciprocal relationship that exists between the parts of creation; and how each part of creation may become "fruitful." Fertility is likened to the moistened earth, which brings forth the growth of plant life and pertains to the spiritual as well as to the material realms (Vision 4.22):

> For just as the Word of God has penetrated everything in creation, the soul penetrates the whole body in order to have an effect on it. The soul is the _viriditas_ of the flesh. For indeed, the body grows and progresses through the soul just as the Earth becomes fruitful through moisture.

When virtue is allied to _viriditas_ (greening life force), then a powerful tool for good exists in the world; and virtue is cultivated through a life turned toward God, participating in the Church of Christ and the sacraments in order that one might grow in holiness.

This brings us to the third example we are going to consider from the _De operatione Dei_. At the culmination of the work, in Visions 8 and 10, we have the feminine personifications of three persons shown in these visions, representing Humility, Charity, and Wisdom. These visions are toward the end of the third part (and of the book), after Hildegard has taken quite a bit of time to carefully set up in this part the meaning of history as it is discovered in the coming of Christ. Vision 8 includes a vision of the heavenly city, but its first task is to introduce us to three female figures, standing in and around a fountain:

> I saw three forms in the midst of the above mentioned southern regions. Two of them stood in a very clear well, which was encircled and crowned by a round, porous stone. They seemed rooted in the well, so to speak,

69

just as trees at times seem to grow in water. One form was encircled by such a purple glimmer and the second by such a dazzlingly white brilliance that I could not bear to look fully at them. The third form stood outside the well and on the stone. It was clothed in a dazzlingly white garment, and its countenance radiated such splendor that my own face had to draw back from it. And the first figure said:

I, Love, am the glory of the living God. Wisdom has done her work with me, and Humility rooted in the living fountain is my helper and Peace is her companion. By the splendor that I am the living light of the blessed angels glows for as a ray of light shines from the source so this splendor shines in the blessed angels. Nor could it do otherwise, since no light lacks radiance. It was I who designed humanity, which is rooted in me like a reflection in water. Hence I am the living fountain, because all created things were reflected in me; and according to this reflection humanity was made with fire and water, as I myself am both fire and living water. . . . My splendor overshadowed the prophets, who by holy inspiration foretold the future just as everything God wished to make was a shadow until God made it a reality. But Reason utters her voice, and the sound of the voice is like thought, the spoken word as a deed. Out of this shadow the book *Scivias* emerged, through a woman who was but a shadow of strength and health because these vital forces were not at work in her. But the living well is the Spirit of God, a fountain that he distributes among all his works which also draw life from him and possess vitality through him, like reflections in water. No being can plainly see whence it derives life, but each obscurely senses what moves it.

Love, or *Caritas,* is the central figure, explaining the rest to the visionary. It is noteworthy that there is a passing reference to the *Scivias* and the divine inspiration of that work (and by implication, this). The image of the root is again a predominant one. As in the *Liber vitae meritorum* where the figure stands in the waters of the abyss, and as in the previous sections of this visionary treatise, where something is rooted and stands is essential in determining its nature and quality. These personifications of virtue and of the work of the divine are rooted in a well of living water, pure water in whose reflection all things receive life. We again have the image of mirroring and overshadowing, reflecting the divine in the created world. All of the created world appears splendid in that reflection; moreover, Hildegard is pointing to how humility as a virtue, informed by Love and Wisdom, leads human beings to peace. So the virtues a person may possess are rooted in the Spirit of God as though in living water and emanate from Reason, which is the discovered harmony of *Caritas* and *Sapientia.*

In the final vision, 10, the figure of *Caritas* appears alone:

Then I saw, next to the mountain in the middle of the eastern region, a Wheel of wonderful circumference, that seemed like a blinding white cloud.

To the east I saw a dark line on the left, looking like a man's breath and reaching almost all the way to the right. On the middle of the wheel and above this line another line appeared, shimmering like the morning dawn, and it descended from the top of the Wheel down to the middle of the first line. The upper part of this half-wheel emitted a green brilliance from the left side right to the middle, while from the right side there was a reddish sheen, also right to the middle, and it all happened precisely so that both brilliances shared the same space. The halves of the Wheel, however, that lay under the line showed themselves to be a whitish color mixed with black.

And behold! in the middle of this Wheel I saw on top of the line a figure who at the start of these visions was called Love. But now I saw her adorned differently than earlier. Her face lit up like the sun, her clothes shone purplish, and around her neck she had a golden band adorned with costly gems. She wore shoes like lightening bolts.

Before the figure's face appeared a tablet that gleamed like crystal. And on it was inscribed: "I will show myself in beauty, shining like silver; for the Godhead, which is without beginning, shines in ever greater splendor." Everything that has a beginning is contradictory in its fearful thereness; such a thing cannot grasp fully the mysteries of God. The figure looked up at the tablet. And as soon as she did, the line on which she sat began to move. And there where the left side of the Wheel was attached, the outer side of the Wheel became a little watery for a narrow space and then—above the halves of the divided wheel that lay under the line—it became reddish and finally pure and brilliantly clear, but then again became cloudy and stormy near the end of the half of the wheel where the line was linked. And I heard a voice from heaven which said to me: *O Human, hear and understand the Words of the One who was there and Who Is, without suffering the transformations of time.*

If this vision is more difficult to follow, it is necessarily so. For at this juncture Hildegard is struggling to put into words what is clear to her from the start and which she cannot speak of any more than she can fully see or perceive this reality. We have reached the vision of God's plan for the end of time: no matter how much might be revealed to us about the divine plan and our destiny, it will all still remain shrouded in mystery. In this vision Hildegard is linking her extraordinary visual capacities with her visionary insight to show us that just as the picture seemingly comes into focus, the Wheel itself shifts, and we once again must rely on the glimpses we have of the divine life and on the faith of things believed in but not seen.

The *De operatione Dei* ends on a highly affirmative but deeply mystical note. The magnificence and glory of God in the green *(viriditas)* brilliance and the fiery radiance of light and life come together and reflect on the seer until movement prevents us from being fully blinded by the enormity of eternity and the splendor of the Living Light.

The De Operatione Dei: *Observations and Remarks*

The last of Hildegard's theological-visionary treatises embraces the former two, not superseding them but rather bringing their themes to a conclusion at once stunningly abstract and firmly concrete. In this treatise we range from the particular connections within the microcosm that affect the growth of vegetation and human health to the heights of the meaning of the eternal, which is reflected to us in small part through the Light. The tone of the work is calm, almost regal; its structure serves the visionary insights and vice versa. Intuition and rationality seem to come together in harmony, even as Wisdom and Charity do, to the point of melding in our perception of them. The themes of God as the source of all things and all things going back to their source, the theme of the macrocosm and the microcosm and how they are joined, is fraught with the terminology of *viriditas,* light, water, blossoming, and all things that signify the blessings of God to Hildegard. There is a great deal of parallelism in her use of words which is not sufficiently captured by the English translation but which can be perceived only in the Latin; this is true in many of her other works too. *Viriditas* conjoins with *virtus* (virtue), *vis* (strength), and *vivere* (life). This parallelism in language is one of the ways, apart from her theological insights and visual motifs, that she unites in her works yet keeps their distinctness intact.

Holding the center of the work together is the ever more elusive but definite emphasis on the centrality of the incarnation as the method whereby the microcosm and macrocosm meet and are able to establish a form of mutuality. In mentioning this theme we do well also to point to the fact that in any of Hildegard's discussions of the incarnate Word she is also implicitly evoking the feminine imagery of Mary, the Mother of God, through whom the Word was made flesh. This will become much more apparent in a study of her musical works, for example, although it is certainly a major theme in the treatises.

The *De operatione Dei* seamlessly unites word (text) and image (visuals). It does not have the evocative, imaginative language of the *Liber vitae meritorum,* nor does it possess the overwhelming inductive seductiveness of the visions as they are portrayed artistically in the miniatures that accompany the *Scivias.* We might say, if forced to choose, that the last treatise swings over to the primacy of text in its reliance on the Word and its incorporation of the image of Reason.

The Theological-Visionary Treatises and the Mystical Polyphony of Hildegard

One of the only real drawbacks in trying to give the reader a comprehensive view of the intricacies of Hildegard's theological-visionary treatises through the use of examples is the necessity of doing the works an injustice. No selections could possibly tie all of Hildegard's many images and overlapping concerns together completely. In the *Scivias* we have examined the doctrinal elements of her work at the expense of the more cosmic and lofty parts of the treatise; in the *Liber vitae meritorum* we have sacrificed the wider scope of incarnational salvation for a close look at the meaning of virtue and vice; finally, in the *De operatione Dei* we have emphasized the glory of God in the macrocosm who is present to the microcosm at the expense of the detailed, technical, and concrete analysis of the microcosm itself.

However, it is important to note what is overlooked at this stage, since many of these themes will be taken up in detail, as we look at Hildegard through the lens of her other interests and talents. The microcosm is the focus of her works on biology, plants, and healing; the incarnational will be the central theme of her song cycles and letters; the cosmic dimensions have been glimpsed in her final work and will be seen again in her references to the heavenly realms encountered in liturgical practices and song. Despite the shortcomings of any overview of these treatises that attempts to treat their individual characteristics as well, we get the big picture of what Hildegard has seen in her visions and some of the important and idiosyncratic details.

It is exactly the distinct yet united form of the mystical treatises in all their aspects that creates the polyphonic mysticism so typical of Hildegard. Although not focusing on an interior path to God that should be followed in the spiritual life, as many mystics do, she demonstrates what she knows and has been shown of that path. Moreover, that path is accessible and recognizable to a vast number of people in all walks of life: this is the strongest note sounded in the *Liber vitae meritorum*. These virtues and vices would be readily recognizable. In one fashion or another, Hildegard's visions lead the hearer or reader into the center of the divine mystery, which is the Incarnation. All centers on the Word made Flesh and the likeness and image that humankind has to God. In the *De operatione Dei* the revelation and explanation of the cosmos as seen through the lens of John 1:1 is both supremely mystical (as is the Johannine literature) and very tangible in the sacrament of creation itself. For a more particular appeal to sacramentality, especially as brought to us through Christ's salvific actions in human history, we have the approach of the *Scivias,* which enfleshes the whole scope of salvation history in a sequence of arresting visual images and textual commentaries.

The three questions with which we began have also overlapped and yet shown change and permutation. The primacy of image over text moves from the centrality of the illustrations in understanding the *Scivias,* to the more imaginative use of the visual in the *Liber vitae meritorum,* and finally to a meshing of text and image in the *De operatione Dei,* ironically the treatise in which she is first able to contemplate with any equanimity "rationality" and "ecstasy," having seen them united in her visions. The source of her authority remains the same, the words directly from God yet asserted in differing tones; and as we have seen, the medium of the message may herself have been chosen by God precisely to be able to convey things as she saw them. If we take a more secular approach, we still must acknowledge that whatever Hildegard brings to the experience of the visions was, for her, only understood in the context of the authoritative voice of God commanding her to speak and write. The feminine as a theme emerges kaleidoscopically throughout the works, clearly coming to a stronger resolution in the *De operatione Dei* but which she herself says has been present to her in the visions since the earliest times; it is her expression of the feminine that changes, not its essential grasp or content. In the *Liber vitae meritorum* the passages used show women personified in positive and negative contexts; whereas only some of the vices are shown as female all of the virtues appear in feminine form when rebuking them![68]

Hildegard's treatises are obviously visionary, claiming revelation from the Living Light as her source. We have seen that the Light may have been filtered through the constitutive qualities of a particular creature but that it need not invalidate the sense of divine origin. Quite the opposite, if we trace the attitude of Hildegard toward the revelations in these three works: it is only in a woman that an effeminate age is rebuked, to one who is lowly in status that the Most High will be revealed. Hildegard's illness and frailty also stand as a testament to the strength she gained from the presence of the Living Light of God: such things are not revealed through one whose life is easy or peaceful but through one who has experienced a great deal of adversity.

Hildegard's treatises are obviously theological, because they present the Christian faith in ways that could be recognized, understood, and heeded in the world of the twelfth century. Good theology interprets faith for its times; great theology carries over its insights into centuries other than its own. Even if Hildegard will not claim the theological construction of these treatises or the theological insights embedded in them as her own work, they nonetheless stand as creative theological treatises that speak eloquently of God, faith, humanity, creation, and Church.

Hildegard's treatises fit into our schema of mystical polyphony in the way we have just described. Never is a theme submerged or lost in the three treatises, although some motifs or melodies receive more attention at different points in the overall composition. They weave and interweave, coming back with renewed interest and a new way of seeing a theological insight or visionary motif throughout the treatises, and in this way they are polyphonic. There are not only a variety of notes in a single line (chant) but several lines with their own variety of notes that overlap to intentionally create moments of lingering harmony (polyphony). Hildegard does not appear as in hymn form, harmonizing all and using only grand chords, but balances and alternates the solo and plural harmonies of her works. Her mysticism lies not only in her own experience—for which many would prefer to regard her as a visionary or a prophet alone—but in the fact that this experience is for us a glimpse into things unseen, with markers and pathways for finding our own way there. The vivifying forces of greenness, the reflection of the light, the mirroring of the divine in the human in creation and incarnation, the cultivation of virtue and the reason for hating vice, these are all presented to us not as an abstract thesis but as a call to fit into God's overall plan by drinking from the pure fountain of grace.

In the modern attempt to reconcile the strange and alien quality of Hildegard's world with our own, we too often become preoccupied with the familiar ways in which we think and feel to really take in what it is she is trying to convey. For in order to hear the song of her mystical polyphony, all the senses must be attuned to what she presents. What she presents is not merely a text, or a picture, or a vision, or an explanation. It is all of these and more. What she presents is the opportunity to experience and to synthesize all of these—as she does—into something even more sublime: an intuitive if shadowy grasp of the reality and reasons for which the world was created by God. She herself would never belittle the parts as mere means to the whole: after all, she uses them all with great care. But, as we see at the final closing of all the theological-visionary treatises, in the end there is nothing but entrance into the wonderful mystery of God. In the *De operatione Dei* we are brought close to a vision of the heavenly realms; in the *Liber vitae meritorum* we are challenged to ascend to God with the aid of grace and virtue; in the *Scivias* we end by being subsumed into the choir of angels and the heavenly chorus.

Having thoroughly looked at her theological-visionary treatises, we now turn to the heavenly chorus as the work of God. The next chapter explores the role of music and liturgical form in Hildegard's life, the source and connecting strands of her mystical polyphony. Before doing so, however, we should discuss one last concept central to the theological-visionary treatises and her music: the idea and ideal of virginity. It is a concept thought of today in physical rather than spiritual terms, but for Hildegard it was a foreshadowing and celebration of the joining of heaven and earth.

Hildegard held virginity in high esteem. In the case of women in the Middle Ages, it allowed them to be more independent than they otherwise might have been; Hildegard regarded virgins consecrated to God as almost "virile," meaning manly but implying strength and power. Their calling to be virgins wholly set upon Christ as their aim in life set them apart from others. Hildegard admired virginity in men or women. But the combination of her life among women, her strong belief in the special call virginity had for women, and her feminine imagery of the divine, which connected the two, shows us that Hildegard's ideal of virginity was one of her central concepts.

Her celebration of virginity in her own community brought her complaints from others, at least in the form of a letter and a reply that are extant. Her non-traditional and exalted notions seemed to others a result of social class combined with inexcusable excess. She is delicately but definitely challenged about why the sisters do not emulate the poverty of Christ rather than adorn themselves in this excerpt from a letter of Tengswich of Andernach in 1148–1150:

> We have, however, also heard about certain strange and irregular practices that you countenance. They say that on feast days your virgins stand in the church with unbound hair when singing the psalms and that as part of their dress they wear white, silk veils, so long that they touch the floor. Moreover, it is said that they wear crowns of gold filigree, into which are inserted crosses on both sides and the back, with a figure of the Lamb on the front, and that they adorn their fingers with golden rings. . . . Moreover, that which seems no less strange to us is the fact that you admit into your community only those women from noble, well-established families and absolutely reject others who are of lower birth and of less wealth. Thus we are struck with wonder and are reeling in confusion when we ponder quietly in our heart that the Lord himself brought into the primitive Church . . . poor people.[69]

By the end of the letter Tengswich is practically brimming with irony in her "humble" request for Hildegard to explain these marvels to one so simple. Dronke has noted that Tengswich was the mistress of a founder of canonnesses on the Rhine, a type of religious order that by their statutes were usually foundations for the aristocrats of the highest nobility in the empire and greatly exclusive.[70] Yet her challenge and criticisms are very clear; few spoke to Hildegard in this manner. Perhaps as a social "equal" she considered herself suitable to question these practices.

Hildegard's reply is to stress that virgins are unlike other women, since they are betrothed to Christ. Her practices are to be reminders of the time of paradise, when fallen nature was not dominant in the world. It is not worldly vanity that is the cause for adornment, but to mirror the coming splendor of all Christian souls, which can only be imitated here by the splendid brides of Christ. She begins by acknowledging that worldly vanity has no place in the Christian life of women, especially married ones. Then she defends such practices in this way:

> But these strictures do not apply to a virgin, for she stands in the unsullied purity of paradise, lovely and unwithering, and she always remains in the full vitality of the budding rod. A virgin is not commanded to cover up her hair, but she willingly does so out of her great humility, for a person will naturally hide the beauty of her soul, lest, on account of her pride, the hawk carry it off.
>
> Virgins are married with holiness in the Holy Spirit and in the bright dawn of virginity, and so it is proper that they come before the great High Priest as an oblation presented to God. Thus through permission granted her and the revelation of the mystic inspiration of the finger of God, it is appropriate for a virgin to wear a white vestment, the lucent symbol of her betrothal to Christ, considering that her mind is made one with the interwoven whole, and keeping in mind the One to whom she is joined, as it is written: "Having his name, and the name of his Father, written on their foreheads" [Apoc. 14:1] and also "These follow the Lamb withersoever he goeth" [Apoc. 14:14].[71]

As to Tengswich's complaints about the nobility of those she accepts in the convent, she appeals to the fallen state in which we find ourselves and says it is better not to yoke "an ox and ass" together. The mixing of rank might lead to a greater awareness of the worldly privileges of birth rather than assure that no one has cause to compare in this way. It is Hildegard's argument from equality by admitting only the nobility.[72]

Later on, when Guibert of Gembloux was to ask her many things about her visions, her convent, and her life, she sent back a reply to his own questions about dress:

> As for tiaras: I saw that all the ranks of the Church have bright emblems in accord with the heavenly brightness, yet virginity has no bright emblem—nothing but a black veil and an image of the cross. So I saw that this would be the emblem of virginity: that a virgin's head would be covered with a white veil, because of the radiant-white robe that human beings had in paradise, and lost. On her head would be a circlet with three colours conjoined into one—an image of the Trinity—and four roundels attached: the one on the forehead showing the lamb of God, that on the right a cherub, that on the left an angel, and on the back a human being—all these inclining towards the Trinity. This emblem, granted to me, will proclaim blessings to God, because he had clothed the first man in radiant brightness.[73]

By this time in her life, Hildegard has more fully thought out and more carefully explained not only the reasons for a particular style of dress but also the glory intended to give to God through such a symbolic adornment. For Hildegard, so liturgical and so visual, this revelation and its enactment must have been comforting and uplifting in a way difficult to describe. Her sisters are not only being wedded to the Bridegroom but are also imaging what that marriage means, becoming a part of God through virtue. It was obviously of importance to Hildegard that "brightness" be part of the dress of those betrothed to God; they should not always seem as black clouds, which misrepresent their vocation and their purpose. We see this link in a letter describing the figure of *Caritas,* whom she sees in a vision as a girl with a shining face, a white cloak, and golden shoes. The girl holds the moon and sun in her right hand and on her breast there is an ivory tablet with an image of a sapphire man. Every creature called this girl *domina:*

> And I heard a voice saying to me: This girl that you see is Divine Love, and she has her dwelling place in eternity. For when God wished to create the world, He bent down in sweetest love and He provided for all necessary things, just as a father prepares the inheritance for his son. Thus it was that in great ardor He established all His works in order. Then all creation in its various kinds and forms acknowledged the Creator, for in the beginning divine love was the matrix from which He created all things, when He said, Let there be, and it was done. Thus every creature was formed through divine love in the twinkling of an eye.[74]

Hildegard goes on to describe the meaning of the allegory, likening divine love to the Virgin Mary. A further link with virginity in general is made when she describes Hope as the eye of Divine Love, Celestial Love as her heart, and abstinence, which links the two.[75] Here, in her letters, Hildegard reflects in practice the convictions of her theological-visionary treatises. Even if the adornments were only for special occasions or only one special occasion, she has embodied her own vision of paradise to draw people closer to what they were at their creation. The feminine is in the divine, and on earth virginity reflects that splendor in whatever way it is possible in an imperfect world.

This ideal of virginity, its personification in the Virtues, and its link to the Virgin Mary indicate that this was something Hildegard not only believed to be true but sought to enact the meeting between the celestial and terrestrial realms in concrete ways. As we turn to her musical gifts we should bear in mind that it is possible the "costuming" so condemned above may have been a visual accompaniment to her play, the *Ordo virtutum,* with its feminine personification of the virtues, all in an attempt to join the heavenly chorus through musical praise of God.

III

Bringing the Strands Together: The Gift of Music

Hildegard of Bingen is recognizable to many not as an author or medieval visionary but primarily through her musical works. Her difficult theological-visionary works and an interest in the historical woman she was often stems from an interest in her as a composer. Interestingly, Gregorian chant has and is undergoing something of a revival, beginning in the late twentieth century and continuing today. Along with this revival Hildegard's works enjoy a popularity that could hardly have been imagined even a decade ago outside of specialist circles. Granted, those who have popularized Hildegard musically are rarely purists, just as those who popularized her prose works were not. No matter what the cause, those interested at first only in the popular modernized albums, such as *Vision* and *Vox Diadema*,[76] continue on to pursue recordings of Hildegard's music by the less well known classical ensembles (who have been gradually putting out performances of her music for the last decade or so). Despite wrangling about the appropriateness of adaptation and modernization, or scholarly disputes concerning the style in which her works ought to be performed for those attempting to replicate an authentic twelfth-century sound, Hildegard's unusual musical style remains a compelling source of musical creativity and interest.

A constant source of her own inspiration and creativity, her music and the liturgy were pivotal points of Hildegard's complex life. We know that she began to compose music early in her public career, perhaps before, and continued to do so for the rest of her life. As we have seen in the discussion of the shaping forces of her life, liturgical music would have figured prominently among these. By the time Hildegard was inquiring about the veracity of the *Scivias* she had been immersed in liturgical rhythms and liturgical music for over thirty years. There is a temptation, just as there is with all of Hildegard's many works, to examine and appreciate only one part of her work, as if it stood apart from everything else she was as a person. This can be especially true with her musical compositions. Their very loveliness and unusual qualities can be enjoyed by a range of persons, from musicologists to the average listener, without reference to the larger framework of her life or historical setting. But to do so is to miss some of the rich allusiveness of the pieces themselves and to cheat ourselves of placing them within the monastic environment in which they emerged and distinguished themselves. For example, Hildegard's constant allusions to Scripture in her musical works show a woman deeply steeped in the musical and cyclical framework of the liturgical year. She rarely quotes directly from the Scriptures in her music; however, there are echoes of it everywhere in her choice of words and melodies. She is still very much her own self in her musical compositions, though. Her own favorite theological themes and wording come through in the rendering of her song cycle into both poetry and sound. Themes with which we are familiar from the theological-visionary works and from the general movement of her life will obviously be reflected in her own compositions. It may be helpful to remind ourselves once again of the alien quality the Middle Ages presents to us today and to spend a moment explaining exactly how the structure of an agricultural society and the monastic life of the twelfth century could so dominate not only a pattern of living but a way of seeing life.

As we have remarked before, the twelfth century was a time of intense religious turbulence and revival. Although many wrongs were being committed in the name of Christianity (and Hildegard was never hesitant to point them out), there was renewal as well. But neither the crises nor the revivals in spirituality would have the impact they did were the concept of reality not ultimately founded on a totally Christian worldview. Stretching it to the limits, we might say it was a world in which the transcendent and the divine were realities not questioned in and of themselves. Their expressions might vary, including everything from an awareness of the Saracens as pagans (having another religious outlook) to the combat against Christian heresies. It was a profoundly religious outlook and not a separate category from the daily affairs of life. In a monastic setting these assumptions were underlined and reinforced by the daily pattern of life. The *Opus Dei,* the works of God, were the liturgical Hours that structured the monastic day with song, prayer, and praise of God. They began with Matins during the night, then proceeded to Lauds, the praise of God at the dawning of the day. Prime was sung at the first hour of the day, around six A.M.; Terce at the third hour, nine A.M.; Sext at the sixth hour or noon

80

prayer; None at the ninth hour, three P.M.; then Vespers, sung at the time of dusk and parallel to Lauds in purpose and form; finally Compline, night prayer before retiring. This gave a regular and obvious structure to the day, which had an eternally cyclical form. In between the times when the Divine Office was celebrated, the work that supported the inhabitants of the monastery needed to be done, especially during the daylight hours. Time was also to be set aside for individual contemplation or spiritual reading, such as *lectio divina*. In Hildegard's time the Divine Office in Bene-dictine life was structured in such a way that all one hundred and fifty psalms contained in the Psalter would be sung or recited in the period of a single week.[77] Because of the need for introductory pieces and responses to all of these readings, medieval chant and sequences were written with regu-larity by those who were musically talented in order to accommodate and embellish the cycles of divine praise. This required a number of different forms: sequences, antiphons, responsaries, and hymns. In addition there were special holy days (our "holiday") on which a specific saint or liturgi-cal event was to be celebrated and for which specific musical compositions were intended. Thus the praise of God included both repetition and end-less variation; it should have enough familiarity in order for the recitation or singing to have an inner, meditative effect on those occupied in God's praise but enough diversity to celebrate the myriad ways in which God's salvific presence was made manifest in the experience of living.

As we can see, music was a focal point for Hildegard: it grounded her life in its transcendent splendor, praising God each day throughout the liturgical hours, and it allowed another expression of her visionary and intuitive gifts. Because for her singing the praises of God was as natural as breathing, to be deprived of song was a wrenching experience; this happened in a dramatic way toward the end of her life. In an act of conscience and in obedience to the Living Light she refused to accede to the request of the prelates of Mainz concerning the burial of a contrite sinner. In retaliation they placed the convent under interdict, which meant neither singing nor music of any form was allowed. Following the appropri-ate channels of hierarchy, Hildegard repeatedly requested that the ban be lifted. This led to one of her most ardent appeals, which gives us an insight into her own particular theology of music. For Hildegard music was the point at which heaven and earth came in contact, if ever so briefly; it was a necessary part of human life, especially for a religious community who were to remain constantly aware of both their mortal humanity and their glorious destiny in God. It is well worth studying this impassioned defense.

> And I heard a voice coming from the Living Light concerning the various kinds of praises, about which David speaks in the psalm . . . "Let every

spirit praise the Lord" [Ps 150.3, 6]. These words use outward, visible things to teach us about inward things. Thus the material composition and the quality of these instruments instruct us how we ought to give form to the praise of the Creator and turn all the convictions of our inner being to the same. When we consider these things carefully, we recall that man needed the voice of the living Spirit, but Adam lost this divine voice through disobedience. For while he was still innocent, before his transgression, his voice blended fully with the voices of the angels in their praise of God. Angels are called spirits from the Spirit which is God, and thus they have such voices by virtue of the spiritual nature. But Adam lost that angelic voice which he had in paradise, for he fell asleep to that knowledge which he possessed before his sin, just as a person on waking up only dimly remembers what he had seen in his dreams.[78]

Here Hildegard asserts her conviction that the sounds of the voice raised in praise of God by the angels, and by Adam before the Fall, is of great celestial beauty. They are graced by the "living Spirit," which unites the blessed with the Godhead; when this unity is lost, so is the perfection of voice in praise. She begins with the revelation of the Living Light for these insights and mentions that composition and the use of instruments instruct those of us who see but dimly how we should give "form to the praise of the Creator." By doing so we use outward things to turn us inward in prayer and transform our very being. Later in the same letter she invokes the authority of the prophets:

And so the holy prophets, inspired by the Spirit which they had received, were called for this purpose: not only to compose psalms and canticles (by which the hearts of listeners would be inflamed) but also to construct various kinds of musical instruments to enhance these songs of praise with melodic strains. Thereby, both through the form and quality of the instruments, as well as through the meaning of the words which accompany them, those who hear might be taught, as we said above, about inward things . . . these holy prophets get beyond the music of this exile and recall to mind that divine melody of praise which Adam, in company with the angels, enjoyed in God before his fall.[79]

The prophets point the way back to the celestial realms of God through praise in the form of music. We hear the reference to the Psalter here and to the numerous Old Testament passages about praising God with instruments such as the timbrel and the lyre. She goes on to develop the reverse side of this connection that we have with God through music by describing the response of the fallen angels and the devil:

But when the devil, man's great deceiver, learned that man had begun to sing through God's inspiration and, therefore, was being transformed to bring back the sweetness of the songs of heaven, mankind's homeland, he was so terrified at seeing his clever machinations go to ruin that he was greatly tormented. Therefore, he devotes himself continually to thinking up and working out all kinds of wicked contrivances. Thus he never ceases from confounding confession and the sweet beauty of both divine praise and spiritual hymns, eradicating them through wicked suggestions, impure thoughts, or various distractions from the heart of man and even from the mouth of the Church itself, wherever he can, through dissension, scandal, or unjust oppression. Therefore, you and all prelates must exercise the greatest vigilance to clear the air by full and thorough discussion of the justification for such actions before your verdict closes the mouth of any church singing praises to God or suspends it from handling or receiving the divine sacraments.[80]

Those who have fallen away from God, from the devil and his minions on down to the misguided and malicious among human beings, are the enemies of songs of praise and hymns to God because they echo the divine harmony. The divine harmony is disturbing to those who have willingly separated themselves from it; as we shall see, in Hildegard's world the devil is completely without music. In her musical compositions he cannot sing if given a role; if referred to, the music takes on a lower, minor tone or dissonant interruption. She is of course rebuking the prelates who have laid the interdict on her convent, accusing them of being misled by the snares of the devil. For Hildegard, there were very few good reasons why anyone ought to withhold the sacraments from the faithful or dare to forbid the praise of God in song. Together, these form the essence of *Ecclesia,* since they are the tangible means by which humanity can partake, ever so briefly, in the celestial realms of heaven. She mentions here two types of music: songs of praise and spiritual hymns. We will return to a consideration of these kinds of musical composition shortly. Now we pursue her thought to its next logical step. If these tangible things are what connect us to an experience of God in the fallen world, then they are also expressions of the Incarnation as it lives on in the Church:

> Consider, too, that just as the body of Jesus Christ was born of the purity of the Virgin Mary through the operation of the Holy Spirit so, too, the canticle of praise, reflecting celestial harmony, is rooted in the Church through the Holy Spirit. The body is the vestment of the spirit, which has a living voice, and so it is proper for the body, in harmony with the soul, to use its voice to sing praises to God.[81]

The links between the Incarnation, the embodiment of the Spirit in the Church, and the connection of body and soul, which was the case in paradise, are all apparent in musical praise of God. The imagery used here by Hildegard is imagery employed in several of her compositions, especially the metaphors about the Virgin birth and those speaking of the body as the garment of the spirit.[82]

She closes her discussion of music with a recapitulation of themes she has sounded before and appeals to divine authority and precedent before finally condemning those who have taken it away.

> And because sometimes a person sighs and groans at the sound of singing, remembering, as it were the nature of celestial harmony, the prophet, aware that the soul is symphonic and thoughtfully reflecting on the profound nature of the spirit, urges us in the psalm [cf. Ps 32:2, 91:4] to confess to the Lord with the harp and to sing a psalm to Him with the ten-stringed psaltery. His meaning is that the harp, which is plucked from below, relates to the discipline of the body; the psaltery, which is plucked from above, pertains to the exertion of the spirit; the ten chords, to the fulfillment of the law.[83]

Hildegard highlights her major themes here: a person sighs for heaven because reminded of the harmony of heaven in the sound and practice of song; the body needs to move upward toward the celestial, as symbolized by the harp, and is met by the spirit descending on the psaltery from above. The ten chords symbolize the Ten Commandments, which literally find powerful musical resonance in this imagery. The soul is itself "symphonic," expressing the "inner accord of soul and body in human music-making."[84] Moreover, Hildegard has a philosophy of music that is also a way of understanding history, a way of bringing heavenly beauty to earth:

> The symbolism then turns into micro-cosmic allegory—music is the human body and soul, and the principles with which they are informed—an allegory that is dynamic and in no way forced, arising effortlessly out of Hildegard's pattern of thoughts and images.[85]

In a way, we come full circle here in the beginning of a chapter on Hildegard's music to where we left off in the chapter about her theological-visionary works. We have the microcosm of the human sphere represented here, joined with the realm of the macrocosm or the celestial through a natural connection between the two, which is founded in the Word of God, eternally predestined to join human beings once again with their celestial destiny. In this we see a clear reflection of the themes of all her works, but especially those presented in the *De operatione Dei*, which unites these realms through the Incarnation. Both are, of course, works of her later life, the last period of activity, which we referred to on the chart at the beginning of this book, so it is natural to find a resemblance. As with the *De operatione Dei,* we do not have an idea that is new and startling to Hildegard or her readers; rather, we have an idea she expresses in her maturity with its reflections and convictions made clear to her. Hildegard has a consistent philosophy of music, whether or not it is thought out completely at all times. It intuitively guides her in her composition of musical praise and becomes more and more explicit as she organizes her work.

Hildegard's songs are collected and form a lyrical whole in a cycle called the *Symphonia armoniae caelestium revelationum,* or the "symphony of the harmony of celestial revelations." Related to this cycle and present also in an earlier form in the last section of the *Scivias* is a musical morality play called the *Ordo virtutum,* the first of its kind. For the purpose of clarity we will look at the *Symphonia* and the *Ordo virtutum* in two separate sections, bearing in mind that all of Hildegard's music is in some way connected. Just as we see the clear link between her later epistle to the prelates of Mainz and the *De operatione Dei,* we see a similar link between the *Ordo virtutum* and the *Scivias,* modified and refined by the writing of the *Liber vitae meritorum.* In the sixth and thirteenth visions of the *Scivias* we also have a theology of music, expressed by Hildegard at an earlier time in a different manner. Vision 6 is of the choirs of angels, whom she sees as a set of heavenly armies in a circular form. In the final vision we have the symphony of the blessed, which includes those redeemed in body and soul:

> And all these armies were singing with marvelous voices all kinds of music about the wonders that God works in blessed souls, and by this God was magnificently glorified. . . .
>
> Then I saw the lucent sky, in which I heard different kinds of music, marvellously embodying all the meanings I had heard before. I heard the praises of the joyous citizens of Heaven, steadfastly persevering in the ways of Truth; and laments calling people back to those praises and joys; and the exhortations of the virtues, spurring one another on to secure the salvation of the peoples ensnared by the Devil. And the virtues destroyed his snares, so that the faithful at last through repentance passed out of their sins and into Heaven. And their song, like the voice of a multitude, making music in harmony [praised] the ranks of Heaven.[86]

Although less cogently and philosophically worded than the statement in the foregoing letter, she expresses the essence of her theology of music here, too. The angels praise God in marvelous song: in that song at the end of time understanding will accompany praise such that humanity will come to know the meaning of God's revelations. The heavenly choir will comprise the angels and all those who love and turn to God, those who have persevered, and those lured by the virtues. Evil will no longer mar the harmony of all the heavens, for its dissonance and lack of harmony will be utterly cast out and destroyed.

In Hildegard's theology of music we hear again and in different forms the insights gained from the visionary character of her experience. Indeed, Hildegard's music is part of her visionary gifts; she claims to have been no more taught about singing and musical notation than she was about reading and writing Latin or understanding the Scriptures. Music both holds together Hildegard's world and expresses the profound realities she has discovered about that world in its lyrics and forms. Her language, taken as poetry, is among the most unusual in medieval European lyric;[87] she writes in a form of free verse (to use the modern term) rather than in rhymed, metrical patterns. This makes her poetic gift quite extraordinary and at the same time makes it virtually impossible to translate into a language other than the original to hear the frequent use she makes of word sound, such as alliteration and assonance, as well as the music that accompanies the lyrics and from which it cannot be separated. We again will hear the terms and images so meaningful to her in the theological-visionary works: *viriditas* and flowering of all sorts; the use of *sudare* to convey the sense of moisture and freshness; the figures of *Ecclesia* and *Sapientia;* biblical echoes, especially those of the Old Testament in the Song of Songs; and her favorite theme of the Incarnation as the divine plan of God to reverse the transgressions of Adam so that once again all may be united and harmonious. All of these images and their expression in music are grounded in the monastic life and experience that was the core of Hildegard's very being. Anyone involved in the monastic life, particularly as a leader and teacher, would have been immersed in the Divine Office and its structures. But for Hildegard music was a passion; though it is her images that often compel us to see her extraordinary talents, her visionary gift was initially one of sound. She hears the Living Light speak: she experiences melodies and music. Moreover, music had a particular purpose similar to that in the prophetic spoken visions: the uniting of the heavenly and earthly spheres. This experience of sound that translates itself or is immediately experienced in concrete visual form is usually referred to psychologically as "synaesthesia." Authors have referred to Hildegard's many gifts, including her musical talents, as synaesthetic in character. One defines her synaesthesia as "the blurring (or fusion) of sense experiences that are ordinarily distinct."[88] What she heard and saw occurred to her simultaneously; so, as we have seen in the theological-visionary works, the issue of the relationship between image and text is a complex one. In terms of her music we need to be attentive to the fact that it is neither easy nor preferable to separate lyrics from their musical settings. Both are synaesthetic in character.

Hildegard's Musical Style and the Creation of the *Symphonia*

Hildegard composed music throughout much of her lifetime, only collecting her oeuvre into an externally organized body of work later in her life. It is important to recognize that this was an external organization of a body of work that had distinct themes and categories of its own before such organization was made definite. It is likely that the earliest manuscript of her music we possess was the original cause of the organization, since it was sent as a gift to the Cistercians at Villers around 1175. This manuscript is in the library of St. Pieters and Paulusabdij in Dendermonde, Belgium, and referred to as either "V" or "D." Another compilation was made shortly after Hildegard's death in the 1180s, possibly with a view toward her canonization, possibly in order to preserve melodies for future generations of the convent who would not have the immediate familiarity with the texts and tones that Hildegard's own community would have had. This manuscript is designated as "R" for the Reisencodex manuscript, which is held in the Hessische Landesbibliothek at Wiesbaden, Germany. There are fragments remaining in other works that have helped scholars in their attempts to reconstruct the order, musical notation, and phraseology of her compositions.[89] We know that Hildegard was renowned for her music in the 1140s because of a letter in which her compositions are referred to with appreciation. She probably composed the major body of her *Symphonia* during the 1140s and 1150s, although some pieces were undoubtedly written later than this.[90] Internally, it was doubtless organized for the convent in a less formal form of notation than we find in the later manuscripts that are extant. We are fortunate that external organization became necessary, because we hesitate to ascribe to Hildegard the intention of creating a complete cycle of songs like the *Symphonia*. As always, she responded to her visionary voice as it came to her, and it is doubtful she structured her treatises or songs in advance.

Why would the average reader want to know about manuscript tradition at this juncture? Probably the best answer is that it is the comparison of the extant manuscripts that enables us to do several things essential to analyzing Hildegard's music. First, we need to be able to see in which way she organized the song cycle as a whole, for this reflects her theological thinking, and it varies according to the main manuscript used. Second, it enables us to make a fairly accurate count of the number of songs included in the cycle, which again varies. Third, it enables us to say something about the method of notation and style, since the earlier manuscript (D) is not as reliable but is earlier, and the later manuscript (R) has been emended by scribes. This last point is essential in understanding the possibility of variation in recordings and renditions of her works.

Music, Poetry, and Style

Understanding and re-creating Hildegard's music for today's audience or appreciating a contemporary scholarly approach to the *Symphonia* that views it as a major contribution to medieval music is difficult, as the result of several circumstances. Some are the result of historical conditions; others appear convoluted as a result of Hildegard's own methods of composition and performance. We will first look at some of the historically conditioned difficulties, then at some of Hildegard's own idiosyncrasies. Finally, in a later section, we will look at three songs representative of the *Symphonia* that exhibit some of the inherent difficulties and delights in working with her musical compositions.

Historically, performers and students of music or of Hildegard herself are faced with the problem of difference in musical notation. The staff as we know it today did not exist; when early staff notation came into existence, it consisted of a staff of four lines and three spaces, rather than five lines and four spaces, as it is today. Notes were not the customary way of marking (their literal meaning) the value and pitch of a song, even on this staff. Gregorian chant and plainsong were written differently, even when an early staff form was used. The common form of notation used from the thirteenth through the fifteenth century was a series of characters known as "neumes." Neumes were used in several systems of notation and differ from the present system in several salient ways. They usually appeared to be square or diamond in shape, without stems; another type looked almost like a modern script "N," which indicated a slurring of notes with the middle being the lowest in pitch. Sometimes sound was indicated by the size of the neumes; if smaller, the sound was to be softer and gentler, for example. A comparison of modern notation with that in neumes can be seen below (this is not Hildegard's work).

As you can see, the sign values are quite different, although if one becomes accustomed to reading chant it is in many ways as simple or simpler to follow neumes than notes. Despite this fact we face yet an-

The same chant fragment in neumes and in modern notation.

FIGURE 7

other type of notation in the form of neumes when we look at Hildegard's work. This form existed prior to the thirteenth century and is a form of staffless notation, sometimes called "chironomic neumes." They resemble a form of shorthand in appearance and were quite adequate for remembering a melody when it was somewhat known to the singer. It is quite another matter to reconstruct the actual form of the melody when it is *unknown* to the singer. In an atmosphere such as the one in which Hildegard composed her melodies, this form of chironomic neumes was the most expeditious. After all, the abbess composed primarily so that her community could sing God's praises. The exportation of her music elsewhere often was the result of contact or correspondence with someone who also might be familiar with its melodic structure and rhythm. It is fortunate, then, that during Hildegard's lifetime and shortly after she died there were two transcriptions of the work we know as the *Symphonia;* otherwise reconstructing her music from any available fragments might have been a fruitless cause. Both are transcribed with the use of the oldest staff form and in German neumes, similar to the neumes described above.

The importance of notation and the use of neumes without staff as a common practice for Hildegard's compositions makes it possible to interpret the songs. Fortunately, Hildegard's style tended to use the same framework of pitches and intervals in an assortment of ways. Her songs are consistent in some sense, then, despite a degree of uncertainty about elements not contained in the notation: time signatures, for example. Thus in modern reconstructions of Hildegard's songs, we may expect that one of the major variations in performance will be the pacing of the song, where and if one pauses and breathes. Rhythm, which along with melody and harmony are the three most identifiable things in Western music today, is thus rather uncertain. Chant notations generally did not supply note values indicating their length, nor did they indicate any possible instrumental accompaniment.[91] The musician and singer(s) are therefore able to choose with some latitude about the rhythm of early chants, which becomes an even more interesting question in interpreting Hildegard's music, notoriously irregular in its phrasing.

The text and music of Hildegard's songs should be considered together, insofar as one is able. Her poetry with its soaring brilliance of imagery is often mirrored in similar jumps in the intervals sung are a whole; the music and the poetry can be considered separately, but it takes away from both. For the average reader and listener it is far more important to see how the two work together. Hildegard has a definitive style, one that seems to hearken back to previous chant and song forms rather than moving into the innovations of twelfth-century composers. Her work has been compared to the *Liber hymnorum* of Notker of St. Gall, who wrote

in the ninth century and is thereby contrasted with the style of her contemporaries, especially Abelard and the Victorines.[92] One of the intriguing characteristics of Hildegard's musical compositions is their mirroring
of the style we find throughout her life and work: order is paramount,
but within that given structure and order there is a great deal of originality, flexibility, and innovation. One of the ways in which she varies
from the Victorines is in the use of structures in her music:

> The music of Hildegard is remarkable above all for its formulaic nature: it
> is made up of a comparatively small number of formulae, or melodic pat-
> terns, which recur many times under different melodic and modal condi-
> tions and are the common property of her poetic output. These formulae
> differ from the recurrent melodic elements [timbres] of Adam of St. Vic-
> tor's work. While the latter are fixed phrases which are assembled and re-
> assembled in a patchwork quilt manner, Hildegard's formulae are melodic
> "frameworks" which occur in innumerable different guises.[93]

Thus while Hildegard's structures are set into frameworks, she feels
free to move them about in terms of her poetic inspiration, in terms of
mode (a set of pitches), and where they are used. Her poetry does not
rhyme in a conventional manner, and the free-verse style lends itself well
to this type of musical accompaniment and vice versa. She creates melodies
primarily by alternating two types of passages, the syllabic and the melismatic, and by utilizing intervals of a fifth and a fourth frequently, which
often then move up (or down) into the octave. Davidson calls the rising
fifth followed by the immediate move to the octave Hildegard's "musical
thumbprint."[94] What does this mean to the non-specialist?

Essentially, what it means is that Hildegard likes to use the same
conventions in singing, whether or not they are in a different mode (key,
tonality) or placement. So, for example, she will often choose a final tone
that sets the pitch for the entire piece. She will then use intervals between
tones for expression and what is called "tone-painting." Her favorite interval was a fifth from the main pitch tone which then often would jump
to the octave for embellishment or to represent a dramatic, celestial moment. For example, if the final tone is D, then the fifth would land on A
and the octave on d. There were eight church modes or scales for creating chant, but Hildegard tended to use only three tonalities in her works,
limiting the modes and composing using variations on d, e, and c.

> Hildegard drew on a relatively small number of motifs that she repeated,
> with ingenious variation, in every piece composed in that mode. This qual-
> ity of repetition restores some of the musical stability she sacrificed in aban-
> doning strophic [having the same music for all stanzas] construction.[95]

Despite this small number of motifs and tonalities, Hildegard uses an extremely wide vocal range: some songs span two octaves or more, which places strain on any average singer. We do well to remember that many of her compositions were also meant for choral singing, which would have made this use of a wide range even more difficult to sing. Stylistically, she probably wrote this way in order to give an emphasis to her words with the use of the extreme upper and lower ranges of the tonalities in which she composed.

Her alternation between the syllabic and the melismatic is characteristic of her work, especially the ornate use of the melismatic. Both are essential to draw attention to the meaning of the text by way of the musical setting.[96] The syllabic, as in the word "syllable," says that these tones correspond to a whole word or to a part of a word. The melismatic, meaning "florid," refers to the occurrence of many notes sung on the same word or partial word. Although she uses both forms consistently, Hildegard is very fond of melismatic structures. In one instance her use of melisma extends to eighty tones sounded on a single syllable.[97] In Hildegard's case, the use of melismas is not to create a florid style but to move to a celestial one. Melismatic phrases were common to the alleluia verses sung during the Mass and thus had a solemn or ethereal connotation to them. Some have conjectured, whether or not their origin is based in the writing of alleluias, that these melismatic phrases are essentially an expression of Hildegard's mysticism.[98] This certainly seems plausible when we listen to recordings of her music, because the use of melismas in key portions of the text leads us into the realm of transcendent mystery and theological depth. We will see this in the examples that follow this section.

What about the words, the poetic themes that accompany these musical practices? It is the interweaving of the musical structures and the manner of writing the lyrics that make Hildegard's songs special. She could be considered a poet apart from the musical setting of the songs, although this would do violence to her intent. Ostensibly, as in her visions, the sound and the image are one. Some have not even considered her compositions to be poetic but rather a form of prose; this is due to a proselike quality that comes from the irregularity of the lines and creates a certain asymmetry in their expression. This is not verse as many have defined it. Yet the songs have an undeniably poetic expression to them. Although they are not metrically consistent or rhymed they resemble a poem written in free verse in their fantastic imagery. Largely due to the efforts of medievalist Peter Dronke, Hildegard's songs have been accepted as a form of poetry rather than a lesser prose form.[99] He refers to her songs as containing "some of the most unusual, subtle, and exciting poetry of the twelfth century."[100] As it is generally easier to see how her poetic style works within the musical structures by example, we will confine ourselves here to briefly describing some of the more outstanding features of her poetic expression.

Hildegard is using an older form of poetry than was usual for the twelfth century, which saw great advances in the use of regular meter and rhyme. It is both innovative and primitive, depending on how one looks at it: she is hearkening back not only to the chant compositions of a few centuries earlier but to the form and expression she experienced through reading biblical texts in the Office. Since it is likely that Hildegard wrote from inspiration and by ear, it is likely that her compositions were modeled on how the songs of praise she had been immersed in for years "sounded" to her. Even had they been written in regular, rhymed verse, she probably would not have heard or phrased them in the same way.[101] She rarely uses direct quotations from Scripture, although allusions to it are everywhere; sometimes they are paraphrased, but in most cases they are references that subtly appear in the context of her own wording and development of an idea. This subtlety does assume a lot about the reader or listener, since she is expecting them to pick up on what are, for us, rather distant allusions. Even once explained, they put us at one remove from the immediacy of her complex imagery. Her imagery is much as it is in the theological-visionary works but in a less declamatory form. We have mentioned above some of her favorite words and references these poems contain. In the songs she tends to compress and expand her imagery rather suddenly for the effect this produces. In describing this poetic effect, we can see how similar this is to her musical style. Both compress and extend for tonal color, poetic expression, and impact on the singer and listener. She does this with both biblical and natural images, imitating the precipitous fall of Adam or the swoop of birds with the same musical jump in interval and sudden juxtaposition of images. The result is that of a startling immediacy characteristic of Hildegard and probably reflective of her intent and her visionary gift. Despite her individuality of expression, her songs are never written in the first person but move from the second person singular to the third person singular: they are meant to be communal and used for public worship, and writing in the first person would have been inappropriate and out of character.

Perhaps our greatest difficulty in assessing the power of Hildegard's style is one that always remains a problem: translation. This is complicated by Hildegard's use of a single term to carry a diversity of meanings. Since the songs are written in Latin, all of the word play, alliteration, assonance, and echoing or mirroring of sounds are irretrievably lost when we take them out of the original language. Although we can reconstruct what they say, we lose the flavor of the songs themselves. Therefore, when discussing the three examples below, we will supply the Latin as well as two versions of English translation so as to better convey the style in which she wrote the songs.

Structure, Organization, and Number of Songs in the Cycle

The number of songs that make up the *Symphonia* is usually said to be between seventy-one and seventy-seven due to manuscript variations and confusion between song forms (such as sequences with hymns). For our purposes we will follow the schema outlined, well defined and set with considerable justification by Barbara Newman in her critical edition of the *Symphonia*. Newman counts sixty-nine songs in the cycle (plus four songs without music, totaling seventy-three).[102] They are organized hierarchically into the following pattern:

Father and Son	Seven Songs
Mother and Son	Sixteen Songs
The Holy Spirit	Five Songs
The Celestial Hierarchy	Twelve Songs
Patron Saints	Fourteen Songs
Virgins, Widows, and Innocents	Five Songs
St. Ursula and Companions	Six Songs
Ecclesia/Church	Four Songs

This hierarchy reflects Hildegard's sense of order and the appropriate place given to rank and honor. The only disputed part of the hierarchy is the interpolation of the songs about the Virgin between the songs about the Father and Son and those concerning the Holy Spirit. Whereas Hildegard was acutely sensitive to the fact that God was one yet three and trinitarian in her theology, I agree with Newman's reading here. Mary plays a unique role in Hildegard's theological cosmos, but she is not elevated for honor alone. Mary's function is to give the Word flesh, to make the Incarnation possible and so to redeem human beings from the errors of Adam and Eve. Thus, Mother and Son have the connotation of moving from the eternal Word with the Father to the incarnate Word through the Virgin Mother. As Hildegard makes a great deal theologically out of the reversal between Mary *(Ave)*, who brings new life in Jesus, and Eve *(Eva)*, in whom all things were lost, this placement seems appropriate. If the songs to the Virgin were placed after those honoring the Spirit, the imbalance of numbers as well as content would tend to indicate something amiss. The placement also sounds Hildegard's central theological concern: the meeting of heaven and earth, the ability for the created to rise up to the Uncreated and for the Uncreated to become part of creation.

The structure and number of songs in the *Symphonia* cycle would not hold any great interest were it not for the salient fact that they reflect similar theological themes in Hildegard's *Opus Dei* that might not otherwise be apparent. Using what we have discussed above, we can see there are sixteen songs devoted to the theme of Mother and Son, the highest number in any category. When we add these to the songs concerning Father and Son and Holy Spirit, we end up with a total of twenty-eight songs. For Hildegard, as we have seen in previous chapters, it is the mystery and joyous occasion of the incarnation of the Word, predestined from all time, that overshadows and gives significance to all the other works of salvation history. This emphasis is not limited to the Word becoming flesh but has echoes in her other theological themes. It is there when she speaks of the essential unity of body and spirit in human persons; when she stresses the redemption far more than the sin of Adam, for it was through this sin that all creation is brought even closer to God; the triumphant reversal of the role of woman in the Virgin Mary, almost obscuring the errors of Eve; the reverence for all creation and the special place human beings have in creation, being in God's image and likeness. In the numbering of songs, we also notice the predominance of songs written about female figures or personifications; this is striking about Hildegard's work, although the feminine does not consequently appear only in a positive light.

The organization and structure of the *Symphonia* reflect Hildegard's natural assumption that society, both in heaven and on earth, was rightly stratified into different orders or classes. Thus songs pertaining to God and divinity appear first (the interpolation of the Marian songs being a tribute to the divinity of God); next come angels, prophets, patriarchs, and apostles; they are followed by the saints, especially the patron saints of the monasteries and convents of Hildegard's community or commissioned by others for their patrons; virgins, widows, and innocents in their ability to devote their lives to God; St. Ursula as the preeminent example of virginity along with the Virgin Mary and also as an example of the slaughter of the innocents; and finally the Church itself, comprising all those people who belong to her.

Examples from the *Symphonia*

As we turn to some specific examples to illustrate the descriptions in this chapter, we limit them to three in order to get a deeper perspective on each one. The reasons for each choice will be stated and will hopefully become apparent in the explanation itself. One of the criteria is purely for the patient general reader: the song must be recorded somewhere and be available today, preferably in more than one version. In this way, since a picture—in this case a musical selection—is worth a thousand words, the interested reader can listen to Hildegard along with reading the commentary provided both by the recording artists and here in this book. We will begin with a long and unusual piece that shows the range of Hildegard's abilities and imagery. It has received scholarly attention, it includes several of her most important theological themes, and it has been recorded by four different labels and groups, so we can bring in the dimension of contemporary performance as well. The other examples, which are also representative, are considerably shorter, and we will not need to deal with them in such elaborate form once the reader is aware of the type of translations, phrasing, and comparison possible in Hildegard's musical works.

O Ecclesia

This piece is a sequence that unites several of Hildegard's themes, as we shall see. It is part of the Ursula group, despite the title, which echoes the first line. First we will present the piece in its wording, its Latin and English translations, and then will discuss it. It has been recorded by three ensembles and one soloist: Gothic Voices, Sequentia, The Early Music Institute, and Ellen Oak.[103]

Latin Original	Literalist Translation[104]	Poetic Translation[105]
O Ecclesia, *oculi tui similes saphiro sunt,* *et aures tue monti Bethel,* *et nasus tuus est* *sicut mons mirre et thuris* *et os tuum quasi sonus* *aquarum multarum.*	Ecclesia, your eyes are sapphire-like, your ears are as the mountain of Bethel, your nose is as a mountain of myrrh and incense, and your mouth is like the roar of many waters.	Ecclesia! your eyes are like sapphires, your ears like Mount Bethel, your nose like a mountain of incense and myrrh, your voice like the sound of many waters.

Latin Original	Literalist Translation[104]	Poetic Translation[105]
In visione vere fidei Ursula Filium Dei amavit et virum cum hoc seculo reliquit et in solem aspexit atque pulcherrimum iuvenem vocavit, dicens:	With the vision of true faith Ursula loved the son of God and left behind bridegroom and world alike and gazed into the Sun and cried out to the young and fairest one:	Ursula fell in love with God's Son in a vision: her faith was true. She rejected her man and all the world and gazed straight into the sun, crying out to her beloved, fairest of the sons of men:
"In multo desiderio desideravi ad te venire et in celestibus nuptiis tecum sedere, per alienam viam ad te currens velut nubes que in purissmo aere currit similis saphiro."	"With great longing I have longed to come to you and to dwell with you in heavenly marriage, racing to you by an unfamiliar way, as a cloud races in the purest air, sapphire-like."	With yearning I have yearned to come to you and sit by you at our wedding in heaven! Let me race to you strangely, chase you like a sapphire cloud where the sky is purest.
Et postquam Ursula sic dixerunt, rumor iste per omnes populos exüt. Et dixerunt: "Innocentia puellaris ignorantie nescit quid dicit."	When Ursula had spoken so, this report went out among all the peoples, so that they said "The innocence of girlish ignorance knows not what it says."	When Ursula had spoken, all people heard her and answered: how naive she is! The girl has no notion of what she means!
Et ceperunt ludere cum illa in magna symphonia, usque dum ignea sarcina super eam cecedit. Unde omnes cognoscebant quia contemptus mundi est sicut mons Bethel.	And they began to play with her amid great bursts of music— until the burden of fire fell upon her. Through this, all could see that counting the world as nothing is like the mountain of Bethel.	And they began to mock her in harmony— until the burden of flame fell upon her. Then they learned how scorn for the world is like Mount Bethel.

Latin Original	Literalist Translation[104]	Poetic Translation[105]
Et cognoverunt etiam suavissimum odorem mirre et thuris, quoniam contemptus mundi super omnia ascendit.	And they too were aware of the most sweet odor of myrrh and incense, for despising the world rises above all things.	And they discovered the fragrance of incense and myrrh because scorn for the world mounts above all.
Tunc diabolus membra sua invasit, que nobilissimos mores in corporibus istis occiderunt.	Then the devil entered his minions, and these destroyed the eminently noble virtues in those bodies.	Then the devil possessed his own. In those virgin bodies they slaughtered nobility.
Et hoc in alta voce omnia elementa audierunt et ante thronum Dei dixerunt:	And all the elements heard the high cry, and before the throne of God, they said:	And all the elements heard the clamor of their blood and cried before the throne of God:
"Wach! rubicundus sanguis innocentis agni in desponsatione sua effusus est."	"Ah! the red blood of the innocent Lamb has been shed on her wedding-day!"	Ach! the scarlet blood of an innocent lamb is spilled at her wedding.
Hoc audiant omnes celi et in summa symphonia laudent Agnum Dei, quia guttur serpentis antiqui in istis margaritis materie Verbi Dei suffocatum est.	Let all the heavens hear this and in consummate music praise the Lamb of God, for in these pearls of the substance of the Word of God the ancient serpent has been strangled.	Let all the heavens hear it and praise God's Lamb in great harmony—for the neck of the ancient serpent is choked in these pearls strung on the Word of God.

At first glance it might appear that this sequence is more of a ballad, as it tells a particular story. Indeed, that is partially its intention, for the story is that of Ursula and her martyred companions, a story that had gripped the people of twelfth-century Germany particularly because of a recent discovery of "relics" in Cologne. Ursula's story is fairly simple. According to legend she was a British princess who, in order to avoid marriage, asked to go on a pilgrimage to Rome with some companions. These companions—probably eleven, but inflated to eleven thousand by scribal error—were said to be all virgins. On their way home they were confronted by the Huns (sometimes Attila himself), and rather than surrender their faith and virginity they were martyred. With the discovery of a potential site of this martyrdom, the legend underwent some modifications, as the bones of men and children were found as well. In a vision Elisabeth of Schönau confirmed the authenticity of the relics, intimating that the male companions were holy men protecting the virgins. In Hildegard's hands, however, it becomes multivalent in meaning and dense with stunning images.

There are so many things one could say about this song it is difficult to determine appropriate limits in commentating on its content. First, there are the rich biblical allusions, here rather direct. The sapphire of the eyes of Ecclesia and the cloud that becomes sapphire-like all refer to one of Hildegard's favorite Old Testament passages, Ezekiel's vision of the Son of Man on a sapphire throne (Ezek 1:26). We will recall that in her imagery of the Trinity in the *Scivias* the human figure is sapphire in color. Mount Bethel recalls the vision of Jacob in Gen 28:1-22, and as in Hildegard's other visions, the mountain is that which stretches up to the divine because it is "Heaven's Gate." The opening reference to the eyes and the use of imagery of perfume are taken from the Song of Songs and may also symbolize the anointing of Christ in death and as king. The "sound of many waters" is a multivalent reference to the book of Revelation, or the Apocalypse: it reminds us both of the marriage feast of the Lamb, which is described there, and of the coming divine Judgment. Second, there is the identification of Ursula with various female figures and roles throughout the song: she is the Church, the one knocking on the gate of heaven to become the bride of the Lamb, a lamb or an innocent herself. In the final stanzas after martyrdom, the use of blood in the images reminds us of the passion of Christ, of the martyrs, and of the consummation of a marriage. Like the Church, the bride of Christ, she longs to be with the Bridegroom looking toward heaven (the sun, the mountain). There is even a reference to the "contempt of the world," which is featured as one of the virtues assisting Christians to their celestial destiny in the *Liber vitae meritorum*.

The legend of a naive princess and her companions is thereby transformed into a prophetic vision and celebration of the Church, the bride of Christ, who will partake in the heavenly things yearned for with the coming of the Bridegroom. With the shedding of blood there is always the echo of martyrdom and a reminder of the wine of the Eucharist in addition to the images mentioned above. Moreover, we have two effective reversals in this sequence that are of importance theologically and existentially. The first is the attempt to ridicule Ursula for her longing for heaven and contempt for the world as naive, something Hildegard may well have identified with herself. This is proved false when it comes to the test: although it is not as sweet as Ursula imagines, she is steadfast like Mount Bethel, and everyone acknowledges that she is in the right. The second is the amazing language used at the very end of the sequence in which the Christian conviction that the triumph of the Word and the Church over the devil and the serpent will come at the end of time. Even though the devil introduces, literally, a dissonance into the proceedings, there is nothing to be accomplished. The nobility of Ursula and her companions will live on forever, and the elements themselves (showing Hildegard's concern for the cosmos) shout out against such desecration. The song ends with the startling imagery of the serpent being choked or strangled with the pearls (the martyrs), which are made of *materia,* a term used in reference to the incarnation of the Word. Thus the pearls are made out of the substance of the divine Word, and Satan is throttled in triumph. The celestial harmony or symphony can be heard in its fullness as it sings of this triumph, which is the triumph of the whole Church.

The musical score is reflective of the imagery and the tones of the piece: we are jarred at the outcry of the elements by a dissonant, drawn-out sound, which also occurs at the moment when the devil and his minions enter (the lowest note in the piece); we soar toward the heavens with Ursula in syllabic forms and melismas written in a high register. There is a great contrast between the upper and lower registers, which usually signifies heavenly and earthly activity. The story is told in a middle range, mostly consisting of syllabic tones; however, it has both a dominant tone (A) and a tonality for contrast (G). Whenever we touch the celestial realms the music jumps and soars (this is especially true of the decorative melisma surrounding the image of the pearls choking the serpent). There is a sense of a narrative interpolated by quotations, just as we see in the wording and the poetry. This is tone-painting at its best and is responsible for the fact that this sequence is somewhat irregular in form.[106]

O Viridissima Virga

If we were to take an example from each type of composition used in the celebration of the Liturgy of the Hours, we ought to take a responsory next. However, this composition, described as a "free song"[107] to the Virgin, is so like Hildegard that its inclusion is a welcome example of her style. What you may find interesting in the text—besides the text itself—is the range of translations from the Latin for this particular song. Of the three, this is where they vary the most widely because of the tension between the poetic Latin and its literal translation. Dronke believes that despite the large number of sequences and hymns to the Virgin, Hildegard

Latin Original	Literalist Translation[109]	Poetic Translation[110]
O viridissima virga, ave, *que in ventoso flabro* *sciscitationis* *sanctorum prodisti.*	Hail, O greenest branch! You came forth in the windy blast of the questioning of saints.	Never was a leaf so green, for you branched from the spirited blast of the quest of the saints.
Cum venit tempus *quod tu floruisti in ramis* *tuis;* *ave, ave fuit tibi,* *quia calor solis in te sudavit* *sicut odor balsami.*	When the time came for you to blossom in your branches, "hail" was the word to you, for the heat of the sun distilled in you a fragrance like balsam.	When it came time for your boughs to blossom (I salute you!) your scent was like balsam distilled in the sun.
Nam in te floruit pulcher *flos* *qui oderem dedit omnibus* *aromatibus que arida erant.* *Et illa apparuerunt omnia* *in viridate plena.*	For you bloomed the beautiful flower that gave fragrance to all the spices that had grown dry. And they all appeared in full verdure.	And your flower made all spices fragrant dry though they were: they burst into verdure.
Unde celi dederunt rorem *super gramen* *et omnis terra leta facta est,* *quoniam viscera ipsius* *frumentum protulerunt,* *et quoniam volucres celi* *nidos in ipsa habuerunt.*	So the skies rained dew on the grass and the whole earth exulted, for her womb brought forth wheat, and the birds of heaven made their nests in it.	So the skies rained dew on the grass and the whole earth exulted, for her womb brought forth wheat for the birds of heaven made their nests in it.
Deinde facta est esca *hominibus et* *gaudium magnum* *epulantium.* *Unde, o suavis virgo,* *in te non deficit ullum* *gaudium.*	Then food was prepared for humans and great joy for the banqueters. So in you, sweet Virgin, no joy ever fails.	Keepers of the feast, rejoice! The banquet's ready. And you sweet maid-child are a fount of gladness.
Hec omnia Eva contempsit. *Nunc autem laus sit Altissimo.*	Eve despised all these things! But now, praise be to the Most High.	But Eve? She despised every joy. Praise nonetheless, praise to the highest.

chose to include this particular one because it is her masterpiece on the theme. He also concludes that because of the subject matter and the imagery prevalent throughout this song, it may have been composed while she was at work on the *De operatione Dei* or perhaps afterward; therefore it would be a late composition.[108]

In this composition we encounter once again the vibrancy of Hildegard's nature imagery intertwined simultaneously with her theological convictions. This is most striking in the center of the piece, when the Virgin's womb brings forth the earthly material for the Eucharist as well as the Word of God. In the entire work Mary is likened to the tree of Jesse, pointing to the ancestry of Christ. Musically and poetically it is a work in complete control of this central image. The tree is perhaps one of the most profound symbols Hildegard uses to connect heaven and earth, for it is rooted deep within the earth (and here the Old Testament) and reaches up to the heavens (the revelations in the New Testament). The song opens with a recollection of this image in Mary, who is the greenest branch, the one with the life-giving *viriditas* of heaven. The saints have awaited this moment in the history of salvation, when the heavenly meal will be offered to the human race, despite the rejection of Adam and Eve. Eve is singled out here as the reverse of everything Mary represents. The song is full of biblical resonance almost to the point of quotation but not quite. There is the reminiscent flavor of the Song of Songs in the imagery of the aroma and perfume that this blossoming has brought about. The somewhat odd-sounding section where the birds make their nest in Mary's womb is a reference to the birds nesting in the tree of the kingdom to come in the Gospel of Matthew. The freshness and dew may be reminiscent of the Advent antiphon based on Isaiah 45, in which dew is called down from the heavens.[111] The poetic wording is tight, and careful, with similar words creating a rhythm and at times a contrast: *tuis/tibi; quia, qui, que; arida, omnia, plena, leta, facta; quoniam, epulantium, gaudium; ipsius/ipsa*, and so on. We should make a point of noting that the Marian songs, whatever styles they are written in, celebrate the coming of the incarnate Word of God into the world. They are not hymns to Mary herself but to the great event she enables to come to pass. The source of Hildegard's reverence for Mary is twofold: her role in salvation history and her nearness to God through virginity. This latter theme is present and celebrated in this song in its use of *virga, virgo*, and *viriditas* and by the fact that redemption comes from a virgin who is like a fresh, moist flower that perfumes the air—a whole host of Hildegard's favorite images used in this one piece. Hildegard's preferred images are incarnational in nature: they span the distance between heaven and earth and create a bridge to paradise.[112] We also have a short summary of theology in this song: Eve and the Fall are mentioned, and this event is overcome and reversed by the fruitfulness of the Virgin in giving birth to the Word; through Christ's resurrection the Church is gathered and nourished by the Eucharist, the world is replenished in its freshness, and the possibility of renewal abounds. We can see the similarity to the microcosm-macrocosm theme in the *De operatione Dei;* also noteworthy is that it is typical of Hildegard to stress God made man rather than Christ crucified in her imagery, both early and late. Her characteristic celebration of the Eucharist– "wheat" or "corn"–is also connected to the praise of the virginity of Mary, who actually *became* the bridge between heaven and earth.

Musically this song reflects its themes and provides these themes through the use of mostly syllabic phrases with melismas reaching into the upper ranges on certain important words (such as *plena*) or selected passages. The opening section is pitched quite high and melismatically, which is replicated in the tonality used for the musical phrase speaking of the fruit of the Virgin's womb, which ties the Church and the Eucharist firmly together theologically in the music, centering on the incarnation and its effects. The last two lines contrast each other strongly, with the line about Eve beginning in a higher range and with a sweet sound, descending only at the end of the line; the line about praise starts and stays surprisingly low in pitch until the ascending passage at the end on *Altissimo*.

O Virtus Sapientiae

This piece is an antiphon, meant to be both brief and filled with praise.[113] Its subject is one that is closest to Hildegard's heart: the virtue of Wisdom, which, in her works is, along with Charity, the feminine personification of the divine or the divine power.[114]

What we notice in this antiphon in particular are the abstract images reflected in the wording of the piece and also the sense of joy that pervades it. The play on words in section 1 about the wings circling is a powerful one, and we can see that it gains even more from its compression and allusion in Latin. There are echoes of Isa 6:2-3 and the circling, singing seraphim here. The image of a winged figure with three wings is reminiscent of one of the visions in the third part of the *Scivias,* but there the figure is identified as the "zeal of God."[115] Here we have the germ of a similar idea in the omnipresence of Wisdom in the cosmos, less protective than all-encompassing. One of Hildegard's favorite words, *sudat,* appears in section 2, which along with *viriditas* connotes moisture that is life-giving. *Sudare,* or moisture, is necessary for the life of the world and is reminiscent of the use of moisture in Isaiah 45. Newman suggests in her commentary on this piece that *sudat* has a double meaning, suggesting not only the fruitfulness of nature but also "Christ's agonized sweat

Latin Original	Literalist Translation	Poetic Translation
O virtus Sapientiae, *que circuiens circuisti* *comprehendendo omnia* *in una via que habet vitam,* *tres alas habens—*	O energy of Wisdom! you circled, circling encompassing all things in one path possessed of life. Three wings you have:	Sophia! you of the whirling wings, circling encompassing energy of God: you quicken the world in your clasp.
quarum una in altum volat *et altera de terra sudat* *et tercia undique volat—*	one of them soars on high, the second exudes from the earth, and the third flutters everywhere.	One wing soars in heaven one wing sweeps the earth and a third flies all around us.
Laus tibi sit, sicut te decet, *o Sapientia!*	Praise to you, as befits you, O Wisdom!	Praise to Sophia! Let all the earth praise her!

in Gethsemane (Luke 22:44)";[116] Dronke thinks that for Hildegard *sudare* does not recall the sweat of effort but instead is associated with the "distillation of a perfume, a heavenly quality."[117] Finally, the exuberance of the praise signifies the identification of this personification with the divine, and the three wings symbolize the triune presence in the whole cosmos.

The music is characterized by a long opening melismatic phrase emphasizing "O" and continuing through the line. Its tonality is somewhat minor in sound, underscoring the solemnity of Wisdom being praised and as befits one of the mysteries of God. The entire antiphon is more melismatic than syllabic and has a stately quality that contrasts somewhat with the imagery.

In the rest of the *Symphonia* there is a wealth of music and poetry to be explored. Because of the songs chosen here as illustrations, we have had to set aside others. While this is acceptable, there are a few major elements of Hildegard's imagery that appear in the songs, the theological-visionary works, and the scientific works that we have not investigated.

The first of these is her use of buildings and stones for imagery concerning the Church. She frequently uses the image of gemstones, which we briefly glimpsed in the use of "sapphire." However, she goes further than a reference to sapphire: those participating in celestial realms are often adorned with sparkling jewels; wounds are transformed by God into gems that adorn the building of Christ's Church; and the virtues dazzle not only by their radiance but by their adornment. In her sequence to St. Rupert, *O Ierusalem*, the city is built of fiery, living stones *(torrentibus lapidus, vivis lapidibus)*, which in the sunlight gleam like gems.[118] In addition, the Latin *gemma* can have several denotations: aside from referring to gemstones, it is also used to describe a budding plant. Since both flowers and precious stones represent for Hildegard the paradisal realm, her use of *gemma* has a compound meaning.[119] Because this theme is one frequently used in her poetry in the song cycle, it needs to be mentioned. Moreover, we have seen that Hildegard has a heightened awareness and sensitivity to color, perceived in the miniatures accompanying her other works and unmistakable in her use of color as a key image.

Second, we have mentioned another theme we have neglected somewhat in the analysis of the theological-visionary works: that of the centrality of Mary as the means by which the Word is made flesh. At times the figures of the Virgin, the Bride, the Church, Wisdom, and Charity all seem to be interchangeable, or at least caught up inextricably in one another. We should appreciate the fact that for Hildegard the Virgin Mary is a symbol of personal importance: for the incarnation is the axis around which the Church and the Christian faith revolve, and virginity is a way of life that brings one closer to the realms of heaven. Since Hildegard and her virgins are celebrating in these songs, it is appropriate to remember their personal as well as ecclesial significance.

Musically, we should point out the frequent use of "O" as an exclamation to begin her songs, especially in the case of antiphons. This recalls the "O antiphons" of Advent, which look toward the final coming of Christ and the renewal of heaven and earth, yet another of Hildegard's famous themes. We have mentioned her use of intervals, but many musicologists trace her songs mathematically in such a way that we can see that the numbers resolve into the "perfect" intervals of fourth, fifth, and octave; they also reflect a consistent use of the three classical mathematical means: the arithmetical, the geometric, and the harmonic.[120] In addition, Hildegard is daring within the few motifs she employs: a piece composed for the Holy Spirit, *O Ignis Spiritus Paracliti*, dares to end on a half-step, which usually signified the inharmonious rather than the harmony of heaven.[121]

Once again, it ought to be stressed that for Hildegard the lyric and music were inseparably intertwined; discussing the music textually poses problems in that it severely limits the ability of the reader to grasp this mutual interdependency and reliance that exists between words and tones.

We now move to a different type of musical composition: her play about the virtues, which is a singular combination of drama, poetry, music, and imagery. Nonetheless, it is integrally connected with the *Symphonia* in the sources we have for it but more significantly in the fusion of text and music that it represents.

The *Ordo Virtutum*: The First Morality Play

The *Ordo virtutum* can be found in outline or fragmentary form at the end of the *Scivias,* leading us to conjecture that it was completed at a relatively early date compared to other forms of musical composition by Hildegard. At least in the form of a sketch, its appearance in the *Scivias* indicates that the basic idea of a play of the virtues that is in some way involved with the celestial praises at the culmination of time was in her mind. The pictorial appearance of the visions in the treatise seems to have played a part in Hildegard's visualization of the character and costumes of the virtues. The finished work does make several departures from what seems to be its outline in the theological-visionary treatise, however. The all-important second section of the play is absent, even in the form of an idea, unless we want to take the sketchy portraits of some of the virtues in earlier visions of the treatise as the framework around which these were built. Although the *Liber vitae meritorum* is not often mentioned in conjunction with the *Ordo virtutum,* the play skillfully manages to convey to the listener, reader, or audience the overarching theme of predestined salvation history we find in *Scivias* with the idea that it is the practice of virtue that enables the soul to be saved in the *Liber vitae meritorum.* Conversely, it is the very lack of the opposition of virtue to vice in the *Ordo virtutum* that is one of its most distinctive qualities and that differentiates it from the later tradition of medieval morality plays. It is unquestionably a struggle between good and evil: with the exception of the figure of the Devil, all of the personifications are of virtues (except for the central character, the Soul). There are no personified vices, and we do not see any of the suggestive imagery about vice that is present in abundance in the *Liber vitae meritorum.* Vice is limited to the taunts and snares of the Devil and actions that take place entirely offstage. Besides the fragment in the *Scivias* there are only two extant copies of the manuscript, one of which is unreliable and copied at a later date. The authoritative manuscript for the *Ordo virtutum* is to be found in the Wiesbaden Reisencodex and was compiled shortly after Hildegard's death (1180–1190).[122] Because of the *Scivias* fragments this leaves us considerable latitude in dating the play in its final form, although it undoubtedly was performed at least once in the active middle period of Hildegard's life.

As we look at the *Ordo virtutum* we need to look at several factors involving its composition before turning to the content and structure of the play itself. The first factor to be addressed is whether the *Ordo* is indeed a play, and if so, is it a morality play. There has been a plethora of discussion concerning Hildegard's inclusion in the history of the development of drama. Until recently, and even now, writers exclude her in discussions of the evolution of dramatic forms, including the medieval morality play.[123] Quite rightly this tends to appall Hildegard scholars, who see the question of whether the *Ordo* is a play a moot one, given the weight of the evidence in favor of its performance as a play. Criteria given for excluding it usually include the lack of a history of performances, the fact that only men were involved in the staging of drama at this time and for centuries afterward, and that it has no elaborate set of stage directions that would signify the author's intent. Furthermore, it is difficult to situate this work of Hildegard's, considering where she falls chronologically. How much of the work is reliant on reacting to the *Psychomachia* of Prudentius or on the works of Hrosvit of Gandersheim who preceded her? How could she fit into a tradition of public medieval morality plays that clearly come after her? To what extent does her allegory resemble that used by other writers? Defenders of the play point out that from its very beginning and considering the title bestowed upon it, the inevitable inference is that it is indeed intended as a play; that it was carefully recorded and transcribed in a way that would appear unnecessary if Hildegard had not conceived it in such a way; and that simply because it does not fit a modern definition of what a drama should be should by no means exclude it, especially if that exclusion might well be based on misogynistic grounds.[124] Her allegorization is striking, because it is taking allegory a bit further to personification, and predominantly female personification. We will assume that the *Ordo virtutum* in its final form, not in the sketch found in the *Scivias,* was indeed intended to be the play it appears to be from the very start, since the evidence for this is quite sufficient and the "irregular" qualities of the play can be attributed to Hildegard's uniqueness rather than to its lack of dramatic structure.

The next factor to be taken into account is the time at which the finished play was written, and in conjunction with this, the occasion(s) for which it might have been performed. Those who discount Hildegard's work as a drama often include in their reasoning process the fact that women, especially cloistered women, could hardly have been expected to give public performances in the Middle Ages. This point makes sense, only overlooking that such a drama could be staged in a liturgical context or within the community itself without violating the norms of behavior for the twelfth century. If aspects of Hildegard's drama are unusual, then we also have to accept, as Dronke points out, that Hildegard was unusual *herself.* She was acutely aware of social station and norms, however, and is unlikely to have staged the play outside a religious or monastic context.

Is the *Ordo virtutum* a liturgical cantata rather than a morality play?[125] The answer seems to lie between these two options. It is a liturgical morality play. It shares with the morality plays the common desire to teach a didactic lesson about right and wrong and the way life should be lived out; it shares with liturgical pieces a more transcendent concern with bringing the audience to a fuller experience of the heavenly realms. Because of the inherent action implied by the play itself it is unlikely to have been a formal cantata or recital piece because it would lose much of its dramatic qualities in this form. Despite the large number of solo voices used it would be very static sung in this way, which is contrary to the natural action arising from the situations presented in the *Ordo virtutum*, in which interaction between personified roles takes place consistently. It would have been designed to be performed at a liturgical festival or occasion, and within the confines of an ecclesial environment. An added factor that would support this is the difference between the work of Hildegard and her dramatic predecessors and successors: unlike Prudentius and unlike the medieval morality plays in later centuries, the *Ordo* is not a staged combat between the virtues and vices but is rather a play organized around the struggle between the Devil and the Virtues for one single Soul.[126]

We turn now to the date and occasion for which the *Ordo virtutum* may have been composed. The most frequent suggestion is that it was composed for and performed at the dedication of Hildegard's foundation and the dedication of the Rupertsberg convent, which would have meant a very special liturgical celebration and one of great importance for her nuns. This would be in accord with an early date for the manuscript, for it would then have been completed before 1152 and able to be staged appropriately. It has been noted that the number of the Virtues in the play (around twenty) coincides with the approximate number of sisters who set out to found the Rupertsberg. The Devil could have been played by Volmar or another priest, and the first section could easily have been sung by several dignitaries or by male adjuncts to the convent from Rupertsberg or Disibodenberg. Perhaps the most intriguing suggestion comes from Pamela Sheingorn, who suggests that in keeping with one of the major themes of the play, virginity, the play was staged for the occasion on which those entering the convent in their profession would leave the world behind and embrace the virtues they aspired to follow. This would argue for a somewhat later date of completion, although it would leave it open to speculation. She has a very interesting explanation for this: she compares the striking parallelism between the liturgical ritual *(Ordo)* for consecrated virgins and the text of Hildegard's play.[127] Whether or not the argument holds, the parallelism is significant in confirming that the *Ordo virtutum* did have a liturgical place and a ritual significance as well as a dramatic one. Sheingorn suggests that one of the reasons it has been overlooked as ritual and as drama is that they have been defined as distinctive from each other, whereas Hildegard is fusing the two genres[128] (which at her time may not have been set genres as they are defined in hindsight today).

The Musical and Poetic Structure of the Ordo Virtutum

The structure of the play is not clearly set out in the manuscript, yet the play falls roughly into the following divisions or scenes of unequal duration:

> Prologue or Introduction
> Scene 1, The Complaints of Souls Trapped in Bodies
> Scene 2, The Self-Definition of the Virtues
> Scene 3, The Return of the Penitent Soul
> Scene 4, The Triumph over Satan
> Finale/Processional

This structure is generally agreed upon as containing the major shifts in the play, even if the stage directions are not present. Details of organization may be argued diversely, but as a whole these divisions are agreed upon at large.

The Prologue begins with the Patriarchs and Prophets asking "who are these who are like clouds?" Their function is to introduce us to the Virtues, who immediately reply. The sung part for the Patriarchs and Prophets in actuality is minimal and intended for the male voice; it does, however, make the important connection for Hildegard with the roots of the meaning of salvation firmly grounded in the prefiguring of the Old Testament and covenant. This is reflected in the text, where the Patriarchs and Prophets observe their relation to the Virtues by saying: *Nos sumus radices et vos rami / fructus viventis oculi, / et nos umbra in illo fuimus* (We are the roots and you the boughs, fruits of the living eye [or bud], and in that eye we were the shadow.) Although brief, the speech is an important one. We observe the sharp and compact way in which Hildegard uses her images: *oculi* with its double meaning of "eye" and "bud" is a play on words that renders the image of the tree here even more powerful; the Old Testament figures represent the deep and ancient roots of God's design. The tree grows to its maturity in Christ Jesus, who is referred to by the Virtues as the boughs of this tree. If we look even further into this compressed image, it is possible to distinguish a possible reference to the Trinity: the living eye as the Father; the Word of God as the flourishing of the tree (and referring to the speech of the Virtues, made just previously, equating Christ's limbs and the boughs); and the Spirit in the "fruits" of the living Eye, with which the Virtues are identified (the "fruits" of the Spirit are expressed in the virtuous Christian life). In this Prologue Hildegard has managed in the short space of three speeches and eight lines to outline the context for her play theologically. It will revolve around the Virtues, who are referred to as "shining with the Word of God" and who thus participate in the light of the Godhead; the history of salvation was in shadow but can now be seen clearly as a result of the incarnation. Musically, Hildegard is using the standard ecclesial modes of chant, although with some interesting shifts and juxtapositions.[129] The play begins in the Dorian mode, as if in a sequence, with melismatic sections that parallel each other in the personifications of the Patriarchs and Prophets and of the Virtues. Hildegard's characteristic use of rising fifths and fourths to the octave is present from the very beginning of this play.

The first and third scenes have most of the action in the play. While the second scene is vital to the play and its composition, there is not much plot development in it; there is not much plot development in the Prologue or the Finale, for that matter, whose concerns are more theological and mystical than plot driven. **Scene 1** opens with the lament of the Souls/Virtues about the condition of the fallen world in which they are surrounded by the "shadow" and "realms" of sin and into which they have strayed from their proper place as "daughters of the King." Here Hildegard sets up the condition of the world as we know and lament it ourselves, considering the difficulty of living a life totally set upon God and reliant on the practice of virtue. In this scene we are also introduced to *Anima* (the Soul), who seems to be more cheerful than the others but mainly as a result of naïveté. The Virtues are well aware of the things the Embodied Soul must come across and combat. They mention this to the "happy Soul" in this scene, which results in the Soul suffering progressively from disappointment, depression, and a desire to flee the realm of the virtues in order to experience the world. The Soul moves from her initial happiness in contemplating the "garment" God has prepared for her to a desire to discard that garment altogether. The image of the garment and the dialogue between the Virtues and the Soul indicate their deeper understanding of what and who they are; the Soul plunges from rapture to depression because she does not want this temporary, imperfect garment in which she was created, she wants to be clothed in the resplendent garment of salvation in all its final brilliance. She does not accept the conditions of her creation in the fallen world. Ulrike Wiethaus remarks that Hildegard means to take an anti-Catharist stand in this play and that this is the purpose for which Hildegard composed it.[130] If this is even just a part of the reasoning behind Hildegard's writing, we see it reflected here in the first scene, where the Soul will not accept her present condition or the intended goodness of her creation and embodiment. She wants to exist as human beings were meant to before the Fall; the Virtues realize that the Fall has only been reversed in Christ, and to be restored to an even greater glory in re-created splendor one must fight and persevere. They exhort the Soul, saying that she must fight with them. But the now unhappy Soul resists this idea because of her desire for bliss without struggle, failing to recognize her own weakness, which can only be supplanted by God's assistance. Musically, there is a distinct contrast between the happy and unhappy Soul that underlines the change in mood; instead of soaring notes rising in intervals of perfect fourths and fifths, the music reflects the Soul's uncertainty syllabically. Knowledge of God (the first of the personified Virtues to speak independently in the play) points out her lack of acknowledgment of who she is, directly: "Look at the dress you are wearing, daughter of salvation: be steadfast and you'll never fall. / You do not know or see or taste the One who has set you here."

The lament of the unhappy Soul that she only wants to enjoy herself exposes her weakness concerning worldly pleasures, and immediately afterward the Devil enters, promising her all the honors the world can bestow upon her. The Devil cannot sing; he can barely speak mellifluously. The *Ordo* calls for the Devil to speak in a voice that is *strepitus* (grating, shouting, growling). Despite the clear contrast with the musicality of the Virtues, this Soul succumbs to the lures of the Devil, unlike Christ in the desert (to which the Devil's speech is a reference). Innocence is asked by the other Virtues to lament the loss of the Soul, and Humility, Queen of the Virtues, points out that they are immune to these deceiving ways, since they recognize the true nature of the Devil as the "dragon of old" (Lucifer). Nevertheless, the Soul departs.

Scene 2 consists of the Virtues introducing themselves, explaining their characteristics, and pointing out what each Virtue can do for all the other Virtues and Souls. It is full of implied movement and activity; it has been suggested that in this section there is a type of dance.[131] This scene is uniquely Hildegardian both in the text exposition and in its inseparable musical characteristics. The center of the play is to be found here, despite the lack of forward movement in the plot. It is the dramatic center in its liturgical nature, for it is the celebration and explanation of the connected virtues that enable us to dwell with and in God. The musical capstone comes approximately halfway through the entire *Ordo,* in the thirty-eighth item, which contains the amazingly high and transcendent song in response to the introduction and contribution of *Casistas* (Chastity), extremely melismatic in character.[132] This entire scene includes some of the richest and most striking melismas in the piece, although syllabic constructions are used also. Each Virtue is unique in textual expression with its inseparable musical setting, which is virtually impossible to describe without hearing the piece itself. Whether pitched in a higher or lower range, there is a characteristic sound of the heavenly and transcendent in each of the Virtues' songs; the text is unique to each Virtue, mirroring each one's particular qualities. The structure of this section is engaging in its pattern too: each of the Virtues declares herself (I am . . .), describes her characteristics, and goes on to say how it is she supports all the others or can assist them in living the life of grace. The rest of the Virtues all then respond in chorus, affirming what has been declared. It is a genuine celebration of virtue in a way that is neither sentimental nor abstract but hopeful and practical. This does not mean the *imagery* is not abstract, for we are speaking of a play that Hildegard composed. It is filled with densely packed metaphors and frequent scriptural allusions, especially to the Song of Songs. There are martial metaphors in which the Virtues trample on those things that are unworthy; at such moments the music takes on a regular syllabic quality to underline the action suggested by the text. The Virtues personified in this section, to whom we have not been introduced, are Humility, Queen of the Virtues; Heavenly Love; Modesty; Mercy; Charity; Fear of God; Obedience; Faith; Patience; Discretion; Contempt for the World; Chastity; and (probably)[133] Discipline. Innocence and Knowledge of God take part, but we have heard from them before. Humility has spoken before but now clarifies her status as the Queen of the Virtues and shares with Chastity the identification with the Virgin Mary (who was humble and chaste). There is also an echoing of the stepping on the serpent usually attributed to Mary in a reversal of Eve's downfall, which appears in the section when Victory is singing. The call of Humility to joy at the end of this section of the celestial dance ends on a note of sadness as the Virtues mourn for the Lost Soul (echoing the parable of the prodigal son).

Scene 3 consists of the return of the Soul to the area in which the Virtues have remained. She appears weak, beaten down, and penitent. She approaches the Virtues asking for help in her ailing condition, and the Virtues keep calling her back to themselves. "Her melody wanders up and down in the Phrygian mode, and coupled with the lamenting words, is affectingly sorrowful."[134] It is of interest that the Soul must make a decisive move toward the Virtues (they admonish her to "run to them quickly") before she can be truly assisted by them. Their exhortations occur in three separate musical phrases: it is the last of these that is the one quoted above. Her wounds and her illness are likened to the wounds of Christ, and healing is only found in Christ through the aid of the Virtues, freely embraced by the repentant sinner. The Soul feels tarnished by the sweetness of sin and is afraid to approach the Virtues, whom she has told at the outset she never should have left. There are reverberations of the resurrection in the Virtues' exhorting the Soul not to be afraid *(noli timere)*. The Soul appeals finally to Humility, who orders the others to help her up, an allegorical interpretation of the virtue that must first be embraced to truly learn the others. Humility embraces the Soul and helps her "for the sake of Christ," who has suffered for the Soul.

Scene 4 opens with the Devil demanding that the Soul return to him, for she belongs to him. The now Penitent Soul is strong enough to resist and defy the Devil; she recognizes him for what he truly is, a "trickster" and a liar. She casts off her miseries in the form of her stained "garment," representing the flesh, and takes on a new "garment" of holiness. She determines to fight the Devil and challenges him, and the music syllabically reinforces that determination. Humility calls on Victory to bring in her warriors and bind the Devil and chain him underfoot. The triumph over Satan is, as Ekdahl so concisely remarks, "one of the most glorious moments in all of medieval music drama"; for the female voice, the music is set in a ringing, high pitch, ecstatically phrased and embellished melismatically. The Devil, never one to give up, attacks Chastity, saying that since she has never had a sexual relationship with a man she knows nothing of God's intention in creation; her refutation of him textually underlines the truth and triumph of the Virgin birth and, both in wording and music, reminds us of the earlier scene in which Victory symbolically (and now actually) treads upon the serpent. The scene ends with a triumphant hymn to God, from whom "a fountain in fiery love" has flowed so that all may enter the heavenly Jerusalem.

The **Finale**, which has often been envisioned as a processional, is a mystical hymn focused on Christ's salvific act. It begins with a reminder of a time when all things flourished and flowered in the *viriditas* of God. Later, when the freshness had vanished, a champion arose to defend the dry world by taking its wounds into himself. Hildegard uses here some of her favorite images, juxtaposing freshness and dryness, speaking of the Son as a "mirror of [your] fatherhood," and once again using the image of the eye. This eye could not be satisfied until Christ's body was "full of jewels." We have the double meaning of Christ's suffering body and the suffering body of the people of the Church, who at the end of the hymn are called on to bend the knee to the Father so that God may stretch out his hand to them. The entire section is mystical in its style, musically as well as textually; it is full of melismas, and the play ends in a particularly long melismatic phrase on the Latin *porrigat* that underlines the power and length of God's reach (see example below for this phrase).

por rí–gat.

FIGURE 8

The Significance of the Ordo Virtutum

The *Ordo virtutum* is a work that celebrates the themes dearest to Hildegard's heart. In her theological vision the most important factors are the incarnation of the Word; the virginity by way of which this event became possible; the reality of suffering and evil but the inevitable triumph of the good through God's predestination; and the re-creation of the world into a creation gorgeous beyond all imagining. Because all of these themes are touched upon, it is a type of *summa* of Hildegard's theological outlook. Despite her affirmation of creation, old and renewed, we also sense the tension between her positive view of the Mother of God and her negative view of the sexual act; Hildegard's writings always indicate a tension between the triumphant state of virginity and the realities of sexual reproduction. She is no dualist, however; she accepts the realities of creation as it is now but believed, as many did during her century, that virginity, especially in women, made a person able to come closer to God. Virgins were the spouses of the heavenly Bridegroom and no other, with no divided loyalties and away from the temptations of the world. In this context, Sheingorn's suggestion that the play was intended for liturgical use on the occasion of the consecration of virgins is an apt one, whether this was the actual case or not. She outlines in her article specific moments in the ritual that would accord well with its performance before the ceremony. Each "soul" would be given over in marriage by the person responsible for her to the Bridegroom (the bishop standing in Christ's stead). The veiling of the virgins, done in a special way in Hildegard's convent to represent the heavenly light, would parallel the action when the Repentant Soul casts off her tarnished garment to be replaced by a clean and white one. Even the wording of the consecration rite resembles the words found in Hildegard's musical morality play. The processional ending, as envisioned by Sheingorn, only ratifies the whole process:

> In Hildegard's play the Soul recognizes the folly and danger of life in the world and receives medicine from the Virtues that heals her wounds. The dominant presence of Chastity toward the end of the play and her identification with the Virgin Mary reinforce the idea that the Soul must persist in virginity. Then the Virtues address God, both as Christ and Father. . . . This ending provided a perfect transition to the *Ordo* for the Consecration of Virgins; in this *Ordo* the bishop speaks as Christ—and I would suggest that his role begins here, at the end of Hildegard's play.[135]

The *Ordo virtutum* is a celebration of virginity and virtue, giving the strength to come to new life in Christ. The alliteration of the English words resonate even more strongly in the Latin: *virginitas, virtus, vis, viriditas.*

Musically and poetically the *Ordo virtutum* is an achievement of reciprocity: they are inseparable from each other. When we pause to consider also the multivalence of the subject she is treating, this symmetry becomes even more impressive. Besides giving us fuller insight into Hildegard's vision and her visions, it is a rare achievement in the twelfth century or in any other. It defies categorization as ritual or as morality play but manages to transcend and include both genres in its structure and execution.

Mystical Polyphony in Hildegard's Music

How can we even introduce the notion of polyphony after spending an entire chapter discussing music that was closest to chant in form, and irregular and idiosyncratic at that? It seems to me that we find her polyphonic gifts expressed through her non-polyphonic compositions. Despite the fact that she does not fit the definition of a composer of polyphony in terms of musical form, she comes close to it in language: the dictionary defines "polyphonic prose" as one that uses all the tools of polyphony *except* metrical consistency. These tools are alliteration, assonance, and rhyme. In an unconventional way we find it in her text and music with their expanded and compressed images, which are mirrored in the use of syllabic and melismatic phrases. We find it in her subject matter, where the dense imagery of the cosmos, incarnation, salvation, and the celestial realm all overlap, creating a deeper, more complete understanding of what could have been simply a trite repetition of conventional Christian doctrinal themes. As with the other visionary works, the treatises, Hildegard has the ability to surpass the form in which she works: although the rudiments and structure are totally orthodox and acceptable theologically, within that order her visionary insight and imagination soar, at times into almost surrealistic imagery. With these gifts she manages to re-present the Christian faith and its mysteries in a way that is engaging but puzzling, leaving the reader or listener breathless and dizzy at the end of them. Upon reflection, as we untangle the various threads so we may look more carefully at her work after our initial exposure, we find that the source of the vertigo comes from the polyphonic quality of her mysticism. Despite the fact that Hildegard does not speak introspectively about her own mystical journey or personal spiritual life, which has led many to doubt her mystical credentials, she accomplishes the same result by taking the other person, the one receiving the form of communication she has designed, *into* the center of the mystical experience. When someone enters that mystical realm, he or she is accosted by the synaesthesis of sound and picture, which Hildegard experienced naturally, plus the added stimuli of the biblical, ecclesial, and liturgical allusions that made up Hildegard's monastic context. The texture of Hildegard's visionary output is dense with mysticism and layers of meaning that, as polyphonic, seem to be dancing with and around one another constantly.

Her music shows us some of her own development spiritually. We see a movement from the simple to the complex to the truly simple reflected in some of the song-cycle pieces and most evidently in the composition of the *Ordo virtutum.* Appearing simply as a sketch and composite part of the process of salvation history in her early work, *Scivias,* she goes on to mature her thoughts on the subject of virtue and vice with the complexity of their characterizations in the *Liber vitae meritorum* and then resolves them into the deeper meaning of virtue in itself that we see in the *Ordo virtutum* and the *De operatione Dei.*

Perhaps it is in her music that we find the central image of Hildegard as a polyphonic mystic. She herself thought sound, especially music, and sight were inseparable in her experience of the Living Light. By listening to her music, however far it departs from the original way in which it may have been sung or presented, we can experience in an aesthetic form what a multivalent and polyphonic mystical vision is like, insofar as we are able to capture it. Hildegard's music is technically fascinating to musicologists. Her theology is engaging to theologians. Her poetry and self-expression in a variety of writings are appealing to the literary scholar. Her uneducated and yet thoroughly liturgical Latin is a puzzle and a fascination to scholars of Latin and monastics alike. Her formation in a totally religious monastic environment fascinates those interested in psychology, history, and spirituality. Yet within a single composition of her music, one is able to experience all of these dimensions at some point, and they do come together sometimes within several lines of one another. We can say (going in reverse) that Hildegard's music was an expression of her spiritual life as a Benedictine nun, the use of chant dictated by time and circumstances, and the subjects in her songs and especially in her play fraught with psychological insights into human character. We can trace the possible sources or lack thereof for her knowledge of Latin and works written in Latin that could have been known to her. We can speak at great length about the style of her poetry and attempt to translate the tone as well as the literal meaning of her words, dwelling also on her contribution to literature. We can spend time benefiting from her theological insights and exploring the fresh way in which they are presented, seeing their relevance for the twelfth and the twenty-first centuries. We can immerse ourselves either in the beauty of the sound of her music or in the beauty of its structure.

What we return to in the end is that Hildegard was also fascinated by all these things and created all her works as an expression of the many gifts she felt she had been graced with through her vision of the Living Light. You cannot become either more mystical or more polyphonic than this.

In the next two chapters we will be looking at ways in which this mystical gift of polyphony expressed itself in an outreach to the world around her. In the next chapter, we consider her works on nature and biology, the *Lingua ignota,* her lives of the saints, and her commentary on the *Rule of Benedict* as expressions of her view of the cosmos through her visionary spirituality. In the chapter following, we look at Hildegard as a prophetess for her times, seeing how this role as the "Sibyl of the Rhine" affected those around her: her vast correspondence, her sermons, and her role in the community. While drawing on what we have discussed before, we will also look at her preaching journeys and her sermons and her relationship to the "effeminate age" in which she lived and felt called upon to confront.

IV

Earth and Heaven in Dialogue

We now shift to a different way of looking at Hildegard and her world: in place of the primarily inspired and visionary works, we move to those without explicit visionary claims or linked with Hildegard's vision and ability to "foresee" the future or interpret the present with the help of the Living Light. These works are much more varied in type than those we looked at in previous chapters. Despite the variation and the lack of visionary status these works remain an important part of Hildegard's life and works. Since we are attempting to look at Hildegard as a whole, these works in some way fit and balance the entire picture.

As a bridge between the preceding chapter and this one and with the subsequent chapter in mind, we will look at this diverse group of written works in the following order: first, we will look at her "unknown language," which she used at times in writing lyrics for her music, and its possible purposes; second, we will look at her lives of the saints and commentaries on the *Rule of Benedict* and the *Athanasian Creed,* the so-called "minor works" of her writings; third, we will go to her "scientific" treatises, which deal with the natural world, biology, and healing. As we shall see, Hildegard's unique way of looking at the visible and invisible worlds as inseparably connected will influence each of these diverse achievements in its own particular way.

We have seen how Hildegard's works attempt to join heaven and earth, usually with her eyes fixed firmly on celestial rather than earthly realms. We recognize in her writings until this point that she has given time to both the macrocosm and the microcosm in her works and that the effort has been to show how they are joined inseparably as a result of the embodiment of God's love in the incarnation and in the Spirit present in *Ecclesia,* the Church; *Sapientia,* Wisdom; and *Caritas,* Love. We have seen her exaltation of the life of virginity as a way in which one can focus all of one's attention toward God. We now consider what this meant for Hildegard in putting her visionary commands and ideals into practice in the context of the convent, the world, and the historical setting of the twelfth century.

The Lingua Ignota

One of the most puzzling of Hildegard's creative ideas, this "unknown language," or *lingua ignota,* is composed of approximately one thousand words formed from a set of letters corresponding to the alphabet and called the *litterae ignotae.* Usually the purpose of an unknown language was to create a parallel form of speech for a particular purpose, such as a utopian language or an ethereal, spiritual language, both of which would transcend ordinary boundaries of language and thought. For Hildegard, we have some evidence that the first use of this created language was musical. In a letter to Pope Anastasius, mostly berating him for his conduct, she mentions this fact:

> But He who is great and without flaw has now touched a humble dwelling, so that it might see a miracle and form unknown letters and utter in an unknown tongue melody and speech.[136]

Moreover, these words appear in her songs. The clearest example of this is in her antiphon written for the dedication of a church, entitled *O Orzchis Ecclesia* (*lingua ignota* appears in italics):

> O *orzchis* Ecclesia, armix divinis praecinta et hyazintho ornata, tu es *caldemia* stigmatum *loifolum* et urbs scientarium. O, o, tu es etiam *crizanta* in alto sono et es *chorzta* gemma.

Despite its appearance in her songs and the extent of the vocabulary itself, there has been relatively little written about this unknown language. What has been said tends to be a reference in passing while speaking about other subjects concerning Hildegard. Some think using this unknown language was another way, in addition to their use of special clothing, in which the aristocratic Rupertsberg nuns could feel set apart from the world and from other convents. Others think it might have been a private language among the sisters to use as a reminder of the unknown and wonderful world to come, or a return to the paradise that had been lost. Its use could have included many or all of these interpretations. Whatever its primary purpose, it is largely lost to us except through speculation. Why would Hildegard create such a language and write it down?

In commenting on the song cited above, Schnapp suggests that these rough, consonantal sounds served musically to "build a ritual bridge between the Mass at Rupertsberg and its heavenly prototype." He is in agreement with those who observe that this would have been connected to the elaborate use of allegorical costuming for festive occasions and says that "these virginal words participate in a delicate blurring of boundaries between *nomen* and *numen,* natural and supernatural, convent and celestial church."[137] Musically, the *Lingua ignota* mirrors Hildegard's use of alliteration and rhythm in the united text and tonality of her songs; like many unknown languages, there is a use of constants of one form or another in a repetitive way. In all of Hildegard's linguistic constructions, 95 percent of these words contain either the grouping *sch, x,* or *z;* only about two hundred of the thousand-word vocabulary do not contain a *z.*[138] Therefore, the link to music and creating a meeting place where heaven and earth can be joined, however briefly, seems one logical meaning for the use of the *Lingua ignota.* One of the fascinating facts about this language, however, is that it is not limited to the celestial or musical spheres. In fact, it virtually forms a connection, albeit a cryptic one, between the subject of Hildegard's music and her scientific works. The unknown language was used for many things within the convent, including words that had very practical meanings. Approximately a quarter of the invented terms (neologisms) refers to the natural world, and nearly 150 terms refer specifically to the human body, which links this language to Hildegard's scientific and medical works.[139] Thus earth as well as heaven is the concern of the *Lingua ignota* and takes well to the structure of the microcosm and the macrocosm, which we saw most fully in *De operatione Dei,* a structure that pervades Hildegard's conscious approach to many different subjects.

We see also the influence of what Hildegard regarded as a natural hierarchy within the grouping of these terms and to a limited extent their use of certain sounds. She begins with God and the supernatural realm; terms for God begin with *a* and end in *z* except when she is referring to the incarnate Word. Logically, the word for the Son begins in the middle of the alphabet with *l,* symbolizing the centrality of the incarnation in the history of salvation and its placement after the old covenant and before the end-time. Heavenly beings again span *a* to *z,* with the obvious exception of the devil or the fallen angels. She moves then to the saints, as we have seen before, and the patriarchs and prophets. Humanity is next and includes a list of kinship terms to identify the relationships between people personally and as groups. The Church follows, then the secular order; after this we move to more concrete items such as time measurements, the socioeconomic sphere, and the natural world.[140] Although organized according to hierarchy, this does not reflect the actual number of words assigned to each. Compared with the number of words coined for the natural world, the number used for the supernatural realms are very few; for example, there are more than sixty entries for birds alone, while there are only nineteen words meant to correspond to the celestial realms. It is interesting that, from the vantage point of semantic analysis, Schnapp speaks of her hierarchical order being disturbed by an internal "turbulence" that disrupts the more obvious ordering of words or the usage of certain suffixes.[141] This "turbulence" has been a factor in all of Hildegard's works and is an expression of her creativity and possibly of the subversive side of her nature: we have seen it in the song cycles, the theological-visionary works, and the order in her life, which was often abruptly disordered (as in the move from Disibodenberg). When we look at the words that cover her scientific and medical interests, we see that together they form the largest part of the vocabulary. Although it has been suggested that terms for the human body were invented to modestly avoid mention of body parts offensive to a virgin, Hildegard's directness in these matters (as we shall see below) belies such an interpretation. Besides, the medieval world necessarily had to be in greater touch with the body and its functions. Unlike the present century, it could hardly hide bodily needs from the world at large.

The *Lingua ignota* (figure 9) is a language with a liturgical purpose of enhancing the mysteries of ritual celebrations; it is a language that was understood in private between the nuns and in this way reminded them of the link between earth and heaven, no matter how mundane the task being performed; it is a language that resonated with rich overtones for those who used it and leaves us puzzling it out etymologically in a way that can only belabor its inner meaning to the point that it becomes a lexical curiosity. For Hildegard and her sisters, however, its very secrecy must have enhanced their sense of a special vocation and life lived in the convent at Rupertsberg, one that affirmed what was central and treasured in their lives.

Other "unknown" or private languages are known to have served the purpose of bonding a group and reminding them of a special task or mission; in this case, it is Hildegard's vision of the intimate connection between the life of the dedicated virgin, the celestial link through music, and the monastic life as a constant place for practicing the presence of God, the Living Light, which eventually after death would come to be known in full.

Codex Vindobonensis.

Codex Wisbadensis.

LINGUA IGNOTA   FIGURE 9

The Lives of Saints, the *Rule of Benedict*, and the Athanasian Creed

In a way, these minor works of Hildegard mirror the coming together of heaven and earth in that their subject is the saints, including the founder of the Benedictine order. The subject unites them, while their reasons for being written vary. The *Life of St. Disibod* was written at the request of the abbot of Disibodenberg; the *Life of Rupert* was undoubtedly a way of pointing to the holy origins of the land on which her own convent was built and was a hymn to its patron saint; the commentaries on the *Rule of Benedict* and on the Athanasian Creed were written for the edification of others, although the final work is more theological in its content than are the previous three. Of these works, only the *Explanation of the Rule of Benedict* has been translated from the Latin;[142] none are very lengthy, particularly when we consider Hildegard's tendency to write voluminous commentaries and treatises. Most authors with an interest in Hildegard have passed over these works with little comment. There is probably good reason for this neglect, since they appear clustered together in a miscellaneous group without a common theme. For Hildegard, they may well have had the common theme of linking the celestial world of the saints with the realities of the present on earth, a reality too obvious to her and others in the twelfth century for her to linger in explanations. Accordingly, we will be concerned as much with her *reasons* for their composition as their *content*. The saints are, in themselves, a way of locating a meeting place between heaven and earth in persons of extraordinary virtue; in the medieval world, the saints could not only intercede in prayer but left behind them visible traces of their lives (relics, buildings) and their influence in the places in which they lived out their earthly lives.

The *Life of St. Rupert* was undoubtedly written around the time of the move from Disibodenberg to Rupertsberg. It is an attempt by Hildegard to revive the cult of St. Rupert and to legitimate the vision that called her to move there. According to her account Rupert was a young man disposed to goodness from the start, supported by the aid and counsel of his mother, Bertha. Bertha was a Christian, but Rupert's father, Robolaus, was a pagan. These and other hagiographic passages are rather reminiscent of the life of St. Augustine. Hildegard claimed that Rupert (or Robert) was the grandson of a Carolingian prince who owned vast estates around the area of Bingen. His pagan father died at an early age, and Rupert came into great wealth. Bertha, however, raised her son to fear and love God; at the age of thirteen, when she suggested that they build an oratory to pray for their souls' salvation, Rupert quoted the gospel and the prophets and suggested that their first task was to share with those who were homeless and in want. So instead of an oratory, Bertha built hospices to care for the sick. At the age of fifteen Rupert went on a pilgrimage to Rome. Upon his return he began to give alms and property to the poor, and he built many churches on his lands. When he was twenty he died, for it was the will of God that he not be corrupted by worldly companions who wished to take advantage of him. Thus his goodness and purity were preserved, and his good works were carried on by Bertha, who survived him by twenty-five years. She founded a monastery on the site of her son's tomb, which was destroyed by the Normans in the ninth century and "remained desolate" until the twelfth century, when God guided Hildegard in a vision to restore the cult of St. Rupert by establishing a convent on the monastery's remains. His feast day, on the fifteenth of May, reflected for Hildegard a saint who was still full of purity and freshness *(viriditas)* when he died,[143] his goodness a beacon to all.

The *Life of St. Disibod* also celebrates a saint's early dedication to goodness, although this is probably a hagiographic convention. Hildegard most often compares him with John the Baptist, wandering in the wilderness and preaching God's word to all who would listen. Disibod's life was one of a holy ascetic and wandering pilgrim. According to his legend he was an Irish bishop who was exiled from his diocese and traveled to Germany with three companions to keep him company. When he arrived, he built himself a hermitage on the side of a wooded mountain near where the rivers Nahe and Glan run together. Later, he established a monastery at that location, but on the summit of the same mountain. While he himself never entered the community, preferring to live the life of an ascetic hermit, St. Disibod was renowned for his gifts of healing and spiritual direction. Unlike St. Rupert, he had a long life; after living this life of rigorous and solitary asceticism he died at the age of eighty-one, and the perfumed odor of the saints rose from his tomb when he was buried. Many recorded miracles occurred at the site of his tomb. Apart from his ascetic life, Hildegard seems to have admired St. Disibod, her first patron, for his humility. Humility, as we have seen, was a key virtue for Hildegard. Some time before composing the *Life* she sent hymns to the saint written by Hildegard at the request of Abbot Kuno, accompanied by a letter of rebuke. In the hymns she speaks of Disibod as "God's life-creating finger" *(viriditas),* who blessed all with whom he came in contact. It may well be that the letter accompanying these compositions was a direct command from Hildegard for the abbot and the community of Disibodenberg to emulate the founder more closely in both his asceticism and his practice of humility. The *Life* itself was composed almost twenty years later at the request of Kuno's successor, Helenger, as abbot of Disibodenberg. From the date of the letter accompanying the *Life,* it belongs to the latter period of Hildegard's life, probably around 1170.

The *Explanation of the Rule of Benedict* is of interest because although she lived in accordance with the Benedictine Rule, St. Benedict is rarely referred to in any of Hildegard's other works. There is the possible exception of the *Letters,* although the Rule is more often alluded to than discussed; however, we have seen her internalization of some of the central virtues Benedict sought to cultivate. This explanation was intended as a commentary on the Rule intended for an unknown group of recipients who requested Hildegard's enlightened commentary in order to see if they might better understand the intent and meaning of the Rule and whether they were observing it properly. As was common at the time, the request is worded formally in the style of the era; it is unclear where this religious community was located, and it is even unsure whether they were a group of women or of men. They identify themselves as the *congregatio Hunniensis,* and scholars have suggested several communities of the time as possibilities: a community of nuns at Liege, one in Heningense, and Ravengiersburg at Trier.[144] It seems far more likely that whatever group was petitioning Hildegard was a smaller canonical house, since they mention that they have been accused of lax observance of the Rule in the letter requesting her help. In any event, their identity does not alter the style or content of the reply. It was probably composed during the late 1150s or early 1160s.

Hildegard's style in this exposition is much simpler and to the point than in many of her other writings. Although the petitioners were asking her as both a visionary and a Benedictine authority to guide them, there is less interpolation of the direct visions or words of God revealed to Hildegard about this matter. Those that appear are at the beginning and the end, which could be as much a formalized style of writing as it is to any claim of prophetic insight. It begins, as do so many of Hildegard's writings, with her appeal to herself as merely a "poor little female in form" who must depend on the light of God for any teaching she might be able to offer (1);[145] it concludes with a repetition of this humility formula and a statement that what she has written was heard by her "from Wisdom who taught me the obscure things in the rule of blessed father Benedict so that I could present them openly" (38). Curiously, she chooses to comment in detail on many chapters of the Rule while omitting others completely. Some of these omissions are noteworthy; for example the chapters Benedict wrote specifically concerning the role of the abbot, of obedience, and of taking counsel from the community. However, we see her interpretation in her elaboration of the virtues important in her own life that appear also to be central in the Rule: she speaks at some length about the virtues of discretion, humility, and obedience.

We also see some of her own assumptions in the reading of the Rule. For example, discretion rather than literal observance is important so that all might live in harmony, which for Hildegard includes both physical and spiritual health (2). She clearly observes the Rule with the hermeneutic of moderation and discretion: where Benedict has not clearly commanded or forbidden certain things, they are then left open to the discretion of the abbot or superior of the community. For Hildegard, this is why Benedict does not discuss certain points or issues (12). She allows for the wearing of undergarments, as an example of moderation, pointing out that these are customarily worn in their time, unlike the time of St. Benedict himself; it may even further the goal of suppressing lustful thoughts and feelings that is the spiritual meaning behind Benedict's orders about clothing (15, 28). Since she takes an active interest in the liturgy, the sections about the rules concerning time and type of worship are slightly adapted to her understanding: she widens the meaning of Benedict's rules concerning the divine service and the way the canonical Hours should be celebrated by combining several of the principles found in the Rule itself (11–14). She underlines the reverence that should be given to guests that is central to the Benedictine Rule and its innate concern for hospitality, where the guest is treated as Christ himself would be welcomed (26). Here Hildegard's virtue of "contempt of the world" joins with humility in recommending that the community be examples for one another and for monastic guests. She reiterates Benedict's concern for the vow of stability, but cleverly manages to avoid the awkward question of transfer to another monastery that keeps the Rule more strictly, a much debated issue in the course of the twelfth-century monastic reforms (32). Each person wishing to remain in a monastery other than the one at which they were professed must be handled individually, asking practical questions such as the circumstances of their arrival, the possibility of a safe return, and whether they have had leave from their original monastery for travel. All of this is interesting to us because Hildegard held some interesting ideas for both a Benedictine and an oblate: she disapproved of the oblation of children, surprisingly, and the vow of stability to one monastery hardly kept her from separating from Disibodenberg and founding her own convent! She discusses the procedure for oblation in (30) and hints at the tensions between oblates and those who join the monastery later, especially in the case of priests (31). She is expansive in her interpretation of diet and the type of dishes that may be offered at table, which reflects her medical opinion that food should sustain and nourish the health of each person; abstention from food and fasting can only be undertaken with the appropriate permission and mainly for purposes of health (21, 23).

What do we learn about Hildegard and her relationship to the Benedictine Rule in her commentary? We hear familiar themes repeated and probably instilled by the Rule itself, such as the concern for the practice of certain virtues, especially humility, reverence, obedience, and discretion. She reflects the moderation present in the Rule and probably stretches it to lengths other Benedictines would not. She is a strict observer of the Rule in its outline, but in its specific prescriptions she saw it would be necessary to adapt to the concerns of health and illness, the character of the particular community, and the difference between the time when the Rule was written and its contemporary practice. Here we see her mature evaluation and departure from her teacher, Jutta, in taking a moderate and occasionally elastic interpretation of the Rule in favor of moderation over asceticism. However, she is not lax in its observation, nor does this document support such an interpretation; aside from those virtues mentioned above, she prizes the Benedictine observance of stability highly, as we shall see in her answers to many of her correspondents in the *Letters*.

The *Explanation of the Creed of St. Athanasius* was specifically directed toward her sisters in the Rupertsberg and is a combination of a commentary and a homily on the Athanasian Creed. This Creed, although attributed to Athanasius, was not written by him but appears and is influential from the sixth through the ninth centuries. Its cadence, which was perfectly suited to liturgical recitation, made it a favorite for the

Divine Office. The Creed itself is a stern and clear warning to heed the orthodox teachings of the Catholic faith, probably in response to Arian heresies. Its central themes are the Trinity and the Incarnation; the trinitarian section seems to reflect the work of Augustine in his *De Trinitate* or at least to share some of its ideas. This text is difficult to date, since its introduction would argue for a date in the 1150s, but Hildegard's correspondence during that period argues for a later date, maybe around 1170. The fact that in one of her letters to Bishop Eberhard of Bamberg she speaks about the Trinity in similar fashion may argue for either dating or one in between: this letter is dated 1163 or 1164. This treatise has many things in common with her explanation of the *Rule of Benedict* in its form as a commentary and in the approach and language used. It begins with an exhortation to her sisters before it moves into the realm of commentary. This transition is handled by the linking of two virtues, Charity and Wisdom. It is through Wisdom that Charity speaks, and as in so many of Hildegard's works the two virtues are closely linked. Once linked they incline humanity toward humility and obedience to God; but since the Fall confusion has been rife among humanity, and evil exists in the form of the fallen angels. Hildegard summarizes the plan of salvation, closely echoing the form of the *Scivias*. She uses the example of the Gospel of John as a defender of the Church against divisive forces (as in the *Liber vitae meritorum*) and then transitions into her discussion of Athanasius by citing him as a great defender of the Church against the Arian heretics.

Hildegard will use her own imagery to expound on the major themes of Athanasius: the Trinity, the Incarnation, the relationship of the divine Persons to the human soul, and admonitions to avoid falling into error. She primarily uses an image of fire, although as in *Scivias* she will also liken the triune God to the metaphor of stone and tree.[146] The image of fire unites the themes she wants to speak about into a whole, however. It links us to Jesus as the "Sun of Justice"[147] earlier in the text, and then to metaphors about the Trinity. The Father is fire itself, "the flame of life," in whom all things have their being. Flames burn brightly with "the color of gold" as they are ignited by the wind, and here we see the unity of the triune Persons. If the Father is the fire, the fire is inseparable from its perceivable color, the Son (the use of a golden color here is interesting as another link to the *Scivias,* where the pictures of Jesus and *Ecclesia* in their perfection are always portrayed in gold leaf in the miniatures), and the wind that ignites, moves, and makes the fire spread is the Holy Spirit. In turn, this sets our souls on fire for God: indeed, the soul is fiery, representing its rationality and ability to speak, or "breathe the Word." In this way, the human being is indeed the fiery image and likeness of God. Movement is the emphasis throughout this analogy and its use of metaphor, but movement does not come from the power or merits of the human person but through the grace and movement of God. The fiery Word, one with the Godhead, heated up the womb of the Virgin Mary; the Son of God was conceived in fire by the movement of the Spirit joined with the will of the Father and the expression of the Word. When she speaks of the effect of God's fiery movement in the ordinary person through the spirit, when describing the human body, Hildegard uses her characteristic expression of *"livores"* and speaks of the elements as she does in her scientific works.

Much of the work is repetitive, with the sole purpose of reiterating the orthodox idea of the Trinity inherited by *Ecclesia* from the true prophets and the saints of God. There is only one God, indivisible in unity, three in Persons yet one in substance and in action. Later in the commentary she uses another metaphor that employs some of her favorite imagery: she likens the unity and trinity of the Godhead to the source of life. God the Father represents the root of all, of which the Son is the fruit, and the Spirit is known through the life force[148] in the world *(per viriditatem intelliengenda est)*. The Persons are one Triune God, not separated in any way; there is no temporal distinction between the Persons in eternity, whether prior or subsequent. The equality and eternity of the Trinity is assured. Her point is to exhort the "lukewarm" and the indifferent, those whose "coldness" make the viridity and fire of life flicker and fade in themselves. If they fail to express this power of life and accept this fiery movement, then at the time of judgment God will not fail to hold them accountable for it. Wicked men "flee from the fire of the Holy Spirit," yet can always return to God's mercy as did the prodigal son.[149] As with the Athanasian Creed itself, Hildegard praises God but warns her human audience: be open to the Triune God through the virtues and through the Church, do not stray from the truth itself but cling to the truth as it has been revealed.

As we shall see in the next chapter, Hildegard herself was seen as a true prophet for her times, and she is also a champion of orthodoxy in her doctrinal positions. The Church (in its spiritual form) and the virtues are pathways to living in accordance with God's will, and to stray from them is to open oneself to the evils of the century and the temptations of the devil.

Hildegard and the World of Creation

We turn now to what may seem a very different set of treatises and subjects, although the link to the other works in this chapter is Hildegard's overriding concern with the Incarnation: we are fallen humanity, in need of spiritual and physical assistance in the lives we live on earth.

One of the facets of Hildegard's thirst for knowledge and her creative spin on what she knew that fascinates and divides people today is
the literature she wrote concerning the natural world and the scientific
approach she takes. Unlike her other works, the medical-scientific works
do not claim to have any form of divine illumination but contain her
own records, cures, and observations. When we reach the subject of cures,
the line between what is "scientific" in the modern understanding of the
word and the realm of the "supernatural" becomes less clear. Nonetheless, these copious works on science, medicine, nature, and healing are of
great interest to people today, many of whom want to literally use her
books as a medical encyclopedia for holistic health and healing.

We do not know how much Hildegard relied on ancient and medieval sources for her compendium of knowledge, although it is certain
there is some borrowing from other sources and an adaptation of previous medical knowledge gleaned from monastic libraries. There is considerable debate on the extent of her knowledge of medical writings
previous to and written in the twelfth century as well as her "unique" use
of them.[150] Some call her the first German woman to be both a physician
and a scientist, whereas others say this may be overstating the case. These
works are some of the first in which Hildegard's authorship is challenged,[151] and the manuscript tradition has not made it easier to disen-
tangle the problems it has created.[152] For now, we will regard them as
authentic in their origins, although both the subject of these treatises and
their dubious provenance means we will treat them more warily than
some of Hildegard's other writings.[153] They were probably written during the period after the move to the Rupertsberg and likely completed by
1158, during what we have called "the active life" of Hildegard's development personally and spiritually.

To examine them, we will treat them as two separate treatises as is
usually done now, instead of combining them into one: the *Physica,* which
deals with the natural world as a totality, and the *Causae et curae,* which
deals with recommendations for curing and keeping the human body
healthy. It would be a mistake to think of the treatises as separate, insofar as they are dependent on each other for a greater sense of unity and
purpose. The natural world, while of interest in itself, is also the source
for cures; the cures rely on the natural elements for their implementa-
tion. It is quite believable that a woman who was so afflicted by illness as
was Hildegard would have taken a very active interest in medicines and
their physical properties; aside from her own interests, as *magistra* she
oversaw the healing of those in her care and of all who came to the monastery in search of physical healing. Moreover, as one author points out,
despite the fragmented tradition, these treatises seem to reflect Hilde-

gard's unique imprint on other sources, especially in her assumption of a given hierarchical cosmology.[154] By this, we are going back to Hildegard's notion of the interaction of the macrocosm and the microcosm: all begins with God's creation and ordering of the world. Since humanity was God's image and special creation, other parts of the created world would naturally be of use in the care and healing of human ills after the Fall. Logically, this vision would dictate discussing the *Causae et curae* first, the *Physica* second. But over the centuries, the *Physica*, or "natural history," has generally been placed first, with the causes and cures as a type of practical appendix. If we keep in mind the relationship between the two, the reversal should not confuse the major issues that Hildegard wanted to raise in her study of the world around her and its application to medical treatment.

Physica

The *Physica* is divided into nine sections, each treating a different facet of the physical world: the first is on plants, the second on the elements, the third on trees, the fourth on precious stones and gems, the fifth on fish, the sixth on birds, the seventh on animals, the eighth on reptiles, and the ninth on metals. Altogether, it is a collection of more than two hundred short chapters or commentaries; underlying its exposition there is a pervasive interest in the healing properties of these physical, created things, although this is not its sole subject.[155] The *Physica* has less contemporary appeal, as it is mainly a digest of observations common in the Middle Ages. Hildegard's compendium does not show too many traces of her own particular style except perhaps in the section making detailed observations on the types of fish that could be found in the nearby rivers, the Nahe and the Glan. Also, it demonstrates her impatience with describing things that are not of practical or cosmological significance. Alternatively, if she deems them useful they are recorded in great detail. For example, the section on plants is so extensive that it leads us to believe she had a real use for and interest in their qualities and properties. This section describes the advantages of 213 varieties of plants. She considers fifty-five kinds of trees, twenty-six precious stones, thirty-seven types of fish, sixty-eight kinds of birds, forty-three varieties of animals, eighteen types of reptiles, and eight different metals.[156] This gives the reader some idea of the size and the comprehensiveness of the *Physica*.

It is the section on plants, elements, gems, and metals that holds the most interest for us. Hildegard is using medical and physiological theories picked up from other sources that were commonly held beliefs. With others in the twelfth century, she began theologically with Genesis, declaring that the earth and its contents were put there for the use of human beings. Thus their useful qualities and their attractive qualities were part of God's design. She would also have shared and inherited certain ways of looking at human beings and how they interacted with the larger world. For example, it was common at this time to have certain theories about the influence of the elements, the stars (astrology), and the fluids of the body. All of these things required balance and were found in groups of four: four elements, four seasons, four humors, and the four zones of the earth.[157] In the *Physica* she uses the four basic elements in her analysis of the natural world: hot, cold, wet, and dry. These elements were predominant at certain times of year and were discovered in different combinations in plants, trees, minerals, and so on. The combination of these elements with the natural properties of whatever was being examined determined its positive and negative qualities vis-à-vis human beings. The elements, which were external, connected to the inner physiological theory of the human body, which was determined by the four "humors." The balance of elements and humors was the determining factor for health and illness, formation of character, and many other things. The humors and their importance in Hildegard's eyes form a large part of the subject matter in the *Causae et curae*. How did the elements influence the balance of the human body, and what did natural phenomena have to do with all of this?

Certain elements caused certain illnesses or effects. They could be neutral; natural things were composed of the elements in various proportions suited to their species and type. However, to counteract the imbalance in the elements, these natural resources could be used to temper the effects of such an imbalance. When she is describing plants, trees, gems, minerals, and animals, Hildegard will pay special attention to their "elemental" properties. Hot and cold are the main subjects addressed in a vast proportion of these observations, despite Hildegard's concentration on "moisture" and "dryness" in her theological treatises. For example,

> *Dornella* (tormentil) is cold, and that coldness is good and healthy and useful against fever that arises from bad food. Take tormentil, therefore, and cook it in wine with a little honey added . . . and drink it fasting at night and you will be cured of the fever.[158]

Tormentil is a plant which, when combined with other substances, can use its property of coldness to drain excess heat away from a person. Fruit trees are cold, and depending on the season, moist; many other trees are hot. Here we can cross over into folklore as well as observation; trees that hold great heat, such as evergreens, are very hot and keep evil spirits away.[159] Leaves also have particular properties and can be useful to wrap around a sick person or distill into a remedy.

Gems and jewels seem largely to be taken from the Bible, and the theory behind their practical uses is even more complex because of Hildegard's theory that they are formed in the hot sun of the east inside the mountains when this coincides with the rising of cold river water. The reaction is a foam that hardens into gems. Therefore precious stones have qualities based on the time they took to harden and form. Naturally, with Hildegard's image of *viriditas,* the emerald is of the widest use:

> The emerald is formed early in the morning, at sunrise, when the sun is positioned powerfully in its circle ready for its journey. Then the fresh greenness of the earth and crops is at its strongest, since the air is still cold and the sun already hot; and then the plants suck up the green freshness like a lamb sucking milk, since the heat of the day is scarcely sufficient to dry up the greenness of the day and nourish the things that are fertile to produce fruit.
>
> And so the emerald is strong against all human debility and weakness, since the sun conditions it and all its matter is from the fresh greenness of the air. So let whoever has a pain in the heart or stomach or side have an emerald with them so they can warm the flesh of their body with it, and they will be better. But if those diseases overwhelm them so that they cannot escape their storm, then let the person place an emerald in the mouth and wet it with saliva, and thus as the saliva is made warm by the stone repeatedly being put in and taken out, the recurrent waves of the illness will surely cease.[160]

Gems are of great importance in Hildegard's union of the celestial and the terrestrial, as we have seen in her poetry, her songs, and her descriptions of events in her theological-visionary treatises. The emphasis on gems and their specific colors and qualities argues for a consistency with Hildegard's other works that supports the contention that her style is apparent in her medical works, and least in certain passages.

Animals and fish are often good or bad for human beings relative to what they eat along with their elemental composition. So if it is hot and eats clean food, it may be good for eating. Among the animals described are both ones encountered everyday (mouse, mole) and ones Hildegard could not have observed for herself (ostrich, unicorn). The section on reptiles supplies us with a cure for swellings: since vipers are hot, then dead vipers, burned and made into a poultice, can draw heat away from a swelling.

Metals are either hot (copper and gold) or cold (tin, lead, silver) and are classified by coloring. She recognizes the danger of using lead in utensils, which is interesting in light of more recent discoveries in our century about the deleterious effects of lead, especially in utensils. She also is concerned with the purity of metals in the use of healing, since as with gems how they are made is of supreme importance. Gold, in its purity, has many uses. But beware of mixed metals:

> Brass is hot and is made from something else–like limestone from stone– since brass is not of its own nature but made from another metal, like a knight who is not a knight by his own birth but is made a knight. Therefore it is not good for medicine but rather harms than heals. So if a person were to put a brass ring on their finger, or if they were to warm any other part of their body with it, they would attract greater infirmity than health to themselves.[161]

Aside from its characteristic layout as a compendium with its goal of inclusivity, clearly the *Physica* is concerned with remedies as well as observations, with utility as well as description. Although there is less medical theory developed here than in *Causae et curae,* there are still complex remedies contained in this book.[162] From the quotations above we can hear the resonance of Hildegard's voice in the texts selected: they are visual, practical, and fit into her concept of the cosmos. Others, not quoted, show less of the flavor of this author. However, these quotes alone would lend credence to the authenticity of the work.

Before turning to her medical treatise, it may be helpful to visualize the layout of the elements and the humors as done by Isidore of Seville, since Hildegard puts "the doctrine of the fours"[163] in both the *Physica* and *Causae et curae.*

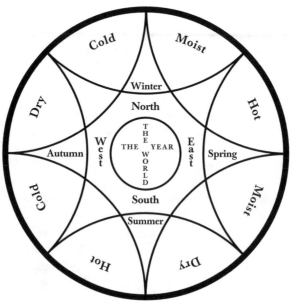

FIGURE 10

Portrait of the Months of the Year

	January	February	March	April	May	June
The Elements	Ice	Water	Storms, Thunder	Earth and Soil	Earth and Soil	Air and Breeze
Qualities	Clammy	Wet	Wet	Dewy and Sticky	Warm	Dry
Parts of the Body	Brain	Eyes	Ears	Nose	Mouth	Shoulders
Senses				Sight	Hearing	Smell
Time of Life	Childhood	Puberty	Puberty	Ripening	Maturation	Youth
Inner Life	Innocence	Split in Two		Pain of the World	Reason	Planning
The Life of Grace	Longing or Yearning	Sin and Offense	Repentance and Penitence	Conscience	Discretion	Judgment, Decision

	July	August	September	October	November	December
The Elements	Fire	Dew	Ripeness, Maturity	Earth	Earth	Snow
Qualities	Warm and Dry	Hot	Dry	Cold	Cold	Cold and Moist
Parts of the Body	Arms	Hands	Stomach	Buttocks	Knees	Feet
Senses	Touch	Taste				
Time of Life	Youth	Manhood	Manhood	Aging	Embryo	Embryo
Inner Life	Precaution, and Provision	Strength, Power	Moderation	Fatigue	Melancholy, Sadness	Hate
The Life of Grace	Bravery, Valour	Pleasure, Joy	Patience	Wisdom	Sorrow, Misery	Anger, Fury

Adapted and translated from the German edition of *Naturkunde*.

FIGURE 11

We see here an elaborate working out of the correspondence of the seasons, the elements, the humors, and the personalities that will undergird Hildegard's approach to compiling remedies in both the *Physica* and the *Causae et curae*.

Causae et Curae

Unlike the *Physica, Causae et curae* presents its healing remedies in the setting of a developed outlook on human physiology and the needs of the body. For this reason it is usually the more appealing of the two works at the moment; its contents and suggestions have been adapted widely by practitioners of holistic medicine with varying degrees of reliability or success.[164] In Germany many of the products associated with her cures and her recommendations for a healthy diet are available to consumers and gradually have become more accessible in other parts of the world. Her medical works appeal more to the practitioners and advocates of homeopathic medicine than to those practicing a more technological form of medicine.

Despite the fact that the *Causae et curae* is mainly concerned with the healing of the body, it begins with a larger, macrocosmic context in which these healings must take place. Again, in her time and in her mind the ordinary and the extraordinary tend to blend together, but there is generally a reciprocity between them. Sin is not the total cause of affliction, but neither are physical causes determinative of health or wellness in their entirety. Many commentators on the scientific treatises are confronted with the seemingly contradictory threads we find in both works: determinism and materialism on the one hand, the power of God and the effects of sin and evil on the other. Dronke finds Manichean strains in Hildegard's works, particular in dealing with the unity of the soul and the body;[165] others see inconsistencies of seeming determinism versus human freedom as the result of her not creating a treatise as much as a practical work, with the tension as accidental;[166] others see the differences in attitude, especially in regard to sexual matters, but view Hildegard as including all of these for a more balanced perspective through a series of observations.[167] *Causae et curae* has received a wider audience than the *Physica,* but it has not been without controversy.

Apart from the actual descriptions in the work, it is this manuscript that is hardest to trace for authenticity and later interpolations. It was arbitrarily divided into five sections in the thirteenth century, often without regard to the meaning of the paragraphs and text division. The authenticity of the fifth and final section is a matter of debate, and much depends on this. This section is devoted to the astrological prediction of human personality depending on the phase of the moon during which the child is conceived. If this is authentic, it strengthens the argument for a deterministic, Manichean view that argues a lesser degree of theological cogency than we see in Hildegard's other works; it may indicate a tension in the way she herself viewed the body. Conversely, if it is a later and spurious addition, it results in making the rest of the text altogether more coherent. Then it implies interdependence when one considers the forces that affect health and illness in human beings. Because of the corrupt state of the manuscript tradition many have opted to assume the genuineness of the document, with cautious warnings about its contradictory statements.

> The last part of the *Causae et curae* is devoted to the *lunaria*[168] mentioned earlier. It is perhaps better to see these as an exercise in the description of various types of men and women rather than the working out of a particular theory. There is, for instance, some difficulty in trying to accommodate Hildegard's earlier investigations of male and female temperaments to this later account. . . . Once more we are faced in the *Causae et curae* with an embarrassment of theories, not all of which seem to be fully integrated with each other. However, the presence of many of Hildegard's typical preoccupations, her style and vocabulary throughout the work make it inadvisable to discard any particular sections of it.[169]

As Flanagan observes, it would be difficult to decide what to keep and what to discard. For our purposes we will look at the *Causae et curae* as a book of cures and observations deliberately set within a theoretical framework that may or may not be consistent throughout.

Hildegard opens this work with the theoretical frameworks necessary to understanding the remedies contained in the book, and it corresponds to what we have seen in the relationship between the macrocosm and the microcosm in the *De operatione Dei*. Section 1 starts with a description of the account of the creation in Genesis and the reasons for and effects of the Fall on humanity. This is not merely a convention of Hildegard's but was the common starting point for the medieval scientist.[170] It is still typical of Hildegard to set up the macrocosmic structure first before discussing the microcosm. She establishes a close link between the workings of the macrocosm and microcosm in this first section. It contrasts with the *De operatione Dei* in that her focus is on the medical and physiological matters with which the book is concerned. Interspersed between practical suggestions and remedies in the subsequent books will always be references to its theological and cosmological undergirding; sometimes this is disconcerting, such as when we jump rapidly from the loss of perfection in Adam's fall to the constitution of semen, and the nature of reptiles (sec. 2). There is a great use of analogy in the *Causae et curae,* and Hildegard does not always elaborate the connections between microcosm and macrocosm but infers them, sometimes vaguely. She describes the aspects of the cosmos after describing the Fall—the various types of weather, the firmament and the stars, the winds and the air, the sun and moon, the constellations and the planets (astrology), and the four elements and all their powers. She shows her views to be in accord with those commonly held at the time, received through various modes of transmission but originating in antiquity with Galen and more contemporaneously with the theories of Isidore of Seville (described above). Despite what we have said about the fragmentary and contradictory nature of advice in the *Causae et curae,* Hildegard attempts to make positive statements about the relationship between the macrocosm and microcosm:

> Just as body and soul are one and mutually strengthen one another, so it is with the firmament and the planets. They warm and mutually strengthen one another. As the soul enlivens and strengthens the body, so do the sun, the moon, and the other planets warm and strengthen the firmament with their fire.

In addition to the positive statement here about body and soul, we see the beginning of Hildegard's extensive use of analogies in the third sentence. She continues after this by likening the firmament to a man's head; the sun, moon, and stars to the eyes; the air to the ears; the wind to the sense of smell; the dew to the sense of taste; and the directions of the world to the limbs or the sense of touch.[171] Direction plays a part here we do not see in the *Physica:* the traditional direction of paradise, the east, tends to produce plants good for healing, for example.

In section 2 she connects this cosmology to the actual effects the macrocosm has on the microcosm in terms of health or illness in the human body. It is the event of the Fall that is responsible for a disruption in the harmonies between the spheres; in this section we have the most fully developed theory of the microcosm and the macrocosm, which is clearly Hildegard's work and her vision. The descriptions of the Fall and its effects on health are telling and parallel to things said in her theological-visionary treatises:

> From tasting evil, the blood of the sons of Adam was turned into the poison of semen, out of which the sons of man are begotten. And therefore their flesh is ulcerated and permeable [to disease]. These sores and openings create a certain storm and smoky moisture in men, from which the *flegmata* arise and coagulate, which then introduce diverse infirmities to the human body. All this arose from the first evil, which man began at the

start, because if Adam had remained in paradise, he would have had the sweetest health, and the best dwelling-place, just as the strongest balsam emits the best odor; but on the contrary man now has within himself poison and phlegm and diverse illnesses.[172]

With her contemporaries, Hildegard related the four elements to the four humors found in the human body. Like the elements, the humors needed to stay in balance in order for a person to experience health; imbalances in the humors resulted in illness or disproportionate tendencies to certain types of temperament or behavior. Because of the imperfection of a fallen world, most people had a chronic imbalance of the humors in one direction, which accounted for certain personal characteristics and for their general constitutions. The received wisdom on which Hildegard bases her physiology can be charted as follows:

Basic Element	In Nature	Type of Humor	Temperament
Hot	Fire	Yellow bile (choler)	Choleric
Dry	Air	Blood	Sanguine
Moist	Water	Phlegm	Phlegmatic
Cold	Earth	Black bile	Melancholic

Interestingly, Hildegard uses slightly different terminology than the teaching of her time, although the theory remains the same. She describes the elements as the forces that hold the universe together and the humors as that force that influences and holds human beings together, so to speak. She speaks of fire as providing warmth and linked to sight; it produces a dry phlegm *(siccum)*. Air provides breath and hearing; it produces a moist phlegm *(humidum)*. The liquidity of blood is associated with mobility; and it produces a frothy phlegm *(spumaticum)*. The earthy quality includes human tissues, bones, and posture; it produces a tepid phlegm *(tepidum)*. This corresponds closely to the humoral theories above, as does her analysis that balance and moderation are the key to ordering the humors so that one may be healthy. She uses particularly animated language in describing what happens when the imbalance of humors sets in: the humors "congeal" and disturb the equilibrium, caused by an "overabundance" of any of the four.[173] She also uses the terms *flegmata* and *livores* to describe the imbalance, terms almost untranslatable but referring to a hierarchical relationship between the humors:

While "humours" appears to be the most general term, the latter two are used in a relational sense according to the relative strengths of the humours in the body. Thus any of the four humours can be referred to at different times as either *"flegmata"* or *"livores."* At any particular time the dominant two humours are called *"flegmata"* and the subordinate ones *"livores."* Finally, it appears that a state of balance in Hildegard's scheme is not one of strict equality, but one where the superior humours maintain the right measure of dominance over their inferiors.[174]

An extreme example of this is her commentary on "raving":

> If one humour overcomes the others in a person and does not observe its proper limits, that man becomes sick and weak. However, if two such humours arise simultaneously *against the order in a person,* he cannot endure it; he will then be destroyed either physically or mentally, now that the proper proportion is missing.[175]

This type of usage can also lead to passages in which the body and soul do tend toward dualism and move away from the body-soul, microcosmic-macrocosmic unity for which Hildegard is striving. Compare, for example, the two competing ideas in this passage:

> The soul is a breath that strives after good; the body, however, inclines toward sin. Only occasionally and with great effort can the soul keep the body from sin, just as the sun cannot prevent little insects from crawling onto those places on the earth that it has heated with its brilliance and warmth. However, the soul is also a breath for the body as the bellows are for fire. For if split logs and glowing coals are laid on it, the bellows ignite the fire. So the soul, which is tightly bound with the body, leads the bones, the nerves, and the flesh to all kinds of activities and cannot refrain from them as long as it is in the body.

This passage continues to ramble on, asserting the good qualities of the soul and the lesser qualities of the body, yet affirming their inseparable nature in the human person. Section 2 is concerned not only to outline theories, therefore, but to describe illnesses and maladies that can be cured by means of the remedies offered in sections 3 and 4. It will wander from the theoretical and cosmological to the descriptive and empirical (at least in the twelfth-century sense) for the entirety of section 2.

Perhaps one of the most interesting things in *Causae et curae* is the attention paid to women's problems in particular, whether they are problems from which the nuns would have suffered or problems that afflict laywomen, such as childbirth and conception. Hildegard shows an extraordinary interest in and a frankness about gynecological matters, whatever her varying views about the practice of sexual intercourse may be. She treats the four humoral temperaments of women separately from their treatment in men, allowing for differences the humors have in each of the sexes. Newman comments in summary about Hildegard's attitude toward the body and sexuality:

> Taken together, Hildegard's medical works and her reputed miracles reveal a solicitude for all the afflictions of women—in physical and mental illness, in barrenness and childbirth, in the throes of passion and the trials of marriage. In her writings, she concerned herself no less zealously with the ills of men. . . . Nor did she seem unduly troubled by the discrepancies in her view of sex. Behind them we glimpse a woman capable of astonishing empathy with her married sisters as well as with men, and willing to observe the sexual comedy from above, from below, and from within. If she never quite decided how much was due to God or to Satan, to human passions, natural powers, or magical interference, her very indecision kept her from false simplicities.[176]

Even Dronke concurs with this, despite his suspicion of a deep-seated conflict in Hildegard's attitude toward the body and soul, as he speaks of medical passages in which Hildegard captures the essential beauty of the sexual act, thus balancing the tendency toward viewing it as unclean. He quotes this passage:

> When a woman is making love with a man, a sense of heat in her brain, which brings with it sensual delight, communicates the taste of that delight during the act and summons forth the emission of the man's seed. And when the seed has fallen into its place, that vehement heat descending from her brain draws the seed to itself and holds it, and soon the woman's sexual organs contract, and all the parts that are ready to open up during the time of menstruation now close, in the same way as a strong man can hold something enclosed in his fist.[177]

There are several notable points we should observe in this passage. First, this is a positive account of sensuality and the sexual act. Second, it is a graphically correct description of the act of lovemaking. Third, this description argues that Hildegard was not isolated from the realities of procreation. Fourth, she uses the traditional categories of the elements of heat in her description, but we could translate this description easily into modern medical terminology because of the empirical observations she is making.

Causae et curae is the work of a woman deeply interested in the welfare of particular human beings, and simultaneously one who wants to find intelligible explanations, medical and theological, for her general observations about human life. Because of her own illnesses she did not regard illness as a punishment for sin but rather as a test from God; the challenge in healing was both to bring the body back into balance and to bring the spirit into harmony with the body. While she relied on specific herbal remedies for a variety of diseases, physical and psychological complaints, and chronic conditions, she also admitted and realized there was a limit to what these remedies could do. God was in control of all of destiny; human beings could merely do the best they could and identify themselves with Christ's desire to heal in the use of the elements of creation God had made for them. Hildegard is not unwilling to say that her own medical theories can be displaced by a higher power, in which a cure can be effected spiritually. In this quote we hear strains of Hildegard's plight of chronic illness, placed triumphantly in the care of God for relief if not for cure:

> If one of the *livores* extends itself beyond measure in superfluity in any human being, the *humores* cannot be at peace in him, save only in those human beings whom God's grace has infused. . . . [W]here others in such cases go mad, these will in this situation be bravest in excellence through the grace of God, for this grace allows them to be in a certain changeable condition, so that they are now ill, now well, now afraid, now strong, now in sadness, now in joy. And God brings about the relief in them, so that when they are ill he makes them well, when fearful, he makes them strong, when sad, he makes them joyful.[178]

There is no more fitting conclusion to our study of Hildegard's medical and scientific works than a quotation that shows both her reliance and trust in the natural world and her trust in the spiritual and transcendent influence of God in that world. Despite the problems with the manuscripts and their authenticity, there remain many characteristics typical of Hildegard. This includes her difficult syntax and running sentences as well as her attitudes toward the microcosm and the macrocosm. There are fascinating sections of the work we have not looked at here, as the text is readily available in English. We would only be quoting things of interest—such as her classification of the types of men and women according to the balance of humors in them—rather than analyzing and presenting her work in the context of her whole life.

Hildegard's concern with the natural world and her desire to describe it underlines for us her vibrant interest in practical matters and in the natural world around her. She has a lively curiosity about things in themselves because they are created by God but also because they catch her interest. She is interested in health and sickness and their place in the meaning of a person's life and their relationship with God. Even though she includes strange remedies made of ingredients that are both ordinary and fantastic in origin and theories that include medical and theological reflections, she remains intensely interested in how the created universe fits together and influences the separate parts of the whole. Because of their content and focus on the microcosm, she does not claim the type of authority for these works as she does for others. Although she claims no visionary authority for these works, we may take her ambivalence about separating the spheres of Creator and created to be a sincere acknowledgment of her limitations as well as of her talents, natural and supernatural.

Earth meets heaven in the unity of the microcosm and the macrocosm with an emphasis on where these meetings take place: in the *Lingua ignota,* a reminder of the celestial realm in the everyday life of the convent; in the lives of extraordinary people dedicated to God, the saints; in those saints who also guide us in how to live (Benedict) and toward correct doctrine (Athanasius); and finally, in the unity between God's creation of the world and humanity, meant to rely on each other for sustenance and healing. In the next chapter we turn to the prophesying of God's words to the human community, specifically as we examine Hildegard's role as a prophetess and an enormous influence on her society and her times.

V

From Mystical Vision to Prophetic Witness

Hildegard's mystical and polyphonic life expressed itself in outward action, as we have seen in the previous chapter, but this is especially true of her prophetic role. At the outset, then, the intentional link between these aspects of Hildegard's life must be stressed. It is possible to become so overwhelmed by her prophetic presence that we disregard the source and support for these prophetic utterances: her inner life of prayer, the Liturgy of the Hours, her community's support, her sense of closeness to God, and her awareness of her special gift and calling. Paradoxically, it is Hildegard's writing as a prophetic visionary that inclines people to place her *outside* the mystical tradition, defining mysticism as only an inner life and path to God. Ironically, it is Hildegard's mystical life that enables her to write at all and to become outwardly rather than inwardly directed. Later mysticism and Cistercian mysticism in the twelfth century were looking for the affective tie with God that many associate with pure mysticism. But Hildegard is a mystic who reluctantly became a prophet through the relentless call of her mystical visions to speak and teach about these revelations of the Living Light. This is Hildegard's contribution to the understanding of a spiritual pathway to God: that a person must trust in the Living Light with the gifts and tasks set before each Christian. She believed that in her own case the Lord called her to prophecy because only in the weak could strength be seen, and hers were troubled times. We have a rare instance of her own testimony about her gifts, written for Guibert of Gembloux, found in her *Vita* and in her *Letters*. In looking specifically at how Hildegard dealt with people, we need to look at a lengthy selection from the *Vita* that summarizes Hildegard's conviction that it is her precious gift of vision that makes all her activities possible:

God works wherever he wills for the honor of his name and not for the honor of earthly creatures. I, however, am constantly full of trembling fear. For I find no assurance of power in myself. Still, I stretch out my hands to God that I will be held by him like a feather which, without an ounce of power, can be blown away by the wind. That which I see, I cannot know completely as long as I am in the condition of the body and in my invisible soul; for human beings stand in need of both.

From my early childhood, before my bones, nerves and veins were fully strengthened, I have always seen this vision in my soul, even to the present time, when I am more than seventy years old. In this vision my soul, as God would have it, rises up high into the vault of heaven and into the changing sky and spreads itself out among different peoples, although they are far away from me in distant lands and places. And because I see them this way in my soul, I observe them in accord with the shifting of clouds and other created things. I do not hear them with my outward ears, nor do I perceive them by the thoughts of my own heart or by any combination of my five senses, but in my soul alone, while my outward eyes are open. So I never suffer the loss of consciousness of my senses in the visions, but I see them wide awake, day and night. And I am constantly oppressed by sickness, and often in the grip of pain so intense that it threatens to kill me; but God has sustained me until now. The light that I see is not spatial, but it is far, far brighter than a cloud that carries the sun. I can measure neither height, nor length, nor breadth in it; and I call it "the shadow of the living Light." And as the sun, the moon, and the stars appear in water, so writings, sermons, virtues and certain human actions take form for me and gleam within it.

Now whatever I have seen or learned in this vision remains in my memory for a long time, so that, when I have seen and heard it, I remember; and I see, hear and know all at once, and as if in an instant I learn what I know. But what I do not see, I do not know, for I am not learned, but I have simply been taught how to read. And what I write is what I see and hear in the vision. I compose no other words than those I hear, and I utter them in unpolished Latin just as I hear them in the vision, for I am not taught in this vision to write as philosophers do. And the words in this vision are not like words uttered by human lips, but like a shimmering flame, or a cloud floating in a clear sky.

Moreover, I can no more recognize the form of this light than I can gaze directly on the sphere of the sun. Sometimes—but not often—I see within this light another light, which I call "the living Light." And I cannot describe when and how I see it, but while I see it all sorrow and anguish leave me, so that then I feel like an innocent young girl and not like a little old woman.

But because of the constant sickness that I suffer, I sometimes get tired of writing the words and visions that are there revealed to me. Yet

143

when my soul tastes and sees them, I am so transformed that, as I say, I forget all pain and trouble. And when I see and hear things in this vision, my soul drinks them in as from a fountain, which yet remains full and unexhausted. At no time is my soul deprived of that light which I call the reflection of the living Light, and I see it as if I were gazing at a starless sky in a shining cloud. In it I see the things of which I frequently speak, and I answer my correspondents from the radiance of this living Light.[179]

In this quotation we have in summary not only Hildegard's description of how her visions occur or what they are like; we also have us a more personal and emotional account of these experiences than we can find almost anywhere except in her letters to Guibert. We hear again her characteristic appeal to God alone for authority, and along with it we hear of her own "trembling in fear," accompanied by one of her favorite images, that of the feather carried by the breath of the wind. We have a full account of what she has suffered physically in her lifetime, both as a result of the visions and from her human frailty. We hear the great consolation she receives, especially from the Living Light in its fullness rather than in its reflection, for during those times she feels like a young girl again. We have specific references to how her soul floats, directed by God, to different locales and reveals things to her about them and the persons who dwell in them; at the end she specifically says that in this reflected Light she sees these things and corresponds with others about them. We also see another of her favored images in the letters, that of "clouds"; they will come in all forms as she describes her vision and God's advice to the one asking her advice. Her image of God as fiery, brilliant, and light will also recur. Especially pertinent to this section is the last sentence, where she clearly states that it is in consulting the reflection of the Living Light in the clouds that she is able to answer those who petition her for answers through their letters and requests. Here earthly concerns are predominant, but Hildegard is once again relying mainly on her gift of vision in order to deal with those concerns and to properly point them toward the spiritual, which is the foundation of all situations. In the troubled times in which she lived she relied on her mystical vision to answer the concerns of her contemporaries.

Many in the twelfth century had reform on their minds. The most outstanding example of this is the reforms begun at Cîteaux, but the entire century was preoccupied with the issue of monastic reform and ecclesiastical purity. This generally took one of two forms, or some mixture of both: a desire to return to the "primitive" Church and stringent Rule, or a desire to look to something new and more pristine to evolve from a renewal of the old forms. Although Hildegard is often placed in both categories, we also have to consider her unswerving advice to monastics that they abide by their current callings to certain roles and not give these up for the sake of a movement to a greater simplicity or eremeticism.[180] There were more complex reformist movements within the monastic context that used symbolic language as a means of calling for change with overtones of Old Testament biblical prophecy. Hildegard's style falls within this last type of reform movement, yet we should not limit her prophetic vision to this school of thought, which lent itself to positions with which she herself would not have agreed.[181] Hildegard saw herself as a prophet, essentially by "sharing" what she heard from the voice of the Living Light, whether in answer to requests in letters, direct commands from God to speak out on certain topics or about her visions, or to talk about the turbulent world around her from the "God's eye" point of view when she felt herself instructed to do so.

Our understanding of Hildegard's prophetic role and her prophetic voice in her own times is clouded by her later popularization as a prophetess by the Prior of Eberbach, Gebeno, in an edited work called the *Pentachronon,* where her writings were compiled after her death in the thirteenth century. Gebeno's personal emphasis was on the sorry state of the Church and on the apocalyptic predictions of what was soon to come if this was not recognized. He also places an unfortunate and inordinate stress on the idea of prophecy as heralding future events.[182] He edited and popularized Hildegard by selecting and emphasizing the apocalyptic dimension of her works. From the number of extant copies of Gebeno's version versus those of Hildegard's own works, it is clear that it must have circulated quite successfully.[183] For most readers from the thirteenth century onwards Gebeno's compilation was the only way in which they were acquainted with Hildegard, her thought, and her prophetic role. This can only lead to a general misunderstanding of Hildegard's intent.[184] There is no denying the apocalyptic bent in her thought; we have seen this in her theological-visionary works. However, it is generally balanced by a very positive view of creation and the sense that paradise is possible, given total devotion to God's will and plan. In her *Letters* her voice is at times harsh and apocalyptic in its warnings, meant to frighten others into proper behavior, yet often the call to justice is tempered by an appeal to mercy and moderation in all things.

In order to facilitate a comprehensive look at Hildegard as the *prophetissa Teutonica,* as she is often called, we need to look at the various aspects of her role as a prophet for her times.

First, we will take another look at her initial vision, in which she was commanded by God to speak and to write, focusing on the prophetic qualities of that command as Hildegard understood it.

Second, we will consider how the role of prophetess necessarily involved political ties to the world, for better and for worse.

Third, we will look at her role as prophetess through what we hear directly from her in her *Letters.* This will be the longest section and shows us Hildegard not only as a prophetic voice but as a correspondent, giving us insight into her interaction with other people and the world around her.

Fourth, we will look at the preaching tours she undertook and the content of the preaching she presented in homilies and sermons.

Fifth, we will sum up why Hildegard the visionary was compelled to become Hildegard the prophet.

The Prophetic Calling

As we have discussed in chapter 2, Hildegard's visions impelled her to speak to others, beginning at the age of about forty-three. Until her work was scrutinized and supported by the church authorities of abbey, diocese, archdiocese, and papacy, Hildegard felt some constraint about this sudden calling to reveal not only that she *had* visionary experiences but that she was to *proclaim* them. The introductory section of the *Scivias,* often referred to as the *Protestificatio* (Declaration, or more literally, "protest"), makes it abundantly clear she is to "speak and write" the things she "sees and hears." Like many historical prophets, Hildegard was unsure this was what God was really calling her to do. Although we see the fiery prophet in the strong, uncompromising woman who emerged from her inner conflict, this outcome was not apparent to Hildegard or to others from the beginning but becomes clear only in hindsight.

Up to the point of this call to speak and write the words God gave her, Hildegard had led a secluded and outwardly uneventful life. She had been at Disibodenberg for thirty-five years, professed for twenty-eight years, and had been *magistra* of the convent for four to five years before she began the struggle with her prophetic calling. Very little in her former life would have predicted the type and volume of work this woman would produce, most of it after the age of forty-nine. Hildegard had been subject to constant pain and illness throughout her life, as she has told us; although the visions seemed to alleviate the pain in themselves, their occurrence often left her drained and weak.[185] Resistance to the visionary gift or prophetic command resulted in debilitating illnesses, according to Hildegard. We may wonder if the illness that prevented her from rising from her bed in Disibodenberg until she was permitted to found her own convent on the Rupertsberg was partially psychological, yet it thoroughly convinced Abbot Kuno. Kuno resisted Hildegard's move in every way possible, using every avenue to block her, and resented the move when it did come. To convince Abbot Kuno that the move was the will of God is not a situation in which she was preaching to the converted, as it were, but to someone bitterly opposed to the idea. And it is this move to the Rupertsberg that seals her independence from both ecclesial and secular authorities, as we shall see.

Relations between Rupertsberg and Disibodenberg, which should have maintained a certain cordiality, degenerated and were often strained, achieving reconciliation only around 1170. While we often pay attention to her correspondence with Kuno and Helenger, the abbots, perhaps one of the most poignant letters comes from the prior of the community. He describes how many of the ordinary monks felt:

> To Hildegard, truly filled with the grace of the Holy Spirit, Adelbert, monk (though unworthy) and prior at Mount St. Disibod, along with the brothers of that same monastery, sends our prayers that you may ascend from virtue unto virtue and may see the God of gods in Zion [cf. Ps 83:8].
>
> Since you send the words of your admonition into foreign regions and cause large numbers of people to desire the paths of righteousness, we (who have known you almost from the cradle and with whom you lived for many years) wonder why you have withdrawn the words of your celestial visions from us who thirst for them.
>
> We remember how you were educated among us, how you were taught, how you were established in the religious life. For your instruction was that appropriate only to a woman, and a simple psalter was your only schoolbook. Yet without complaint you embraced the good and holy religious life. But the will of God filled you with celestial dew [cf. Gen 27:28] and opened up to you the magnitude of its secrets. And just as we were set to rejoice in these things with you, God took you away from us against our will, and gave you to other people. We cannot fathom why God did this, but, willy-nilly, we are suffering great distress from the deed. For we had hoped that the salvation of our monastery rested with you, but God disposed matters differently than we wished. Now, however, since we cannot stand against the will of God, we have yielded to it and rejoice with you, for through divine revelation you make many things clear that were closed before. Indeed, filled, as you are, with the Holy Spirit, you write many things which you never learned from people, things that holy and learned men marvel at.
>
> Wherefore, although we are far from holy (because we remain sinners), we beseech you, both for the glory of God and for old and true fellowship, to remember us and to offer us some words of consolation. We ask also that you seek God's help for us, so that which is least in us God may deign to supplement through the merits of your prayers. Farewell.[186]

This letter was written to Hildegard sometime in the period between 1150 and 1155, early in her public career. It is a stimulating letter in several respects. First, it corroborates Hildegard's own claims about her education and environment at Disibodenberg; since the letter is public and meant to please, the prior could have said these things to agree with Hildegard's own account, but he is likely to have avoided that with one who knew well what her community education had been like. Second, it gives us one of the less official accounts of the hopes, fears, and upsets of Hildegard's original community: they obviously hoped her gifts would help save the monastery in spiritual ways, in prestige, and in secular support through donations. The prior admits, albeit reluctantly, that it is the will of God that Hildegard left. He and the others seem sorry on their own account but also for more substantive reasons. Because of the discord between the two communities, a valuable link had been lost. And because this is indeed the community in which Hildegard was nurtured, it was natural for the monks to be taken aback and not pleased with her departure. They expected to live out the Benedictine vow of stability and obviously thought the same about her. Aside from God's command to her, the truth of the matter was that the number of postulants Hildegard attracted to the convent made the space there much too small for them. There would have had to be major modifications to the monastery to accommodate them, although building of one type or another had been constantly going on since Hildegard resided there. There is a distinct sense of personal loss in this letter, too, and pain over the dissension between themselves and Hildegard's convent. Speaking for the community, the prior accepts the will of God and asks only that they may remain part of the focus of her life and newly appointed prophetic mission. We sense a request for special consideration in the appeal to "old and true fellowship."

Hildegard's reply to this letter is to send a sermon to the monks, in which we clearly hear her admonitory and prophetic voice.[187] She invokes the figure of Justice allegorically, and speaks of the days when they were as eagles; now they are asleep, and when awake they are meddlesome, sighing, and tossed about. She calls them to hear this admonition about falling away from their obligations and to return to God.[188] Despite the likelihood that Hildegard may have had personal feelings and opinions about this in a way that colors her reply, she speaks with the authority of the visionary. This is clear from the opening:

> In a true vision I heard a voice saying these things against the injuries done to Justice by both spiritual and secular people: O Justice, you are a pilgrim and a stranger in the city of those people who make up fables to justify their own misguided will, and although you are the purple-clad friend of the king, they long neither to learn your mysteries nor to obtain your friendship. Thus you cry out against that fate, against which no real justice can keep quiet, and you say in grief: I am so terribly ashamed that

I hide my face in my cloak, lest my betrayers see me. They, however, say: Whatever we devise is good for everyone. And, therefore, O Justice, you are zealous to see to it that whoever resists you is liable to judgment.[189]

A prophetess may not be without honor in her own country, but near enough to it. Hildegard obviously felt that the monks she was raised among had been diverted into other interests, including secular ones, and that this distraction may have been one of the reasons God called her to leave them. In her sermon to the monks, she tries to persuade them that fixing their eyes on God and their own community rather than on worldly renown and regrets will do the community the most good. Justice, in the form of God's judgment rather than that of men, must be reestablished, for this virtue has been abused and ignored. Although other prophetesses, such as Hildegard's contemporary Elisabeth of Schönau, were able to maintain friendly and supportive ties with the abbey community, this was neither Hildegard's situation nor her fate.[190] By virtue of their gender, both were hampered in delivering their messages. Although Elisabeth's style and way were less confrontational than Hildegard's, she too experienced her own difficulties in being allowed to speak those things God revealed to her.[191]

The question of gender is directly relevant to the discussion at this point. To claim a prophetic role was unusual enough in the early Middle Ages without it coming from the mouths of women who were not even to preach in church, according to St. Paul. For a woman to do so and to be allowed to speak, even commanded to speak as Hildegard was, required a very special set of circumstances. The fact that God chose to speak through a woman (or women) meant a radical role reversal that is nonetheless consistent with the need for prophecy. Prophets arose during times of great turmoil and trouble, when the people (usually Israel) were not seeking the ways of the Lord but going through the motions instead. Many must have felt that in their time the Church was in a real crisis of faith and practice in order for a woman to be allowed the range of authority that Hildegard eventually wielded. To a curious extent, the very impossibility of a woman speaking authoritatively to men gave consolation both to the speaker and to the listener. What was so improbable must indeed be the will of God, particularly when it was endorsed by the Church of the time. Hildegard's confirmation by not only the leaders of her local and global ecclesial superiors but by the recommendation of Bernard of Clairvaux, often regarded as the foremost spiritual authority of the times, confirmed that even as a woman she could challenge anyone with the words God granted to her in her visions. This is, of course, one of the reasons Hildegard speaks so carefully about her utterances coming directly, virtually inerrantly, from God. The fact that she initially found it unsettling, and did at a later date as well, bespoke the same qualms of her contemporaries, male and female. What is astonishing is the strength, vigor, and uncompromising stance she took in delivering these prophetic utterances, considering her own misgivings and that of others. She received criticism as well as praise for her gifts, and many thought her deranged or possessed by evil spirits. Despite all of this, she was widely regarded as the best source of prophetic enlightenment in her age, and in her maturity she was called on to speak her advice not only by means of letters that could be copied and read but to proclaim it in person to large groups of people.

Even though this was the situation for Hildegard, we should not overlook the dangers faced by women who dared to speak out in a society that regarded this as abnormal, not just unusual. Hildegard passed the tests set before her and was lucky enough to have been examined by an enlightened pope when another might have had a very different reaction to her gifts. We do know that despite her fame, her endorsement by the ecclesiastical authorities, and her orthodox approach to faith, rumors still circulated that this woman was possessed by evil spirits or merely puffed up in her own vanity. Such rumors did not bother Hildegard as she became more confident in her prophetic role, but the murmurs must have been unsettling anyway. Other women who followed her suffered and were disciplined and even put to death for actions that were approved and sanctioned for Hildegard in her lifetime.

Prophetic Authority and the Ecclesial and Secular Authorities

The burden of prophecy brought with it certain responsibilities. Hildegard's command to speak what she saw in her visions was validated by the church authorities, spiritual people, and her own experience. As she became more accustomed to being consulted about her gift of vision and translating it into advice, she became much more confident in her movement from vision to proclamation. We will see this indisputably in our examination of her correspondence. She acquitted herself surprisingly well at the task of being the famous "seer" of the Rhine, lapsing only occasionally into predicting the future instead of proclaiming the message of prophecy; and even when she did this, it was couched in terms of what was foreseen by the God who knew all from the very beginning.

What kind of prophet did Hildegard understand herself to be? What did she consider the prophetic call in her case? She avoids all use of the name "prophet" in her works, preferring instead to stress that she is the vessel used by the Living Light, the feather borne up on the breath of the

Spirit, the fragile human vessel through whom He Who Is speaks definitively in his words, not hers. It is abundantly clear from the references to Scripture, which Hildegard uses constantly in her works, that her understanding to "speak and write" was probably based on an understanding of the Scriptures.[192] Her letters are peppered with biblical quotations and allusions. These quotes from Scripture—or paraphrases from it—are natural to Hildegard and, it must be said, to many of her correspondents. Hildegard is especially fond of quoting the Old Testament, especially the books of Genesis, Exodus, the Psalms, the Song of Songs, Isaiah, Ezekiel, and various prophets. In the New Testament she leans toward quotes from Matthew, Luke, John, a smattering of the Pauline epistles, and the book of Revelation (Apocalypse). By far the greatest number of quotations come from the Psalms. We have seen the importance and preeminent place of the Psalter in Hildegard's life and formation, so it is hardly surprising that these references or analogies come spontaneously to her mind. We also hear the influence of the Benedictine Rule in her replies, a Rule where the *Opus Dei* gave a very specific sense of being immersed in Scripture and in aiming at a virtuous life.

She likens herself to the Old Testament prophets quite consciously. For example, she compares her situations to ones in which Moses found himself; in her lyrical moments she appeals to Elijah; her familiarity and fondness for the book of Jeremiah may indicate she felt beset by forces outside herself in the act of prophesying. Jeremiah never ceased pointing out to the Lord that he was unsuited to be a prophet (this never worked with God in the Bible); that he wanted to speak the words of Yahweh but was sure the people would disregard them, for they were hard of heart; that he was sure that they would blame it all on him and that it would be uncomfortable if not downright perilous to deliver such words to the people. Perhaps Jeremiah, consciously or not, is representative of a number of the feelings and experiences Hildegard had when she was confronted with prophecy. Unlike Jeremiah, she managed to overcome her resistance to her unworthiness for God's task after her initial struggle with it. However, she continued to link the gift of vision, the burden of advice, and the event of illnesses in her life closely to one another. She did receive criticism as well as praise: there were those who thought her a foolish, vain woman, those who believed she was possessed by evil spirits, and those who thought she prophesied for her own gain. She had to endure those who would not listen to her even in the visions she experienced, which we can credit with her own impartiality. She certainly suffered from the situation in which she found herself regarding Richardis von Stade, where the original visions may have been what prompted her resistance but where she found herself later tempted to bend them to suit her own wishes and needs. A prophet had to be able to discern the difference between God's will and the wishes of any human being, even her own.

Because of the model of the biblical prophets and because the visionary gift had been hers practically from birth, Hildegard rarely falls into the trap of thinking the primary task of prophecy is to predict the future. There are exceptions, but her understanding would be that she was called to speak what she saw and heard in her visions to those to whom God wished it delivered. Flanagan has noted that the contemporary understanding of the word leans heavily toward its predictive side.[193] This was part of what many persons expected from Hildegard when they consulted her: when will I die? will I bear children? what is my destiny? Hildegard resisted most of these pleas, replying only what she saw in a vision from God; she also warned some of her correspondents not to test God or themselves by asking about the future but rather to cultivate the life of virtue in themselves and those for whom they had responsibility. Even an appeal from a large number of prelates about a woman nobly born could not force Hildegard's hand; they sent the woman to her because she despaired of having another child and heir after the first ones had died. In her reply to the five concerned abbots, she focuses on a sermon on penitence and mercy. Only at the end of her letter does she indicate that she is willing to receive the woman but that the fertility of this woman is in the power and will of God alone. She will, however, continue to pray for her.[194] Occasionally, she lapses into what we would think of as fortune-telling; whether from fatigue at maintaining the prophetic stance, the urge to please, or the expectation of the medieval world around her is hard to tell. She certainly would have received more pressure and support to be a prophet who foretold specific events than the role she actually espoused—to be a prophet in whatever way God willed to speak to the people through the medium of her visions.

We can regard much of her correspondence as an appeal to her visionary and prophetic gifts, asking Hildegard to share whatever visions she might have that would be pertinent to the correspondent and to his or her community if that was implied. As her fame spread, her correspondence kept pace with it. Not all of the correspondence had happy results for Hildegard or for those who consulted her. The impetus to speak and teach outwardly through prophecy, whether by letter or in person, became stronger as the years went by. Hildegard was forced to confront many figures of authority and rebuke them in the name of God. Sometimes these situations could have been perilous to her own safety and that of her community; sometimes she relied on her authority to reprove those in office with influence in a way that feared no retribution. In other cases, her authority was sought: eventually, she would be requested to go on preaching journeys or tours where people could meet with her, hear her speak to them of the content of her visions as they affected them, and proclaim these visions publicly when it served the need of the people and the will of God.

The Prophetess and Politics: Worldly Ties

Hildegard had established her own convent and wanted more than ever to give herself to the gifts God gave her and the duties to which God called her, including those of superior of her own community; still, even those who were gifted and spiritual had many ties with the world. Abbeys and convents were dependent upon gifts of charity from the wealthy, and the earthly dowries which came with the Brides of Christ supported most convents. One of the reasons behind the bitterness of the monks of Disibodenberg when Hildegard moved to the Rupertsberg was the loss of these dowries, which had helped support the abbey and keep it flourishing. Once Hildegard's visions became widely known she attracted many spiritual seekers; ironically, the reason she needed a larger convent was the greater number of vocations to the community that her presence brought about in Disibodenberg. Nevertheless, even with the abbot's opposition and the support of her vision about the Rupertsberg, founding a community was not an easy thing to do from any point of view. She would need the deed to the lands and was helped by the Marchioness von Stade in this matter, and eventually she had the lands granted to her unconditionally by Barbarossa; she needed ecclesiastical permission, and after much wrangling with Abbot Kuno she managed to force the issue by appealing over his head to the archbishop of Mainz; she needed assurance that she would have the necessary spiritual support given by a priest, both for the sacraments and as spiritual advisor to the monastery—Volmar at first, and then others (contentiously) later.

Not all worldly ties were without reward. One of her benefactors and her husband gave generously to Hildegard in her time of need; Hildegard returned the favor by coming to the aid of her former patroness when she entered religious life after the death of her husband. Hildegard had two nephews with religious responsibilities, one a prior and one an archbishop, with whom she corresponded. Not all worldly ties could be separated from ecclesiastical issues, as we have seen above. She skillfully handled the changing tides of the times when shifting allegiances forced one bishop to leave his see and be replaced by another, as in the case of Conrad of Mainz, whom Frederick replaced with Christian of Mainz for political reasons. Here we have the example of her friend and patroness Gertrude, for whom she intervened with Eberhard, Bishop of Bamberg:

A certain man rose up in the morning and planted a vineyard. Later, because of much dissension, he turned his eyes to foreign places, and his desire was fulfilled.

Now, O father, look to your daughter Gertrude, who was called forth, a pilgrim, from her own country, just like Abraham, who also left his land. She has given up everything and bought the pearl of great price [cf. Matt 13:46]. Now, however, her mind is being squeezed dry by great anxiety, like a grape in the winepress. Therefore, for the love of Him who was before the beginning and has filled all things with compassion, help her as much as you can, so the vineyard in this daughter may not be destroyed.[195]

Despite the brevity of this letter, it is rich with biblical references and allusions, especially the imagery of the vineyard, which Hildegard uses so well in this context. Her concern is motivated by the situation in the concrete and its spiritual implications. The concern for this specific situation is cleverly portrayed by using the image of the grape in the winepress to explain Gertrude's state of mind and anxiety. Eberhard listened to Hildegard's plea and established a larger convent and one well situated for Gertrude, with the happy result that he saw a flourishing spiritual community of nuns grow rapidly in his diocese. Gertrude also writes to Hildegard with great personal affection, not necessarily about this crisis.[196]

On a different note, here is an example of Hildegard's political acumen. Having finally appealed to the Pope after receiving little satisfaction from the monks at Disibodenberg in the matter of replacing Volmar, she kept appealing up the hierarchical ladder until it could be resolved. Finally, in 1173, Pope Alexander III wrote to Wezelinus, a nephew of Hildegard, to intercede for the sisters, yet to look carefully into the position of the monks as well; for Abbot Helenger and Hildegard could hardly be said to have had a mutually rewarding relationship.

Alexander, servant of the servants of God, to our beloved son, abbot of St. Andrew in Cologne, greetings and apostolic blessings.

On behalf of our beloved daughter in Christ, Hildegard, prioress of Mount St. Rupert in Bingen and of the sisters of that place, you should know that it has come to our attention that when, according to their custom, they had elected for themselves a master and provost from the monastery of St. Disibod, the abbot of that place was unwilling to acknowledge the election of the person from his monastery, and even up to the present time still refuses to assign that person to them. Wherefore since it is proper that there be provision for the aforementioned sisters in those things which pertain to the salvation of their souls, we mandate to your discretion through apostolic writings that you call together both sides to your presence once you have made inquiry into this and decide the case with proper justice. And if these sisters cannot have a provost from that monastery, see to it, at least, that they have a competent one from another.[197]

This letter is interesting because it is not a part of the correspondence between Hildegard and someone else but an action taken in a letter as a result of prior correspondence. Hildegard has obviously insisted on what has been their right and custom and has emphasized to all that it has been to no avail; Helenger has proved resistant to her pleas for justice, possibly out of concerns of his own. The Pope cannily requests a person to intervene who is involved with both sides of the dispute, hoping for an amicable resolution. Note how different the tone of the letter is from Hildegard's usual style, which has its origin in papal authority but also points out very well the unusual manner in which she answered her own letters.

In stark contrast, the most wrenching political dispute Hildegard had to face was a personal one involving not only ecclesial politics but her own feelings. Only three confidantes are mentioned by name with affection in Hildegard's works: Jutta, Volmar, and Richardis von Stade. Richardis was mentioned in chapter 2 as instrumental in helping Hildegard with the *Scivias*. Politically, she was of nobler birth than Hildegard, and this became the crux of the problem, as either she or her family had aspirations for her to be an abbess. After the move to Rupertsberg, Richardis was elected abbess of Bassum. It is from the correspondence and in a lesser way from the *Vita* that we discover how bitter a battle was waged over this departure and its consequences. We assume, though we do not know, that Richardis went willingly. Her family may have been influential in persuading her to this move. Her brother Hartwig was archbishop of Bremen, the diocese in which Bassum was located. In the letters concerning Richardis we see Hildegard writing in a way atypical of the rest of her correspondence: no longer the confident voice but one bewailing her fate; using her prophetic gift to intimidate others (whether or not her insights were inspired); using all her political acumen to apply to church authorities up the ladder to have Richardis returned to her, once taken; and all her emotional resources to sway the von Stade family while at the same time practically accusing them of simony (the buying of church offices). There is considerable correspondence here; we will select some parts of letters that illustrate what we have been discussing above. First, Hildegard in a vitriolic strain, in denying that the archbishop of Mainz has a right to demand she surrender Richardis:

> The Bright Fountain, truthful and just, says, "These legal pretexts brought forward to establish authority over this girl have no weight in God's eyes,

for I—high, deep, all-encompassing, a descending light—neither initiated nor wanted them. Rather, they have been manufactured in the conniving audacity of ignorant hearts. Let all the faithful hear these things with the open ears of their hearts, and not with outward ears, like a beast which hears the sound, but not the meaning of a single word. The Spirit of God says earnestly: O shepherds, wail and mourn over the present time, because you do not know what you are doing when you sweep aside the duties established by God in favor of opportunities for money and the foolishness of wicked men who do not fear God. And so your malicious curses and threatening words are not to be obeyed. You have raised up your rods of punishment arrogantly, not to serve God, but to gratify your own perverted will.[198]

We notice here not only the emotional tone of the letter and its accusations, which whether or not they are legitimate, are worded differently than the admonitions we usually see coming from Hildegard in her prophetic mode. Also, it is striking that she would challenge the election, even for good cause. We have seen above her sense that offices should be undertaken and carried out; this one election may not be the will of God, but a result of simony (the reference to money), yet that has not stopped Hildegard in other situations that required delicately balancing worldly concerns and spiritual ones. At the same time, Adelheid, another relation of the von Stades, was appointed abbess in a situation probably far less suitable than that of Richardis: she was young and inexperienced. Yet Hildegard did not put up a fight over her departure from the community as she did with Richardis.[199] Hildegard sweepingly compares this one instance of Richardis' election to the corruption of the times and insists that it comes from a lack of the fear of God. Even a plea to the Pope did not stop the election, and Hildegard was forced to surrender Richardis.

We sense both grief and rebuke in the one extant letter to Richardis after she took up her duties at Bassum:

Daughter, listen to me, your mother, speaking to you in the spirit: my grief flies up to heaven. My sorrow is destroying the great confidence and consolation I once had in mankind. From now on I will say: "It is good to trust in the Lord, rather than to trust in princes" [Ps 117:9]. The point of this Scripture is that a person ought to look to the living height, with vision unobstructed by earthly love and feeble faith, which the airy humor of earth renders transient and short-lived. Thus a person looking at God directs his sight to the sun like an eagle. And for this reason one should not depend on a person of high birth, for such a one inevitably withers like a flower. This was the very transgression I myself committed because of my love for a certain noble individual.

Now I say to you: As often as I sinned in this way, God revealed that sin to me, either through some sort of difficulty or some kind of grief, just as He has done regarding you, as you well know. Now again I say: Woe is me, mother, woe is me, daughter, "Why have you forsaken me" [Ps 21:2; Matt 27:46; Mark 15:34] like an orphan? I so loved the nobility of your character, your wisdom, your chastity, your spirit, and indeed every aspect of your life that many people have said to me: What are you doing?

Now, let all who have grief like mine mourn with me, all who, in the love of God, have had such great love in their hearts and minds for a person—as I had for you—but who was snatched away from them in an instant, as you were from me. But, all the same, may the angel of God go before you, may the Son of God protect you, and may his mother watch over you. Be mindful of your poor desolate mother Hildegard, so that your happiness may not fade.[200]

This emotional outpouring to Richardis (for which we have no reply) shows Hildegard at her most willful and also at her most human. She seems to have accepted that she has relied overly on the friendship between human beings when she should have depended only on God, counsel she gives readily enough to others. She does not stop there, though, for throughout the letter there is a bitterness about being abandoned (like Christ on the cross!), which leads her to speak of persons of high birth as untrustworthy (she otherwise admires social hierarchy) and ends on a note that would induce guilt in almost anyone. She repeats Richardis' virtues, and they are the virtues she will personify and value most highly; she even mentions that others have asked her what she is doing in this excess of grief and recalcitrant behavior. This letter suggests penitence and insight but simultaneously seems also to reprove and lay blame.[201]

Ironically, this dispute only reaches a conclusion with the sudden death of Richardis in 1152. Hildegard was informed of this by Hartwig, archbishop of Bremen, and Richardis' brother. He shares a mutual sense of grief with her and says that at the end Richardis had planned to come to Rupertsberg and that he will come in her stead.[202] Hildegard writes back a lovely letter of consolation praising Richardis, who was so good that God snatched her from the clutches of the world. We sense in this exchange of letters that Hildegard is prepared to be magnanimous but remembers her fundamental grievance and perhaps feels vindicated. Hartwig's letter is poignant also for its use of honorifics, for as an abbess Richardis outranked Hildegard as prioress or mistress and must be mentioned first in the greeting.[203]

Ties to the world could not be renounced; they had to be dealt with even in the comparatively spiritual atmosphere of a religious house. These ties could bring help and assistance or grief and ruin: ultimately they required a sense of moderation and balance in dealing with the political and spiritual turmoil outside the gates of the Rupertsberg. Hildegard proved herself to be an adept politician in almost every aspect of her life; perhaps that is why the attempt to use her prophetic and political talents in the service of her own needs stands in such contrast to the rest of her sense of self as a prophetess only speaking as a vessel of the Living Light. That she had legitimate concerns about simony and preferment in Richardis' case sounds like the prophetess; the personal style, agony, and calumny that are the tone of the letters does not. Even her emphasis on the hierarchical structure of the Church is called into question when her appeal to the Pope failed. Perhaps, however, this crisis early in her prophetic career set the tone for the capable seer and guide she was to be throughout the rest of her life.

The *Letters* as Prophetic Witness

The *Epistolae,* or *Letters,*[204] consist of collections of letters sent by Hildegard and to her during her lifetime. In Hildegard's correspondence with the devoted and persistent admirer, Guibert of Gembloux, we find some rare autobiographical passages that are of immense help in filling out our picture and understanding of Hildegard the woman, as we have seen at the beginning of this chapter. Because the *Letters* are of utmost importance in understanding Hildegard and her interaction with others, not to mention the importance they have in providing information about her mystical and prophetic gifts, it is necessary for us to be as certain as possible of the reliability of the manuscript tradition. Until now that has been quite difficult, due to the unreliability of the tradition, the various locations in which letters have been found, and the spurious nature of some of these letters.[205] The new translations promise to bring us fresh insight into Hildegard's world by pulling many of these sources together.

The *Letters* have to be approached in a way that informs us about their content, because their title implies something more intimate and revealing to the reader than is actually the case. In the twelfth century there was no means of printing, and everything had to be transcribed. Because of this and the contributing societal factors of the time, letters were rarely merely private communications. Indeed, they might be copied and distributed, read aloud to a group, or preserved and used almost as talismans. This was especially true in the case of someone like Hildegard, whose reputation for sanctity and prophecy became extremely widespread. Besides her native area and what we would consider the area covered by Germany today, Hildegard's correspondents included the bishop of Jerusalem and Prague in the East, and much of France and letters to the sovereigns of England in the West. The *Letters* help us to see Hildegard's fame as it spreads, since her exchange of correspondence really begins with her letter to Bernard of Clairvaux in 1146–47 about the content of the *Scivias*. After Bernard's support of her at the Synod of Trier in 1148, Hildegard's reputation was established by this most respected spiritual figure of the time and endorsed by her immediate superiors and the Pope himself. Her correspondents included a vast range of persons, although limited by their ability to either write in some Latin or have someone write for them. The bulk of her nearly four hundred letters are addressed to people with a modicum of education, whether clerical, religious, or lay.[206] From the *Letters*–and to some extent from the medical-scientific works we looked at above–we receive the distinct impression that Hildegard also received and welcomed many guests and visitors. These people need not have been learned in Latin letters, and her encounters with them are lost to us unless by implication or explicitly recorded by others.

First, the form of the letters, whether written by Hildegard or her correspondent, followed traditional formal social forms. Rank was always kept in mind as well as the characteristics or role of the person addressed. Letters sent to Hildegard all spend time in complimenting her on her special gift of seeing the Living Light, addressing her as the leader of her community and as a "worthy Bride of Christ" or some similar form of salutation suitable for a cloistered nun, and begging her favor in attending to them. The section before the actual request or business states the unworthiness of the correspondent or petitioner, often in fulsome language (to the modern ear). Letters to which Hildegard replies include many of the same conventions: she is a *paupercula,* a poor little figure of a woman to whom the Living Light speaks; her authority is only the authority of God's words and will speak through her as a weak vessel; she addresses the recipient by rank, role, and request. We notice that as the correspondence grows with her reputation there is generally less in the way of formal salutation in the letters containing advice from, as she usually puts it, *He Who Is.* These letters come more quickly to the point. Some letters are rendered obscure, either because we do not have the other half of the correspondence or because of their delicacy where the substance of the message or request may have been entrusted to a messenger.[207]

Second, Hildegard employs two devices we are familiar with from her other works. One is the telling of an allegorical story, which is then explained. In the *Letters,* sometimes there is no commentary on the vision's allegory (as there is in *Scivias*), which makes it hard for us to understand if the meaning is not self-evident. The other device she uses frequently is to turn the story into one in which the virtues are personified, as in the *Ordo virtutum.* They may be the center of the story's allegorical meaning, or its mouthpiece, peripheral to the action. But this is a device we see repeated again and again in the *Letters*.

Third, when we recall the times in which she lived we find, quite logically, that there are images of battle and struggle in some of the letters. Usually this is a struggle between virtue and vice, grace and sin, and has a thoroughly spiritual meaning. At times, however, the spiritual meaning is used in conjunction with the very secular realities that confront or surround her correspondent. Hildegard, as we mentioned earlier, spoke of herself as being born in "a womanish time," when the virtues of the world and of the Church were in danger of being lost altogether. She appears to date this from the rule of Henry IV of Germany, the Holy Roman Emperor who began the crisis over lay investiture and other matters of secular versus ecclesiastical power that would lead to attacks in word and deed on the papacy in Rome. We should bear in mind that in the time of the schisms and antipopes of Hildegard's active life there were actual battles fought in which clergymen participated or led opposing forces into battle.[208] Her language reflects the embattled times, even when it is applied to the battle between evil and good. When used to describe the inner state of mind of a person, it is easy to read dualism into Hildegard's thought. While this may be a tension in her thought, we cannot think of it as a simple dualism and must balance it against her overwhelming use of the goodness of the created world to convey spiritual bliss.

Finally, there is as much "admonition" as advice, especially for those persons in greater authority. Sometimes Hildegard's letters are suitably awe inspiring in their prophetic warnings and consolations; it is the nature of speaking the word given to her by the Living Light to point out the way to *He Who Is*. As in other works, she shifts almost seamlessly from the voice of God to her own voice in the *Letters*. This requires some stern language; however, some of the correspondence seems unduly severe in response to the type of letter sent by the petitioner or the request asked of Hildegard. An interesting point emerges here: her tone with women tends to be more sympathetic and contains more affection than her tone with men, although there are notable exceptions, such as Abbot Manegold of Hirsau.[209] This does not mean she does not admonish both when necessary. We find this tonal difference mostly in her letters to abbots and abbesses, whose problems and anxieties she could often identify with, and even when exhorting the recipient she is likely to end these letters on a sympathetic note. She reserves her most strident rebukes for those abusing clerical or societal power, and the higher the rank, the harsher the words, for God did not tolerate laxity and corruption in the leaders of the Church or in supposedly Christian heads of state.

To demonstrate the structure and content of the *Letters* as prophetic utterances, we will look at four examples that were directed to specific persons who held office, supplemented by what we know of the historical circumstances, and three examples of the overall character of her prophetic correspondence.

The Popes

We realize how fortunate Hildegard was to have had the approval and blessing of Pope Eugenius III at the Synod of Trier; it enabled her to exercise her visionary gifts and mandated her to speak publicly about them. There is a very interesting shift in the tones in the letters addressed to the popes. Her first letter to Eugenius is both flattering and tentative; very soon she becomes much more brusque, and she approves of this pope. As the translator observes, in a short time she has gone from the appeal of "a poor little woman" to an acrimonious style, a considerable jump from using such prophetic discourse in a book like *Scivias* to taking this tone in a private letter.[210]

> [H]ear him who is mighty in name and who flows in the torrent: Do not destroy the sight of the eye, nor cut off light from light, but be absolutely equitable, lest you be held accountable for the state of those souls placed in your bosom. And do not allow them to be sunk in the lake of perdition through the power of high-living prelates. A jewel lies on the road, but a bear comes along and seeing that it is very fine stretches out his paw to pick it up and carry it off. But, suddenly, an eagle swoops down and snatches the jewel, wraps it in the covering of his wings, and carries it into the palace of the king. And this jewel shines so splendidly before the king that he sets great store by it, and because of his love of this jewel, he gives the eagle golden slippers, and praises it highly for its uprightness.
>
> Now, you who sit as Christ's representative on the throne of the Church, choose the better part so that you may be the eagle who overcomes the bear.[211]

The allegory in this warning is to the Pope so that he keeps his eyes open in order to guard the jewel of the Church as the eagle who can stare at the Light without fear; for the bear—probably the emperor—seeks to snatch it away with the help of clerics who do not have the best interests of the Church in mind. Before moving on, let us have a brief glimpse of her writing to a pope she does *not* approve of for contrast. This letter to Pope Anastasius was sent sometime between 1153 and 1154, and after a very brief salutation launches into the substance of the criticism:

> You, O man, who are too tired, in the eye of your knowledge, to rein in the pomposity of arrogance among those placed in your bosom, why do

you not call the shipwrecked who cannot rise from the depths without help? And why do you not cut off the root of evil which is choking out the good and beneficial plants of sweet taste and delightful aroma? You are neglecting the King's daughter who was entrusted to you, that is, heavenly Justice herself.[212]

It gets even worse in the language and similes she employs to describe the situation. Eugenius just needed a warning—this Pope needs a command. Note the use of the personification of justice, which is a constant theme of Hildegard's preaching and admonitions; also notice the plea to restore justice and bring back the lost with mercy. These will be recurring images in her prophetic discourse. We move on now to the bear of the first letter, Frederick Barbarossa (the Red-Beard).

Frederick Barbarossa, Holy Roman Emperor (1152–1190)

Hildegard's ability to manage one of the most difficult political figures of her time was nothing short of extraordinary. Considering that Frederick was neither a man of great patience nor of deep respect for the authority of the Church, his relationship with Hildegard was surprisingly smooth. We cannot totally account for this, although one of the letters may give us a clue; and Hildegard's political acumen certainly came into the blend of forces that shaped this relationship. She had written him a letter of congratulation and admonition on his accession to the throne in 1152, where she praises his fitness to be king and yet warns him that the role is a burden to bear, since many evil people and forces will try to draw him apart from the natural justice and temperance a ruler must possess. We know she was summoned to his palace at Ingelheim, probably in the mid-1150s; we do not know what took place at that meeting, but Frederick wrote to Hildegard later to tell her that all her predictions made at that meeting had come true. He was obviously impressed with the seeress, and the combination of her unflinching character, meeting with her personally, and her accurate predictions may well have caused him to treat her as a vessel of God's providence. From Hildegard's vantage point, Frederick would disappoint her and distress her deeply with the creation of new antipopes and political maneuvering to gain supremacy over the Church in order to control or supplant the papacy. She kept silent when Barbarossa endorsed the first of the antipopes, Victor IV. We can only conjecture why she maintained her silence and allegiance at this point, as there are several convincing arguments for doing so. The first was ecclesial: the initial rupture was endorsed but not caused by the emperor; the rupture was due to the factionalism of the cardinals in the papal election. A minority elected Victor IV in opposition to Alexander III, so it could be seen as a disputed election. The second was practical; there was little to be gained and much to be lost by antagonizing the emperor at this stage. The result of Hildegard's silence on the matter and her outward allegiance was a charter of protection, which Frederick granted to the Rupertsberg in perpetuity in 1163. Such a charter was virtually unheard of in those unsettled times, and we wonder how Hildegard managed to get Frederick to even consider it—it bears not only his official seal but that of witnesses to the agreement.[213] She accepted this charter even though Frederick was under the ban of excommunication at the time (from Alexander III), which for Hildegard is a major concession to her sense of the priority of the ecclesial over the secular. The third may be that Hildegard, after her initial legitimation as an authentic visionary, was caught up in the writing of her *Scivias;* her disputes with Disibodenberg, including the one over Richardis; her new foundation and its needs; her other writings; her burgeoning notoriety and expanding correspondence; and her cordial relations with those who endorsed both sides of the argument. This included Conrad III and his wife, Gertrude, who were benefactors of the Rupertsberg and supporters of Hildegard in her time of need, and Frederick, their nephew, who was successor to the kingdom when Conrad died.

Even Frederick was not safe from prophetic rebuke, however politically expedient it might be for Hildegard to refrain. After the death of Victor IV the setting up of a new antipope became the emperor's cause. It could no longer be considered a dispute between the cardinals and their factions but implied the desire of the secular arm to take over the ecclesial power that rested with the papacy. This is something that had always been abhorrent to Hildegard: she associated the investiture controversies of the eleventh century between the Holy Roman Emperor Henry IV and the reforming Pope Gregory VII with the beginning of the turmoil of the times. For Hildegard, Henry IV had ushered in all the troubles and tumult that she experienced between Church and state in her lifetime. So when Frederick decided to take a hand in maintaining another antipope (and yet another after that), Hildegard wrote to him in no uncertain terms in 1164, after the election:

> O King, there is great necessity that you be careful in your dealings. I see you, in mystical vision, like a child playing insanely before the Living Eyes. You have yet time to get earthly things in control. Be wary, lest the highest King strike you to earth for the blindness of your own eyes which do not see rightly how you would hold that scepter in your hand for right ruling. So look to it. Be such that the Mercy of God does not die out in you.

Calling the most feared political figure of the times an "infant" and a "madman" was hardly prudent, and recalling him to a sense of duty and reminding him of the impending judgment of God if he did not return to the path of virtue and responsibility was a dangerous course. After the election of yet a third antipope in 1169 Hildegard throws all caution to the winds and proclaims prophetically and sternly:

> He-Who-Is speaks: "I shall destroy the insolent along with the contradiction of those who despise me, I shall crush them by myself. Pain, Pain to this evil of the evils spurning me. Hear this, King, if you wish to live. Or I will run you through with my sword!"[214]

We have no response from Frederick to these bombastic missives, which in itself is a sign he feared Hildegard's insight into God by means of her vision or merely chose to ignore her warnings beneficiently. There were some advantages to prejudices about gender roles; despite her recognition as God's prophet by her contemporaries she still was a woman. We can only conjecture that what Frederick would not have stood for in a man might have been tolerated in a woman. He could have restricted her activities, but this would not have been politically expedient, since it would create a person around whom Alexander's supporters could rally, one who was believed to be specially blessed by God at that. He could not destroy or humiliate her foundation, since he himself had sworn to protect it. So they reached an impasse until the schism was eventually settled, in 1175. Hildegard had friends and supporters on both sides of the argument throughout this bloody dispute.

Philip of Heinsberg

Philip of Heinsberg was a highly influential nobleman whose career in some facets seems to be like that of Thomas à Becket in England. At the time of their initial acquaintance Philip was a partisan of the emperor and his trusted lieutenant. He had served as imperial chancellor before being appointed first as a deacon and then as archbishop of Cologne. He was a frequent visitor to Mount St. Rupert and a staunch supporter of Hildegard, one whom we will see came to her rescue in an hour of dire need late in her life. Philip was a worldly man whose preferment to the Church was a means to an end for the emperor, who liked to have his loyal supporters in positions of power in the Church. Unlike Becket later on, Philip maintained his allegiance to Frederick. Hildegard was in some ways a spiritual mother to him, admonishing him about his spiritual responsibilities no matter why he undertook them in the first place. For

Hildegard, accepting the office meant carrying it out as God pleased, regardless of human intentions in accepting such a burden.

Because of Philip's request, we have a full copy of the sermon Hildegard preached in Cologne on her third preaching tour. We will treat this at the proper point. In his letter we see Philip's attitude toward Hildegard is one of awe for her gifts, since he refers to her as speaking "as though the oracle of God himself" (Letter 15). She, in turn, never ceases to admonish him for needing to pay attention to his later role as archbishop, calling on him to fulfill the episcopal function by exercising justice, mercy, and good example. The last is a theme Hildegard will have to constantly remind Philip about:

> But you who are called a bright star because of your episcopal office, giving off light through the name of the high priest, you should not be hiding your light (that is, the words of justice) from your subordinates. Still, you frequently say to yourself: If I attempted to discipline my subordinates with fearsome words, they would consider me merely a pest, because I am not strong enough to control them. O how I wish I could have their friendship without having to say anything! But it does you no good to talk and act this way. What should you do then? First of all, what you should *not* do is terrorize them with awesome words stemming from your office as bishop and the aristocracy of your birth, snatching at them like a hawk, nor should you use dangerous words like a club to browbeat them. Rather, temper words of justice with compassion and anoint them with the fear of God, making clear to them how dangerous injustice is to their souls and their felicity. Most certainly, most certainly, most certainly. Then, they will listen to you.[215]

We learn a great deal about Philip from these lines, and about his openness to guidance from Hildegard. He has taken on episcopal office, so she directs him to live up to it. Do not try to make everyone like you because you cannot; moreover it is good neither for you nor for them. On the other hand, do not scare them with rank due to aristocratic birth or with influence ("dangerous words") and power gained by advantage. You must act the bishop to be the bishop. She admonishes him on more than one occasion to be conscious of his faults as well as the sanctity of his office.

> O you who hold that office which is from God and not from men, since God, the director of all things, has established that certain men may serve as His vicars, be ever aware of the way that you represent Christ. . . .
> And I heard a voice from above saying to you: Make your decision, O man, whether you wish to remain in this garden of delights or to lie with the worms in stinking excrement. . . .

O father, I say these things to you in truth that I saw and heard all these words in a true vision, and I have written them to you in response to your command and petition. Therefore, do not be amazed at these things, but reflect on all your life from your childhood up to the present time. Also change your name from wolf to lamb, because wolves gladly seize the sheep. And take part in the banquet prepared for the prodigal son, who ran to his father to confess his sins.

These letters were written sometime during the period from 1167 to 1173, and Philip did indeed request Hildegard's guidance. Whether he was always glad to receive it, especially with imagery such as she uses in the second letter, is another matter altogether!

Whereas Frederick clearly represents Hildegard's prophetic stance toward secular authority, Philip represents a mixture of her stance toward one who represented both types of authority, secular and ecclesial. She is in no doubt as to which should take precedence. Philip is constantly admonished to take the role of bishop to which he has been appointed seriously; it is not an office that reports to secular authorities but is accountable directly to God. However he may have come to inherit it, he is now responsible primarily for the spiritual life of his flock and for his own example as an exemplary churchman. His rank and influence count little in this instance and actually distract him from his duties to the office he fills. Philip and Hildegard had a long-standing correspondence and relationship, and we have much to be grateful for in that. We do not know if Philip helped shield Hildegard from the tempest of the times, but we do know that in the next case we will consider he came to her rescue. It is also probable that it was Philip who commissioned Guibert of Gembloux to write a biography of Hildegard.

Conflict with the Prelates of Mainz

Apart from the disputes concerning her move to Rupertsberg and the loss of Richardis, Hildegard's most traumatic moments came nearly at the end of her life in a dispute with the prelates of Mainz. We have not chosen this conflict primarily for its dramatic and traumatic character, however, but for the way it shows how Hildegard embraced the role of visionary prophet in a way that threatened her very well being and that of the sisters under her care.

Hildegard had buried on the convent grounds a certain nobleman who had been reconciled with the Church after a period as an excommunicate. She received a command from Mainz ordering her to dig up the body, as the man was excommunicate and could not be buried in holy ground. She refused, citing the man's reception of the last rites and his confession and reception into the Church before his death. The prelates remained adamant and threatened to lay an interdict on the convent if she would not comply with their commands. She consulted her visions, and at their behest she refused the authority of her superiors in this matter. As a result the community was placed under interdict. This meant they could not sing the Divine Office but must say it singly in a whisper behind closed doors; they were denied the reception of the Eucharist and hearing Mass. The fact that it is not Hildegard alone who withstood them but her community who suffered with her says much for the loyalty of the sisters and their conviction of the truth of the visions of their prioress. Hildegard, in a famous letter to the prelates of Mainz, begins by summarizing the situation in this way:

> By a vision, which was implanted in my soul by God the Great Artisan before I was born, I have been compelled to write these things because of the interdict by which our superiors have bound us, on account of a certain dead man buried at our monastery, a man buried without any objection, with his own priest officiating. Yet only a few days after his burial, these men ordered us to remove him from our cemetery. Seized by no small terror, as a result, I looked as usual to the True Light, and, with wakeful eyes, I saw in my spirit that if this man were disinterred in accordance with their commands, a terrible and lamentable danger would come upon us like a dark cloud before a threatening thunderstorm.

She is following her visionary gifts here and insisting on her right to do so: these gifts do not supplant the authority of her religious superiors in this world, but they do in God's eyes. Note that she uses the royal "we" to make certain they are fully aware that this is not the complaint of one superior but comes from the Living Light. Hildegard found this situation particularly distressing because of the repercussions; being deprived of the liturgy, music, and the Eucharist was practically more than she could bear. She was eighty or eighty-one at the time of this incident and had never been strong. We have seen in chapter 3 how this incident led her to develop a theology of music and to reproach any who would deprive people from justly singing God's praises, since only evil can result from such a ban. Because Hildegard also had a deep respect for order and hierarchy, she did obey the commanded interdict despite the intense pain it caused her and her sisters. Although she would rebuke her ecclesiastical superiors for their blindness, she did not disobey them. This is also important for her role as prophet: she is to speak forth God's words but to obey the current order; she is to warn and rebuke, not revolutionize the order of things. It is also meaningful in interpreting Hildegard's regard for birth and hierarchy, which we have encountered elsewhere. She may have shared certain ideas and maybe even prejudices when it came to the "natural social order," for which she has been criticized by modern writers and by her own contemporaries. But she was consistent with it, and this crisis shows how deeply this sense of divinely ordered hierarchy mattered to her. We see the rebuke and the submission in the following paragraph:

> Therefore, we have not presumed to remove the body of the deceased inasmuch as he had confessed his sins, had received extreme unction and communion, and had been buried without objection. Furthermore, we have not yielded to those who advised or even commanded this course of action. Not certainly, that we take the counsel of upright men or the orders of our superiors lightly, but we would not have it appear that, out of feminine harshness we did injustice to the sacraments of Christ, with which this man had been fortified while he was still alive. But so that we may not be totally disobedient we have, in accordance with their injunction, ceased from singing the divine praises and from participation in Mass, as has been our regularly monthly custom.

This letter is filled with consummately and purposely mixed messages. Hildegard submits here and later apologizes for not coming "humbly and devoutly" to her superiors to settle the matter of participation in Communion. But she does not give an inch about what to do, because the Living Light in a vision has informed her how to speak and what is right. Above, she asks with ironic emphasis why a group of poor nuns should question what a priest of the Church had performed sacramentally. However, in defense of what is right as revealed in her vision, she takes the prelates to task for hasty action and a disregard for the importance of celebrating the divine praises. Besides her own eloquent defense of music and its theological importance, she cites biblical precedents and the example of the prophets, who themselves created instruments and praised God in song. She even appeals to the justice of God, as revealed through those who speak on God's behalf, as superior to any worldly circumstances by reason of God's predestining the elect to blessedness such as humanity possessed before the Fall.

> God, however, restores the souls of the elect to that pristine blessedness by infusing them with the light of truth. And in accordance with His eternal plan, He does devise it that whenever He renews the hearts of many with the pouring out of the prophetic spirit, they might, by means of His interior illumination, regain some of the knowledge which Adam had before he was punished for his sin.

It is Hildegard speaking as prophet here as well as a woman under the pain of interdict. This is even clearer later in the letter, when the prophetic persona comes to the fore:

> And I heard a Voice which said: Who created heaven? God. Who opened heaven for his faithful? God. Who is like Him? Nobody. And so, faithful ones, let none of you resist him, or oppose him, lest it fall upon you in his strength, and you have no advocate who can defend you before his justice. These times are womanish times when the justice of God seems to wane. But the strength of God's justice still works, and she proves herself a warrior heroine against injustice until it falls down, beaten to the ground.

This is no more and no less than a prophetic warning to the prelates at Mainz to heed the voice of God, which spoke inalterably through her in this matter. Otherwise, she would not have risked so much. The famous phrase of "a womanish time" is repeated here (we will see its initial use in the next section) with a clever twist on the image of Justice (feminine noun) as a female warrior raised up in God's defense.

There was more to endure, for the prelates did not respond favorably to her. Philip of Cologne took it upon himself to champion her cause and lift the interdict, but Archbishop Christian of Mainz, in Italy settling affairs between the emperor and the pope, initially refused to lift it because of what the prelates had told him. Philip produced witnesses to the reconciliation of the man with the Church in the form of another man who was reconciled at the same time but still lived, and a priest who would swear to this fact. When the prelates said that Archbishop Christian must settle the matter, Hildegard wrote to him of the circumstances and asking for justice, since she is obeying Church law despite her inner vision. Christian's reply is careful and hardly supportive of Hildegard, whom he rebukes for not having handled the matter properly in the first place. However, if the correct witnesses could be supplied—and they could—then he would lift the ban of interdict. His reply is a good example of the circumstance in which the authorities were happy to proclaim and acknowledge Hildegard's prophetic visions, that is, as long as it did not conflict with their own sense of spiritual authority and position.[216] This naturally is a prophet's dilemma, whether we speak of Hildegard or other prophetic voices. Accomplishments and gifts were welcomed if they did not challenge anyone too closely. As a result of Philip's intervention and Christian's grudging assent the interdict was lifted, to the great relief of the community, approximately six months before Hildegard's death in 1179.

Responsibilities of Office

One of the most frequently repeated pieces of advice to clergy and religious in Hildegard's letters is that they be mindful of their calling to a position in which they are meant to be examples for others, taking on the burdens God has rightfully set before them. Whether men or women, without exception Hildegard counsels abbesses, abbots, and bishops to live out the role they were given. Some are those who wish to serve God in a more contemplative fashion; some are desirous of putting down the temptations and burdens of office; some are not fulfilling the offices to which they have been called. All are reminded of the virtue of stability and the importance of tending the garden (the people) well. A combination of the first and second types are represented by Abbess Sophia of Altwick, who approaches Hildegard in this manner:

> Sophia, abbess of Altwick in the diocese of Utrecht—abbess in name only—sends greetings to the blessed Hildegard of St. Rupert, with a prayer that she may enter that choir which is illumined by the light of lights.
>
> Because no one is able to renounce the lust of the flesh and pant after the heavenly country with whole heart without Christ's help, I desire to impart to you, devout lady, the idea I have conceived in my heart by the prompting of God and the grace of his Spirit. Our Lord does not wish any of His sheep to go astray, but like a good shepherd desires to call them all back to the way of eternal salvation. This same Lord has inspired me, I believe, to lay down the heavy burden of administration which I bear, and to seek the seclusion of some little cell. I would be happy to follow this way of life, but whether I can successfully fulfill it or not lies in our Lord's power.
>
> Therefore, because you have merit in God's eyes, I know that you can discern a person's proper course of action through the revelation of the Holy Spirit, and so with humble prayers I beseech you, pious lady, to ask the Lord if my contemplated change pleases Him. For I do not want to be among those singled out by Gregory's famous dictum: "It would have been better for them never to have known the way of truth than to have fallen away once having known it."
>
> Finally, farewell in the Lord, and please do not fail to address these matters of concern to me, returning your answer by way of the present messenger, along with whatever else the grace of God is pleased to reveal to you through the Holy Spirit.

We have chosen this exchange because it is a straightforward and brief example of the way letters were worded. Note that the first and last paragraphs are salutation and farewell respectively, with the polite wording required; either or both could stress the urgency or importance of the case. Here, this only occurs in the farewell, while the honorific titles and wish for Hildegard to see heaven are in the opening and repeated with an acknowledgment of Hildegard's special gifts in the third paragraph. The essential part is in the second paragraph, where it sounds as if she is not only asking for advice but intimating that God has made this choice fairly clear to her and wants Hildegard's blessing. She does not receive it:

> In a true vision of the mysteries of God, hear these words: O daughter born from man's side and formed by God as the type of the building up of His kingdom, why are you languishing, so that your mind is like the shifting clouds that the storm blows about, at times bright in the sunlight, at times dark in the shadows. This is true because of the cacophony of the morals of those who do not shine before God.
>
> You say, I long to rest, to seek out a nesting place for my heart, where my soul may find peace. But, O daughter, it is not serving God to cast off your burden and to abandon God's sheepfold, when you have that light through which you may illumine it, so that you may lead the sheep to pasture. Now then, rein yourself in, lest your mind become inflamed with the sweetness which is very harmful to you in the instability of secular life. But be true to your calling, because this is what the grace of God wishes. Beware, therefore, lest you lose that grace through the instability of your mind. May God help you to stay alert through pure knowledge.[217]

We find several things worthy of comment in Hildegard's reply. Here she is acting only in her role as seeress: she speaks the words of God without the usual salutation and farewell that normally accompany letters. Hildegard does use salutations and farewells, but when giving direct advice to those she need not flatter or deals with constantly, she often skips them. Next we see the imagery of clouds: here they are "shifting" and there are storms. She will often speak of clouds as capable of obscuring the light when human flaws seek to hide from God's will. There is very little patience with the desire Sophia has for putting down her burdens and living in solitude. Hildegard believed that once God called rightly, he did not reverse positions of responsibility. We might conjecture also that she knew the solitary life well enough to know it was not a protective nest and that she had labored hard enough herself despite illness and trials to have little personal patience with such a request. "Instability" is a dire accusation from God when spoken through Hildegard and very much in accord with the Benedictine value of stability taken in the vows of profession. Besides the Benedictine value, we should note that this was a time of great spiritual resurgence, which necessarily was plagued by doubt about what type of religious life to follow. Thus instability was in the environment of the times, both secular and religious in origin. In this letter note the use of the biblical and homey example of the sheep, reminding Sophia that there is more peace to be found and good to be done by "illuminating the sheep" and "leading them to pasture" than by abandoning them. Imagery of the Good Shepherd and healthy, robust images of clean and virtuous living are contrasted with Sophia's temptation to give in to her own desires at the expense of her community's welfare.

In the following brief exhortation to Heinrich, bishop of Liege, she is replying to his concerns about his calling but in a slightly different context than in the letter to Sophia. He faces less of a vocational decision than one that pertains to his calling as it is intertwined with the difficulties he is facing in carrying out the tasks of his office:

> The Living Light which reveals miracles says: You who in your calling are a father and shepherd in charge of souls, stretch out your arms, lest your enemy plant tares in your fields [cf. Matt 13:25]. Watch over that garden which the divine gift has planted, and take care that its herbs do not wither. Rather, cut the rottenness out of them, and cast it out, for it chokes off their usefulness. In this way, you will cause them to flourish. For when the sun hides its rays, the earth ceases to rejoice.
>
> And I say: Do not overshadow your garden with the weariness of silence, but in the True Light weed out those things which must be weeded out with discretion. Illuminate your temple with benevolence, and burn incense in you censer, so that its smoke may ascend to the palace of the living God. And you will live forever.[218]

She uses some of her favorite images to convey the need to care for his flock: the tending of the garden and its herbs, the necessity of the sunlight versus the shadow, the likening of a good priest or bishop to a "perfumer" *(pigmentarius)*, which we see in the use of the imagery of incense rising to God. Heinrich is not to communicate his weariness to those he has in his care but to shine like the sun on them and till the garden with care, weeding out the evil with the discretion given him by God.

Other letters on the subject of responsibilities of office repeat the same themes and admonitions; they can be either quite terse or very elaborate in their wording. Good examples of Hildegard's terseness can be found in Letters 35r, 47, 49r; of elaborate imagery in Letters 26r, 27r, 32r. Lest it seem that Hildegard rejected these heartfelt pleas about vocation automatically, it should be noted that she even refused it to an abbess who, much impressed by Hildegard and her community, wanted to leave her own congregation to join theirs.

Care and Cure of Souls

It was a natural course of events for Hildegard to be consulted by many people, lay and religious, once her reputation and fame spread throughout the regions of Europe. Many wrote to her concerning spiritual matters, which is to be expected, humbly asking for her advice. In one case she was asked about exorcism, which was not a normal request to a female religious but the province of priests. In order to get a better sense of Hildegard's use of the allegory of the virtues and the vices, this next letter concerning spiritual advice focuses on her use of such personifications:

> Now, understand, O Man. Two men were sitting in a house, one of whom was a knight, the other a serf. And two wise and beautiful girls came to that house, knocked on the door, and said to them: You have become notorious even in far distant lands, for many people allege that you have slandered the king, and the king has asked, Who are these miscreants to be saying such things about me? Therefore, you two, hear our advice, for it will bring you victory. I am Humility: I have seen life in the incarnation of the Son of God, and I have crushed Death under my heel. The works of obedience are a mountain, and benevolence is a valley lush with flowers, though frequently choked off by nettles and thorns watered by the storm on sins.
>
> Listen, therefore, O man, for it is the house of your heart that the knight and the serf—that is, Obedience and Pride—are sitting in, and it is at the door of your mind that the two girls—that is, Divine Love and Humility—are knocking, to prevent you from committing all the sins that you are capable of. Now, therefore, observe that the knight defeats the serf, lest he trample the beauty of obedience beneath his feet, for Pride says, Those chains with which I bind mankind cannot be broken. But respond to him in the words of Love: I sat unsullied in heaven, and I kissed the earth. Pride swore against me and wanted to fly higher than the stars, but I threw him into the abyss. Now, therefore, join me in trampling the serf underfoot, my son, and take your stand with me, Divine Love, and embrace Humility as your lady. Thus you will escape condemnation and eternal death.[219]

Written in 1169–70, this piece of spiritual admonition and advice uses the personifications of the highest of the virtues, Divine Love and Humility, to explain the spiritual struggle of this person with the sides of his character. Pride must be replaced by Humility and Obedience in order for spiritual growth to take place. Note the biblical echoes of the triumph of Mary over the serpent and the analogy to the trampling of the serf in the allegory. Pride personified is Lucifer, who was thrown into nothingness because of his vain ambitions. Hildegard both uses allegory here to make her point and explains what the import of the story is to her reader; the "king" always stands for God in these stories and allegories in her letters.

A noblewoman named Sigewize was possessed or overshadowed by a demon and had been out of her senses for years. Hildegard is approached in 1169 by Abbot Gedolphus of Brauweiler about this problem, since he is at the end of his own resources about the matter. Hildegard writes back a lengthy letter describing a ceremony of exorcism, which should be carried out by "seven priests of good repute" who will be symbolic representations of Abel, Noah, Abraham, Melchizedech, Jacob, Aaron, and Christ during the ceremony, in which they will invoke what each of these figures symbolizes. Her ceremony works, but only for a brief time, and the demon enters the woman again; so the abbot sends her on to Hildegard.[220] We know no more from the *Letters* but learn more from the *Vita* about what happened next.[221] Apparently she came to the Rupertsberg, for the demon insisted that only in the presence of "Wrinklegard" could the possessed woman have relief. Hildegard takes up the story at this point, explaining how they took in the woman and even allowed the demon to speak, as long as it did not speak falsehood. On Holy Saturday when the holy water was blessed the spirit within her "let out many blasts." At this point, Hildegard states:

> I very soon saw and heard in a true vision that the power of the Almighty, which had always overshadowed holy baptism and had also overshadowed her, spoke to the conglomerate of devils by whom the woman was put in distress: "Withdraw, Satan, from the body of this lady and make room in her for the Holy Spirit!" With that, the unclean spirit withdrew from the woman in an abominable way, with excrement through shameful parts of the lady. She was now freed and remained so in the faculties of her soul and body as long as she lived in this world.[222]

There seems to have been a gradual type of convalescence, which then made the demon depart at the proper time, on the Vigil of the Resurrection. The narrative of the *Vita* by Theodoric embellishes the miraculous qualities surrounding Sigewize's healing,[223] although Hildegard attributes her cure to God alone, one of Hildegard's basic spiritual and theological positions.

Theological Issues

Aside from their spiritual struggles, people came to Hildegard so that she could consult the Living Light about disputed or doubted theological issues. Such issues preoccupied and concerned Hildegard. At the time she was writing the letters the Church had endorsed the idea of transubstantiation as a way of describing the Real Presence of Christ in the bread and wine. This was troubling to some, who wrote to Hildegard for assurance, such as Abbot Wolfard of Albon in 1153–54. Here is her reply:

> The Serene Light which gives words to ruminate upon says: O man, by thinking about the Son of God, you have assurance. Still, however, you hesitate to break the bread which you really wish to eat at the prompting

of your mind. Why do you go around in circles, sifting through all manner of things and casting your gaze every which way, attempting to find out where the reality is to be found in the sacrament? Why are you doing this? God builds his tabernacle on whatever is good and just. Rise up to the light, therefore, and you will live forever. For God has established the means through which He receives his burnt offering. Blessed is the person who clings ever to God in everything, for he will never be deceived by the devil. Live, therefore, O man, and be victorious in this shadowy world.[224]

Notice here that Hildegard is just as concerned to establish what the Abbot's spiritual priorities should be as she is with dealing with the issue of transubstantiation. While she assures him to accept what the human mind cannot grasp, she implies that God speaks to him about the fact that this preoccupation with being certain and figuring it all out is detrimental to him. He should have faith in God and what is revealed by God through the workings of the Church. As for Hildegard herself, we saw in chapter 3 a vivid picture of Christ's blood pouring into the chalice of *Ecclesia* and the bread on the altar in the narrative and miniatures of the *Scivias*.

Hildegard also devotes other of her letters to theological issues, such as the one to Odo of Paris on the nature of divinity, and to Eberhard, bishop of Bamberg, on the Trinity. The latter is important because it has more of the characteristics of a theological treatise. Unfortunately for us, it is also quite long, and in its content it resembles the exposition on the unity of the divine Persons that she discusses in her *Explanation of the Athanasian Creed,* even using the same imagery of brightness and fire to explain how the triune God is One and Three. Images of *viriditas* are invoked, and numerous examples ranging from the abstract (the parts of rationality) to the everyday (the blacksmith). For greater detail it is best to read this letter in full, and it is not in our best interests to reproduce it here.[225] We will see Hildegard's approach to trinitarian theology in the explanation she offers in the next section.

However, the letter to Odo of Paris is interesting for several reasons and can be quoted in part here. Odo of Soissons, as he was first known to Hildegard, is the man from whom we know that Hildegard's music was well known even around the time of the writing of her first theological-visionary treatise. He later took the name of Odo of Paris when he went to study and become a master at the renowned University of Paris. Thus he is a long-standing correspondent of Hildegard's, yet at the time of asking her about a particular theological question he is infinitely better educated in the theology of the time. We see in this attitude the sense that many had about Hildegard's authority coming directly from God; while theology could be inspired and subtle, why not try to inquire directly through the Sibyl of the Rhine? This comes quite early in her letters, in

1148–49, when her reputation was just being established. Odo presents the problem at the end of his letter:

> Despite the fact that we live far away, we have the utmost confidence in you, and, therefore, we would like for you to resolve a certain problem for us. Many contend that God is not both paternity and divinity. Would you please explain to us in a letter what you perceive in the heavens about this matter?

Hildegard consults the Living Light as Odo requests her to, and here we have a letter worth quoting because of its use of allegory, of Hildegard's basic images, and because of the theological content. The humility formulas and honorific sections are omitted, even though there is a fine description of Hildegard herself as a "feather" commanded to fly by God and supported wholly by God's power.

> And I say to you: From a certain very learned man who inquired of me, I heard that the fatherhood of the supreme Father and the divinity of God were not themselves God. And he asked me, a puny little woman, to look very carefully to the true Light concerning this matter. I looked and I learned, seeing in the true Light—certainly not through my own cogitation—that God is indeed both paternity and divinity, for man does not have the capacity to speak of God in the same way that he would speak of the humanness of a human being or the defining characteristic of a work made by human hands.
>
> The Living Light, therefore, says in the secret word of wisdom: God is complete and whole, and has no beginning in time, and so He cannot be divided by a word as man can for God is nothing other than entirety, and for this reason nothing can be added to or subtracted from Him. For He Who Is is both paternity and divinity, as it is written: "I am who I am" [Exod 3:14]. And He Who Is Completeness. How is this true? In the fullness of making, of creating, of perfecting.
>
> Whoever says that God is not paternity and divinity names a point without a circle, and if he wishes to have a point without a circle, he denies Him who is eternal. And whoever denies that God is paternity and divinity denies God, because he wants there to be some void in God. And this is not true. But God is plenitude, and that which is in God is God. For God cannot be shaken out nor strained through a sieve by human argument, because there is nothing in God that is not God. And since creation has a beginning, it follows that man's reason discovers God through names, for reason itself, by its very nature is full of names.[226]

Despite its early date, the image of the circle is reminiscent of the cosmic wheel, which will be the guiding image of the *De operatione Dei*. She makes the point that what is true from God's vantage point provides difficulty for temporal creatures, who are used to a fractured existence rather than the totality that exists in God; then human beings want to name things and distinguish them. This gets them nowhere when misapplied, although it is very natural to their created reason to think in this manner.

Hildegard's approach to theological issues is to trust to her visions and to God for any partial answers to the mystery of God as God can be known and approached in this life. She is not hostile to theological reasoning; she is interested in theological questions if spiritual life is not derailed by such issues. We will see that in her longer writings and sermons she had a good grasp of the fundamental theological principles of the Christian faith and did not hesitate to argue in their favor against any who would challenge them.

We now turn to her identity as a prophet in terms of its formation and its fame, which came to her through the undertaking of preaching tours at the request of her superiors and later at God's behest in a vision.

The Preaching Tours and the Content of Her Preaching

We know from the *Vita,* from confirmation from letters, and from other sources that Hildegard undertook four separate preaching tours (in addition to which she traveled to give homilies to the monks at Disibodenberg and the clergy at Mainz). They took place between 1158 and 1171. Although the *Vita* only names the places where Hildegard went on her preaching tours, the reasons for the stops she made is not clear from this account. Using other sources, we can reconstruct why certain places were on her itinerary and others not. One factor was undoubtedly geographical ease: it is likely that whenever possible, the travel took place on one of the rivers leading from place to place. Otherwise, all overland travel would require riding or walking on foot, a tiring prospect for anyone, let alone an aging prophetess.

First Preaching Tour

Hildegard's first preaching tour follows the Main River to the east and was begun in 1158 and completed in 1161. Sites she visited included Klause,[227] Winkel, Eberbach, Kitzingen, Ebrach, and Bamberg.

Klause was a small foundation of the monks of St. George in Rheingau with an attached cell for a recluse and was the first site visited. We know little of what happened there other than her visit, which is confirmed by a letter in Hildegard's own handwriting.[228] We assume that at Winkel she visited the convent of Wechterswinkel, where Gertrude (her former patroness quoted in the previous chapter) first settled before Hildegard interceded with her to be transferred to another religious community to which she was better suited. Gertrude was the aunt of the emperor and the widow of Conrad III; her requests of Hildegard clearly imply a spiritual friendship and respect, since Gertrude was well enough connected to have worked her way to a solution through secular means. The fact that she did not undoubtedly made her even dearer to Hildegard.

Eberbach, the next stop, was the site of a large and flourishing Cistercian abbey. We know about the abbey and its abbots from Hildegard's correspondence: she wrote to three of their abbots.[229] The abbot at the time of her visit there was Eberhard, and in his letter to her before 1166 we note the very Cistercian flavor of his writing and the influence of St. Bernard. There was a close tie between the two monastic communities from the time of its foundation and growth under the first abbot, Ruthard. They repeatedly offered service and support to Hildegard should she be in need of it; in return, Hildegard graced Eberbach with a precious copy of the *Scivias*. Disaster came upon this sterling community as a result of their stalwart allegiance to the pope rather than to the antipope set up by the emperor; as a result of their political position, their monastery was destroyed and left in ruins in 1166. A few monks remained, the rest returning to Clairvaux.[230] It is a sign of the disturbing times in which Hildegard lived that such things were common; Frederick Barbarossa only avoided destroying the Rupertsberg because of the imperial protection he granted to it and Hildegard in 1163. All of the nearby foundations who resisted the emperor did not fare so well. This was part of the ousting of Conrad of Mainz and his replacement with Christian of Mainz, a political maneuver on Barbarossa's part. Christian of Mainz spent a substantial amount of time fighting for Frederick in Italy rather than being present in his see at Mainz. During her visit there, this disaster had not yet come to the flourishing Cistercian community, and doubtless it was a friendly and pleasant one, since Hildegard had great regard for Cistercian ideals.

Next she came to Kitzingen, which was reputedly founded by St. Thecla on her travels with St. Lioba and was an ancient Benedictine foundation for nuns. This was the residence where Hildegard counseled the abbess, Sophia, to remain in her position, which we read of in the previous chapter; the spirit of the community was apparently a positive one.

Following the route of the Main would have brought her to Ebrach next, a Cistercian monastic foundation since 1127. The abbot Adam received several important letters in Hildegard's correspondence, including one cited in chapter 5 containing the excerpt of the vision of Divine Love, or *Caritas*. From the tone of the letters, the relationship was a mutually satisfying and rewarding one. Aside from counseling Adam to stay in his office as abbot, she wrote letters to him of great lyrical imagery, allegories of virtue and vice (Letters 85r/a and b, 86). Adam was obviously not a passing admirer but a sincere one. We hear this in his words and the replies they elicited:

> When I first heard of your fame, I rejoiced with great joy. Then God added to my joy when, with a gracious and marvellous command, He directed you to come into our land where you might be seen and heard, and, as I could not possibly have hoped, granted to me a meeting face to face with you. . . .
>
> Now I am sending a letter and messenger on your behalf to the lord Emperor, and I hope through the grace of God to be heard. And whenever you have need of our service, we will be prepared to serve you.[231]

Apart from Abbot Adam's regard for Hildegard as a person and as a prophet, it is enticing to think what he spoke to the emperor about that would be of importance to Hildegard. It shows again Hildegard's care not to totally alienate the secular authorities even when compelled to reprove them, as we have seen in her letter to Barbarossa, above. This particular letter was written sometime before 1166. Hildegard obviously made quite an impression on the community; she later received requests and letters from several monks of the community, including the abbot's secretary and the hospitaler. She was held in high esteem by them all, and they felt comfortable in asking her for what turned out to be uncomfortable advice. Her prophetic gifts were well received here.

On her first tour Hildegard preached publicly in two cities, Würzburg and Bamberg. She addressed both the clergy and the laity on these occasions.[232] Many tell us that this public preaching likened Hildegard to the figure of *Sapientia,* for it was apparent to all that God was speaking through this woman as a prophet, urging them to repentance, conversion, and penance.[233] Bamberg was also the site of St. Michael's, a Benedictine community of men, and two monasteries for women, St. Theodore and St. Maria. Hildegard's preaching tour was much concerned at this point with the monastic life, as we can tell from the majority of places she visited. She had been in correspondence with the abbot and monks at St. Michael, and with one of the abbesses, Abbess Lucardis. After her visit there was a serious dispute in the community of St. Michael's, disturbing to the monks and to the abbot alike, who wrote to her for advice. Hildegard's advice was to show justice and mercy to the monks in order to better serve and understand them (Letter 57).[234] Her plea is a moving and ardent tribute to the quality of mercy and uses the personifications Wisdom, Discernment, and Temperance, who decide it is "Mercy [that should] announce salvation to the people." In her letter to the monks she requested their obedience to their superior with an abundance of biblical imagery (Letter 59). She wrote also to the prior of this house at the same time, a man named Dimo, whose letter we quoted in chapter 5 and which uses the allegorical figures of the knight and the serf (Letter 58). In her letter to Abbess Lucardis she repeats some of the favorite themes we have heard in her letters. She exhorts her to nurture "her garden" lest weeds grow among them and threaten their zeal (Letter 61r). Lucardis is the abbess who petitioned not only to give up her office but to join Hildegard's community. She wrote to Hildegard about this, presumably after she met her and heard her preach. Hildegard must have had a profound effect on this abbess:

> To the beloved lady and mother, Hildegard, worthy of respect for her piety and dignity, Lucardis, abbess in name only in Bamberg, although unworthy, along with all the sisters entrusted to her by God, sends whatever the devout and frequent prayers of the humble can accomplish.
>
> With all our hearts, we rejoice in Christ, blessed lady, that *the Lord, who foreknew you and made you His elect has illuminated you and filled you with the spirit of prophecy in our time. Christ has gladdened us especially in this: that He not only foresaw and predestined you, a woman, for this purpose, but also His grace has illumined many through your teaching.* Therefore we offer the most devout thanks to Him for you, and we humbly pray that He mercifully finish that which He began in you, until He brings you to eternal life.
>
> Therefore, we earnestly beseech you to consider receiving us into your fellowship, commending us heartily to your holy community. Please strengthen us with letters of encouragement. Farewell, beloved lady.[235]

This quotation from Lucardis, especially the part we have put in italics, underlines and reinforces the power Hildegard's prophetic preaching and teaching had over people who heard her and met with her. Sometimes, in looking at the stern admonitions, it is hard to see the overwhelming appeal Hildegard had. It is obvious that this abbess was greatly affected by Hildegard and names her a prophet quite directly. Moreover, she rejoices that this has been done "through a woman." She must have been a person Hildegard would otherwise have enjoyed in community, except for her office; we see that she shares Hildegard's sense of the predestination of God of all things for God's glory.

Second Preaching Tour

In 1160 her second missionary journey began, heading southward down the Mosel river valley to the important cities of Metz and Trier. On the way, it is likely she visited Krauftal on the Saar river, and Hördt on the Rhine.[236] Of these visits and journeys, she is best remembered from the ringing prophetic sermon she gave in Trier, which sheltered both heretics and supporters of the antipope who caused schism in the

Church. This sermon is pivotal for understanding and viewing Hildegard in her prophetic role and was preached on the feast of Pentecost, 1160. She begins with the typical protestation:

> I, a poor little figure without health or strength or courage or learning, myself subject to masters, have heard these words addressed to the prelates and clergy of Trier, from the mystical light of the true vision.[237]

They probably never knew what hit them. After this typical disclaimer that it is God, not this figure of a woman speaking to them, she warns the prelates of Trier that they have been completely lax in their duties, failing to sound "the trumpet of justice" and prey to all manner of evils as a result. She sees Trier in a vision, enveloped in pentecostal fire and its streets "glistening like gold," while now all she sees is that the city has become so spiritually and morally corrupt that it will undoubtedly be destroyed like Nineveh. Note the comparison of her warning to the city of Trier with that of Jonah to the city of Nineveh, a likeness to a prophet though she does not directly claim to be one here. She prays that the "frigidity of the city" can still be consumed by the fiery love of the Holy Spirit, though she goes on to say it is a doubtful occurrence. Here we find the origin of one of her most famous sayings about it being "a womanish time," in which they no longer show the merits of men but have to be shown the right path they are studiously ignoring:

> In truth this is a womanish time, with a tyrant at the head, exhorting all sorts of malice forth. I speak to you in a true vision, that many will be disciplined as the head of household, who is God, must treat his children when they act with such reckless provocation.

She is perilously close here to naming the tyrant as the emperor Frederick Barbarossa, and that is surely the implication of her words. Laxity is a result of currying favor with the secular authorities for reasons opposed to the spiritual goal of the Christian people. As a result of their neglect and chasing after wealth and privilege instead of spiritual goods, the shepherds and the people are in danger of great distress; ultimately, their avarice will gain them nothing:

> But now the law is neglected among the spiritual people, who scorn to do and teach what is good. And the masters and prelates sleep, while justice is abandoned. Hence I heard this voice from heaven saying: O daughter of Sion, the crown will tumble from your head, the far-flung pallium of your riches will be drawn in and confined to a narrow measure, and you will be banished from region to region. Many cities and monasteries shall be dispersed by the powerful. And princes will say: Let us take from them the iniquity that turns the whole world upside down among them.[238]

In her letter to Hillinus, the archbishop of Trier, she repeats many of the important themes and images of her sermon, directed to him specifically as the shepherd of the Church. He is the one who is supposed to be "stationed in the tower," guarding the city against attack: he must continue to do so, even if the "wall and the ramparts" (the clergy) and the "streets" (the people) disregard God and rampage through the city. If he does not stand firm all is lost and will be destroyed.

> Wisdom cries out, saying: The present time is a squalid, womanish time. O alas, Adam, the root of the whole human race, was a new testament of all justice. Afterwards, in his race the manly spirit rose up and went out in three throngs like a tree spread out in three branches. The first throng was of such a nature that the sons of Adam chose according to their own capacity. The second was such that men rashly became murderers. The third, that they committed whatever idolatry or similar evils they wished. Now this tree has dried up, and the world has been turned upside down through many dangers. This time looks back to the time when the first woman gave the nod of deception to the first man. But man has more physical strength than woman. Yet woman is a fountain of wisdom and full joy, which man brings to perfection. But, alas, this present time is neither cold nor hot, but it is squalid. After this, a time will come which will bring forth manly strength in the midst of great dangers, fear, injustice, and ferocity. At that time, the error of errors will blow like the four winds which inundate the world with slander amidst great dangers.[239]

In this quotation she repeats the idea of the winds of the devil blowing through the city and the earth, and she laments the loss of manly strength and fortitude. But the compression of themes helps us see other aspects of Hildegard as a prophetess and a theologian too. Here she opposes the masculine and the feminine to the detriment of both, showing that all along they were intended to be complementary. Instead, everything is other than it should be. Even worse, it is a time of "lukewarmness," it is "squalid." To be lukewarm was a terrible state, since it implied complete apathy toward virtue; it is roundly condemned by the Bible (especially the prophets) and every spiritual writer in the Christian tradition. Both man and woman are responsible for the first turning away from God, according to their natures. She praises women in this excerpt for being "a fountain of wisdom and joy" for man, even though these times see nothing of goodness. As in her other works, we need to presuppose with her that the redemption is the prefigured end of time, seen before the fall of humanity; so it is doubly to their discredit not to anticipate the coming of the Lord and the restoration of the paradisal state. Instead, all they may receive are the afflictions and torments of those who will turn against God in the last days, as with the Antichrist. We hear a ringing apocalyptic tone to her sermon as she emphasizes this theme.

Overall the message is one of repentance; she closes both her letter and her sermon with a call to change, to realize and reform the errors of their ways. Then and only then can they know God's mercy. Left to their own devices they are lost.

She did find time to visit St. Eucharius in Trier, where she was on friendly terms with the monks.[240] They exchanged many letters, and she wrote several songs for their community, including a sequence to St. Matthias sent for the rededication ceremony when their monastery was reconsecrated to St. Matthias.[241] She trusted their abbot, Ludwig, to have a copy of her *De operatione Dei,* and since she is without a secretary asks his assistance in editing it.[242]

Ironically, in Metz Hildegard probably chose to visit Frederick's sister, Berta, with whom she corresponded; this just shortly after obliquely referring to her brother as "a tyrant" in Trier. We know little of this trip to Metz except that she is reported to have called the clergy to "sound the trumpet of justice," as she did in Trier. We would expect some record of her sermon if it had the full impact of the one given at Trier.

There was a Benedictine abbey in Krauftal, and Hazzecha often asked Hildegard for admonitory advice. This correspondence between Hildegard and Hazzecha of Krauftal is interesting in its display of compassion, coming right after a display of a prophetic, dispassionate call to justice. Despite Hazzecha's sense of her weaknesses, Hildegard exhorted her sisters to support her because of their abbess' exemplary judgment. Here she may have been trying to get each side to support and balance the other, for in letters to Hildegard, Hazzecha often expressed the desire to flee and live in solitude in a hermitage, perhaps with several loyal companions. Hildegard cites discretion and obedience as the key things for the abbess to attend to; the community should help her remain balanced by countering their unruliness with obedience and respect.[243]

Finally, in Hördt Hildegard made such an impression on the provost that he wrote her afterward about the burden of office, but also with great solicitousness for her health and well-being. Despite the joy he received from her visit, he noticed her infirmities and the toll of travel upon her.[244] As the final stop on this journey, his observations are probably accurate.

Third Preaching Tour

The third journey was undertaken between 1161 and 1163, and this time she traveled northwest, following the Rhine and the smaller tributaries of the Sieg and the Ruhr rivers. The monasteries and cities visited in this preaching tour included Marienberg, Andernach, Siegburg (near Bonn), Werden, and Cologne.

We know nothing of her visit to Marienberg, since nothing remains in the correspondence that speaks of the visit or verifies the relationship. In contrast, we do know about the Canonesses of St. Mary at Andernach, whose superior was Tengswich. Tengswich, we recall is the one who questioned Hildegard's liturgical practices as elitist and lacking in the spirit of poverty. The exchange of letters had taken place in 1148–50, so presumably they had much to talk about on this tour, although nothing is recorded of it.

Siegburg had a Benedictine monastery where she was received with sincere affection, for the monks there regarded her as their "spiritual mother" and maintained a continual correspondence with her.[245] In one such letter, Hildegard speaks to them of a vision in which the bright stars represented spiritual monks, and the darkness of night represented lax monks. All was compared to a cloud, another of Hildegard's favorite images, in its dual capacity to show or cover the light as twilight comes.[246]

In Werden there was another Benedictine monastery to visit, an ancient one built in the eighth century by St. Ludger, whose grave became a center for pilgrimages in the region. This is the most likely location for Hildegard's stay, although there is some dispute about the visit to Werden and little evidence to show for the alternatives.[247]

It is in Cologne, the final stop, that she gave her other famous sermon against the leaders of the city for allowing room for the heresy of Catharism. The Cathars had spread northward from Italy through France and ultimately took hold in the area around Cologne. Cologne meant many things to Hildegard, not least of which was that it was the site of the discovery of the relics of Ursula and her companions, for whom she composed such glorious music. Ursula was likened to *Ecclesia,* as we saw in chapter 3; but the church of Cologne was not in the image of this brave virgin figure. Despite her friendship with the archbishop—and perhaps for his sake—she took as strong a stand in Cologne as she had in Trier. This time the target was not merely the presence of the Cathar heresy, which Hildegard found repugnant in its precepts, but the negligence on the part of the spiritual leaders of the city, which led so many of the laypeople in Cologne to listen to the false preaching of the Cathars. For although completely wrong, in Hildegard's way of thinking, the Cathars did do or appeared to do certain things correctly that the orthodox clergy should have been doing all along. They were not greedy or avaricious; they seemed to lead chaste lives (although Hildegard will say this is just an appearance); they preach with passion and conviction about what they (misguidedly) believe is God's will. In chastising the clergy she points this out:

But you are a bad example to others, since no rivulet of good reputation flows from you, so that, with respect to the soul, you have neither food to eat nor clothes to wear, but only unjust deeds without the good of knowledge. Therefore, your honor will perish and the crown will fall from your head. Thus injustice calls forth justice, and it seeks out and searches for every scandal, just as it is written: "For it must needs be that scandals come: but nevertheless woe to that man by whom scandal cometh [Matt 18:17]." Thus the woes of mankind must be purged through tribulation and contrition, and many woes are laid up for those also who, through their irreligious acts, bring misery upon others.[248]

She squarely fixes the blame for many being won over to the Cathars to the lazy and irreligious clergy of Cologne. Interestingly, she points out especially the danger this presents to women. Since Hildegard and other women who claimed a visionary and prophetic voice were always in danger of being accused of seduction by evil spirits, she is doubly incensed that the supposed "spiritual leaders" of Cologne allow the women of the city to be led astray so easily by the false teachers, who account them as nothing by virtue of their sex anyway! The Cathars "flee" from women, but they are followed by women in droves because of their austere example.

In the beginning of this their seduction into error, they will say to women: it is not permitted for you to be with us, but because you do not have good and upright teachers, obey us and do whatever we say, whatever we command, and then you will be saved. And in this way they draw women to themselves and lead them into their own error. Therefore, they will say in the pride of their puffed-up spirit: We are completely victorious.[249]

Again it is the clergy who are neglecting the flock, not teaching or preaching God's ways, that makes such an incursion of heresy possible. She "sounds the trumpet" of warning:

Wake up! The misguided people of today have no idea what they are doing, no more than those who went before us in times past. For, at that time, others who err in the Catholic faith will fear them and will serve them slavishly, imitating them as much as possible. And when the full gamut of this error has been run, these people will everywhere persecute and exile the teachers and wise men who remain true to the Catholic faith—but not all of them, because some of them are mighty knights for God's justice. Moreover, they will not be able to affect certain congregations of saints, whose way of life is upright.[250]

Those who have a good grasp on their faith in doctrine and practice cannot be misled by the Cathars and their deceptive appearance (for the devil may appear in many guises). So there can be hope for Cologne, but if the rest do not wake up to the situation and lend a hand to correct and drive out this heresy, then there is much to despair of. The Catharist heresy offended Hildegard in two ways especially: it denied the goodness of material creation, declaring that all matter was evil (they were a Gnostic sect); and it denied the unique quality of the Incarnation joining heaven and earth in the two natures of Christ, claiming that he was an angel sent to earth and did not exist before the creation of the world as the Word (the Arian heresy). She begins the entire sermon with an appeal to the beauty of God's creation and an invocation of Christ as "the one who was and is and is to come." In a passionate defense of the natural world she calls creation in its formation by God in "moisture and viridity" the way in which we come to know God:

> These [the created things of God] are the materials for the instruction of mankind, which he comprehends by touching, kissing, and embracing, since they serve human beings: by touching, because a man remains in them; by kissing, because he gains knowledge through them; by embracing, because he exercises his noble power through them. Thus mankind would have no freedom of possibility if they did not exist with him. So, they with mankind, mankind with them.[251]

Catharism attacked Hildegard's very sense of the God who revealed in visions to her the essential teachings of the faith. As we have seen from the theological-visionary treatises, from the text of the scientific works, from the language of the songs and the letters, from the content of her morality play,[252] and, finally, from her sense of the mutual interdependence of all created things, it is only with extreme abhorrence that Hildegard can consider the Catharist heresy.

Despite this innate revulsion and her strong stand against the Cathars, we need to remember the exhortations in this sermon for the clergy to teach proper doctrine and lead upright lives, for historical circumstances would lead to a mass execution in Cologne of these heretics. This is not what Hildegard is calling for in this impassioned speech. Executions make martyrs and do not solve the problem of a lax and lazy clergy who refuse to be a light to the people, leading them to God. Some blame this fiery sermon for the circumstances leading up to the execution of the Cathars, and it may have inadvertently contributed to this event. But no matter how strongly Hildegard felt about them, she nowhere advocates that violence be taken into human hands, for God's judgment and justice are enough. Human beings must set a good example, suppress error, and lead the people in righteousness. But that does not include destroying souls that might well have been saved, from Hildegard's perspective, if their teachers and leaders had more backbone.

For Hildegard, whose faith in God was so rooted in a holistic view of the macrocosm and microcosm and whose theology was so orthodox and focused on the incarnation as the turning point around which history revolved, the Cathar heresy could have been easily beaten by good, heartfelt preaching of the gospel, which to her makes so much sense. How could the people prefer the Cathars, who believed the spiritual to be good but the material world and the body to be evil, over the incarnate Jesus Christ, who redeemed all? How could the people be more attracted by a sect that disdained women, not because they had to fight to attain chastity but because they weren't even interested in sexuality? For Hildegard, the people could only have embraced these tenets, which offended common sense as well as church doctrine, because of their zeal in preaching. Zeal is one of the qualities Hildegard prizes most and is necessary in those who have the care of souls. She will ceaselessly remind the clergy and religious that zeal is required of them in the life they have been called to lead.

The journey to Cologne ended Hildegard's third preaching tour. She concludes the sermon by saying, "I have worn myself out for two whole years so that I might bring this message in person to the magistrates, teachers, and other wise men who hold the higher positions in the Church."

Fourth Preaching Tour

It is very likely that Hildegard had no thought of undertaking a fourth preaching tour: in the interim between the third and fourth tours she was afflicted by two fairly serious illnesses. She reports in an autobiographical section of the *Vita* that the fourth preaching tour took place only because of a vision she had received, in which the Living Light delivered a mandate to make a journey:

> I saw that the departure of my soul had not yet come. I suffered more than forty days and nights with this illness. Meanwhile, in a true vision it was revealed to me that I should search for some cloistered communities of men and women and share with them the words which God had revealed to me. When I finally prepared to do that, although my bodily strength was diminishing, the weakness disappeared somewhat. I revealed the wisdom of God and was able to get rid of some of the discord existing in the cloisters. If because of fear of the people, I took no notice of the ways shown to me by God, my bodily pains took over and did not leave until I had obeyed.[253]

We note here that Hildegard makes a direct connection between her illness and her willingness to carry out God's will as she has seen it revealed by the True Light. What is interesting about this quotation at this time in her life—she would have been seventy-two—is the manner in which this relationship between vision and illness has stayed the same and yet is different. The characteristic difference striking to us should be in her relating the times of pain with her *failure to preach to the people*. We could say this was true in the case of the visionary writings, the move to Disibodenberg, and so on, but that was in the abstract. At this point in her life, the Living Light only afflicts her when she *fails to proclaim* what she must to each community. This is fairly close to an acknowledgment of a truly prophetic mission. Letters were not enough: exhortation and personally delivering the message mattered.

This final preaching tour was begun after a three-year bout of illness between 1167 and 1170. In 1170 Hildegard set off in a southerly direction along the Rhine into the region of Swabia. There she would visit monasteries at Maulbronn, Hirsau, Zweifalten, Rodenkirchen, and Kirchheim. Since she was responding to the call of God, she felt this mission to be one of calling these communities back to renewal and of strengthening their trust in the good news of God so they might proclaim it throughout the area.

Maulbronn was a Cistercian abbey, and she was received with respect because of her connection with their founder, Bernard of Clairvaux, from whom they were now much removed in both time and place. They were building a large church at the time of her visit, and subsequent letters between Hildegard and the community are ones in which prayers are requested by the abbot, Dieter, and one of his monks. In both cases, she responded promptly with words of consolation and advice.[254]

Hirsau was a Benedictine abbey located in the Black Forest that was in a state of gradual decline because of discouragement, dissension, and factionalism. Hildegard tried to get them to overcome their lukewarmness and return to their former state of vigor. But even though she wrote letters to both the community and the abbot, they lacked the zeal she longed to give to them in exhortations such as this:

> The Living Light says: O tumult, which though fragile rages darkly through the world made up of great infirmity; why do you make such noise through your great temerity? Nothing good can come of all this furor, which has embraced worldly ways of injustice and has put off the summit of glorious victory for the tempests of black tyrants!
>
> The mystery of God says: God wants to sustain the heavens. Why? Father, you have slipped from seeing, and so the heavens with its lights. . . . The Lord says to you, serve me well; and you should reply, then nothing shall overcome us. . . . Now, O man, you put yourself permanently in God's eternity and the right will prosper over all.[255]

In these brief letters to the community and to Abbot Manegold of Hirsau, Hildegard repeats her unvarying themes: look at where you are and what your destiny will be, but only put your trust and faith in God and all will be restored. Both justice and mercy have a place in her prophetic words. Despite her efforts Hirsau did not recover its former glory, and we know that it ceded most of its land to secular authorities in the early thirteenth century.

In Zweifalten, a double monastery for Benedictine monks and nuns, Hildegard found a despondent abbot and a lax and disorderly community, as attested to in her correspondence. These letters are a place in which Hildegard's prophetic gifts are most clearly acknowledged.[256] Most of the exchange of letters concerns the fate of the monastery or of a particular member within the monastery. The prior wrote to Hildegard asking what has been revealed to her about how to shore up the failure of discipline in the monastery, and the nuns also ask for her guidance when she consults her divine visions. It is possible that after being besieged with such a set of letters, Hildegard thought they needed a strong taste of prophetic rebuke and exhortation delivered in person. She does address the entire community of monks in a letter that makes up in directness what it lacks in tact and that might have been the substance of her preaching to them:

> Listen, therefore, you who break out in your evil deeds! You were called "Mountain of the Lord" because you should imitate the Son of God through your cloistered behavior. . . . For even though your life in the cloister puts you in the palace of the Divine, you do not want to tame the fire inside you. You were rescued from the stall of an ass and placed by the highest Lord in the exalted service of honor in the festivals of the holy Church. Why then are you not ashamed to run back again like dummies to the stall of the ass?[257]

She continued on to Rodenkirchen, which housed a group of Augustinian Canons in what had formerly been a Premonstratarian monastery. The superior, Stefan, had been a frequent visitor to Rupertsberg and a good friend to Hildegard. It is Stefan who likened Hildegard to other prophetesses spoken of in Scripture, such as Hilda, Deborah, Judith, Jael, Anna, and Elizabeth.[258]

Finally, she arrived at Kirchheim, where she preached publicly for an assembly of priests led by Werner of Kirchheim. We have a copy of the sermon, which Werner requested from Hildegard, and so we have some idea of her intent in visiting this city and community. She conjures up an allegorical picture of the Church, *Ecclesia,* beset and besieged by enemies and lamenting her treatment at the hands of uncaring and unworthy priests and servants of God. Yet there are also beautiful passages in this sermon that point to the beauty of *Ecclesia* as she should appear:

> I . . . saw a most beautiful image. It took the form of a woman, and so exceptional was her sweetness and so rich in delights her beauty, that the human mind was powerless to comprehend her. She stretched in height from earth to heaven. Her face shone with exceeding brightness and her gaze was fixed on heaven. She was dressed in a dazzling robe of white silk and draped in a cloak, adorned with stones of great price—with emerald, with sapphire and with pearls, having about her feet shoes of onyx.

Hildegard's sermon and allegory go further than the laments of the Church above but are more specific and link the birth of Christ and the birth of the Church:

> I lay hidden in the heart of the Father until the Son of Man who was conceived and born in virginity, poured out his blood. With that same blood, he made me his betrothed and furnished me with a dowry, so that in pure and simple regeneration of spirit and water, I might give new life to those constrained and tainted by the serpent's venom.
> But my nurturers, the priests—who ought to make my face glow red like the dawn, my robe gleam like lightning, my cloak sparkle like precious stones and my shoes glisten like whiteness itself—have strewn my face with dust, and torn my robe, and made my cloak a thing of shadows; my shoes they have blackened utterly. The very people who ought to adorn me in every part have left me destitute in all these respects.[259]

Ecclesia has been attacked and abandoned. She ends by enjoining the priests who may be disposed to listen to allow the fire of the Holy Spirit to work among them that the vestments of the Church may be cleaned, renewed, and restored, for not all have destruction on their minds.[260]

With this last stop and a powerful image of *Ecclesia,* with a call for justice ringing in the air, Hildegard finished her fourth and final preaching journey, returning home to stay.

Polyphonic Mysticism and Prophetic Witness

We come full circle to where we began this chapter by considering in what way Hildegard *necessarily* became a prophetic voice as the result of her polyphonic mysticism. It is characteristic of the mystical journey to be inward, but it also directs itself outward; often this is observed in works of charity, as in the example of Catherine of Siena. In Hildegard's case it is more difficult for us to separate the two. Probably we should not even try. If Hildegard's character is synaesthetic, then there is little choice for her to express what she experiences herself as a simultaneity in an outward form in order to come back to its inner origins. She begins with the experience of vision, relates it and learns from it, and returns with that information to add to her own store of spiritual wisdom and to share the fruits of that accomplishment with others. She is necessarily prophetic not because she is a visionary but because she is a visionary with multiple layers of insight. Her visions do not come in dreams or in ecstasies but in a waking state. They are part of the double vision she lived with all her life, and she strove to master its meaning in multitudinous ways. Her interior vision is made of many layers, as we have seen.

In a way, expressing these layers prophetically is merely turning over the tapestry so that it may be viewed by others in the outer world. Her overlapping concerns and standard motifs and personifications in her letters and sermons that are prophetic in tone are the same ones that appear in her other works. *Viriditas* and the greening power of God are something that must be shared and cultivated; otherwise all falls to dust and ashes. To have meaning the world must be seen through the eyes of the visionary who has been privileged to see from God the intentions for creation, centering in love, wisdom, mercy, and justice. The praise of God leads to the practice of virtue, and the practice of virtue leads the soul to praise God. Since praise, prayer, and virtue were the cornerstones of Hildegard's vision of the religious life and central to her understanding of the reflections of the Living Light she was permitted to see, she had no choice but to proclaim this understanding and way of life to others. If for no other reason, she needed to be a prophet out of compassion for her tortured, confused times. She, as a woman, must speak up for the Living Light and dispel the darkness of her "womanish times." As she moved throughout her own life from the complexities with which she dealt to their resolution in a mature simplicity, she was able to convey that to others as well as to rest in that spiritual state herself. We see this in a letter to Ludwig of Trier, written without a secretary and late in her life. It flows naturally from her, the confluence of all the many streams of revelation that have spanned a lifetime. Dronke says of this letter and its mature expression:

> It is an elaborate letter in thought and language. Here, late in life, we see how Hildegard had acquired the power to construct complex, fluent and fluid sentences, apparently quite unaided. . . . At first she makes a series of interleaving parallels between macrocosm and microcosm. The day in the outer world, from the first dawn to nightfall, is like the ages of man, from childhood to senescence. As the sun lights up the world from dawn to twilight, God lights it up with the breath of life. But as "the whole of creation . . . is man," human life also epitomizes that divine light-giving breath. The hours of the human day are both stages of human life and ages of the world.[261]

Hildegard then applies these insights to her friend. But it is not the character of the person with whom we are concerned here, rather the fluency and fluidity of expression. Dronke is speaking from a literary point of view particularly, but her expression extends beyond the consummate skill in using words and images to show us a woman who has matured in the sense of a mystic reaching her destination. She so thoroughly dwells in the Light that is God and reflects that light to others as best she can that she barely notices the complexity and depths of the imagery present here, let alone the view of the cosmos. In her prophetic words she often spoke to a particular audience in fragments of her insight and vision, using the same motifs over and over again. Here we see them joined peacefully together, immeasurably elaborate in imagination and expression, unbelievably simple in their joining together.

Having looked at the many aspects of Hildegard's polyphonic mysticism, which ends here in proclamation, we are finally in a position to try to do what she has done: make the complex less opaque, the simple more than self-evident. In the conclusion, we will strive for the ease and fluency Hildegard attained herself in reaching some conclusions about her life. Her contribution to the history of mysticism is a unique one. Unlike many others, however, Hildegard's recent rediscovery and her complex visionary life have made it difficult until now to situate her within the various ways of the mystics. Hopefully we can rectify that now.

Hildegard has meaning for us in her prophetic role in several ways. First, she is very human in the way she approached the role: even while claiming divine enlightenment she had lingering doubts and fears about speaking to others about what knowledge she had received in her visions. Second, there was no immediate precedent for this prophetic role. We assume too easily that when a long time elapses between the occurrences of a phenomenon, it is in some manner extinct. Hildegard became a prophet in a world that had not seen a prophet in centuries; moreover, a prophet who was also a woman had even less precedent. Third, we tend toward the static view of the medieval world; by this point it should be abundantly clear that many changes were taking place in Hildegard's time. We cannot use the excuse, so easily made, that in an ever-changing, technological world prophecy is an outmoded form of discourse. To the contrary, for if we focus on the type of challenge contained in most prophecy instead of on its potential for telling the future, there certainly seems to be room for a thoroughly modern prophetic voice. Hildegard had to speak out in times of religious and political turmoil, times of apathy as well as of evil actions. It was no easier for her than it was for the Hebrew prophets, and it is not a simple task today.

The prophetic aspects of Hildegard's life demonstrate that it is possible to overcome many obstacles when we are certain of the mission to which we are called. This is even more extraordinary when we realize that Hildegard's preaching tours began after her correspondence, when she was in her sixties and seventies; not everything need be left for youth to accomplish, for age and wisdom have much to offer the world. Hildegard as prophetess is a shining example of that possibility.

VI

Concluding Remarks

Hildegard is one of those unique figures in history who appears to have been supremely talented and prolific at the same time, having her own unique voice yet representative of her time and place. How does one summarize or conclude who she is as a person, a mystic, a spiritual leader, when there is so much to think about? And what can her life tell us for today, taken as a whole and not in parts, selecting out those facets we would appropriate for our own ends?

The metaphor I have used throughout of a mystical polyphony gives us several ways to address these questions. Rather than being overwhelmed by the content of her life and work, we sought to see an emerging pattern, a set of interwoven strands that made this woman a complex and compelling figure. Again, as in the introduction, we must address what it means to say that Hildegard was a mystic and what it means to call her polyphonic in her approach to life, but now with a deeper appreciation of both of those terms and all of her talents. At this juncture it could be beneficial to look at the visual overview of her life provided by the charts as we discuss her mystical polyphony.

Why is Hildegard a mystic? Clearly, her life is lived from start to finish by the direction given her by her visions of the "shadow of the Living Light" or the Living Light itself, God in the fullness of glory. A visionary need not be a mystic in the later sense given to the term, when interiority becomes important; but it was developed as a definition in the sixteenth century, even when explored earlier. Hildegard is a twelfth-century person: what is remarkable about her is the amount we *do* know about her mystical experiences and visions rather than what we *do not* know. While it is only in the letter to Guibert of Gembloux that she lets us inside the experiential part of her visionary life, it is a glimpse that helps define the whole of her mysticism. Hildegard is a mystic because she had a close and constant special relationship with God. Rather than showing itself in ecstasies or being suspended from everyday life while in contact with the Living Light, she had a dual vision of the cosmos for her whole life. This dual vision is the cause of her unique sense of self, and it is on this that her life and message is based. Hildegard's unique mystical gift is the ability to literally *see* the Incarnation at all times: the heavenly realm and the earthly reality co-existed for her in every waking moment, although with varying levels of intensity.

We identify with Hildegard's mysticism today because of its glimpse of the heavenly joined with an appreciation of the earthly. Her imagery alone gives us the sensation of being drawn up to God, while ratifying the goodness of God's creation. Life is *viriditas,* not static but a dynamic, life-giving force of greenness coming from the most High and permeating everything in the created world, the cosmos, the realm of the angels. She manages to heighten our appreciation of the natural world without sentimentality for something separate from us but with joy at its existence and its continual reflection of the Living Light in the smallest of things. In contemporary thought and society we mirror many forms of dualism in our attitudes toward life. Even in the attempt to create a "holistic" approach to life we are tacitly acknowledging that we feel the lack of harmony in our increasingly compartmentalized way of living. Hildegard's dual vision gives us hope for a real, not an artificial, experience of totality, of harmony between all things no matter how different. We need not be a synaesthete as she was nor have her range of abilities in order to experience her joy in the joining of the celestial and terrestrial into one cosmos brought to fullness by a loving God, visualized as blinding, beautiful Light. We can encounter her world through listening to her music, meditating on her lyrics, reading her visionary works, contemplating her view of the natural world and the saints, or in her role as a prophet, one who bridges the gap in communication between the heavenly plan for humankind and its all too earthly realities. One of the advantages of Hildegard's mysticism is that once we understand her as a whole and see the joy that fills her experience of the Living Light we better understand how Incarnation and incarnation is possible. One reason that people are drawn to different parts of her opus is that each person is their own individual incarnate self: the road to Hildegard's mysticism, and thus a pathway to a spiritual relationship with God, is particular to each person.

Her spiritual pathway, as we mentioned at the beginning of this work, follows that of other mystics and spiritual figures. It begins with simplicity, moves to complexity, and then back to a refined simplicity. How is this demonstrated by what has been discussed here? Hildegard starts life with a simple religious vocation about which we know little. She appears to have had a special religious faith on account of her visions but as yet did not understand them; indeed, she was afraid of them. Under Jutta and Volmar's guidance she learned to accept this gift and make it part of her religious life and expression of faith, but one used in private. As *magistra* after Jutta, Hildegard continues in the same pattern for a while. Then her simpler view of faith and life was suddenly overturned by the command to write down what she had seen in visions, a command she perceived as relentlessly coming from the Living Light, from God. Enclosed for years, at the age of forty-two her life became extremely complex. It put her at odds with the monks who oversaw her formation, forced a move to a difficult location to found a new convent, and made her speak out and write about her visions. She became a public figure known all over the medieval world after being enclosed and very private during the first half of her life, took on the burdens of prophecy and preaching as well as that of abbess of her own community, dealt with the ecclesial and political authorities of her day, and presented her complex view of the feminine and the role of women in an "effeminate age," all the while claiming to be "a poor little woman." Hildegard's Living Light demanded much of her, and we should not forget that she was sickly throughout her life. Perhaps in this sense she *was* a poor little person! Just reading about her activities, her talents, her challenges, and her growth is enough to make anyone a little tired and long for simplicity. Yet as we have seen in her works, while she was simultaneously doing many of these different things—composing, preaching, writing, prophesying—she comes to a real sense of her gift, a reliance on God, and a serenity and joy that shines through her life's efforts. This is especially true of the "mature" works later in her life, such as the *De operatione Dei*. What Hildegard does is interweave the strands of her life into a comprehensive whole, thus returning to a mature simplicity with great depth and many layers.

To reach this point of spiritual maturity she learned how to live polyphonically. The many parts of her life song overlapped and harmonized as one, while separate. They blend seamlessly into one another in overall character and purpose, the joining of earth and heaven. Perhaps the polyphonic living of Hildegard can inform us today about what simplicity really means. It is not just going back to a simpler, earlier way of life in the first sense; rather, it means taking the complexity that is the challenge of each of our lives and finding a touchstone, a place of simplicity where the complexities and the tasks fall into a place and where they make sense. It wasn't easy for Hildegard, and it won't be easy for us. She is an example of a woman confronted with what, without hindsight, seem

like insurmountable odds, if we are fair about it. Yet she managed to sur-
prise herself and her world by repeatedly rising to the challenge, based
on faith in her calling and her unswerving faith that the Living Light
would guide her steps as she developed a mature simplicity marked by
serenity and joy. Simplicity for us too often means simply "less," when in
spiritual terms it means "more." Instead of reducing what we do or have—
although these are not bad things in themselves—if we cannot, then simplicity is found in doing, having, and being with serenity and joy. We
envy Hildegard, the polymath, who could do so many things naturally.
Yet we have also seen her very real struggles: with authenticating her visions, with her status as a woman, with her grief over Richardis, with her
recurrent ill health, with her dismay that the world was not getting better
for hearing God's words through her voice but maybe even getting worse.
In this we relate to her humanity and her seemingly insurpassable odds
of success in what she set out to accomplish. The fact that she managed
it is a testimony to her life lived mystically and polyphonically while she
remained one whole person, not a series of attributes. To find the touchstone that brought it all together is what helped her and might be what
attracts us to her when we consider her polyphonic way of living. Having lived with Hildegard for the years it has taken to write this book has
suggested to me that her method in all things of keeping a certain stability while creatively working within the parameters she set is one that
both impressed her contemporaries and remains impressive today.

Hildegard, as many of the other women mystics, shows us that the
mystical and spiritual life is a gift, a grace, not an office. In today's world,
preoccupied with gender roles that center on issues of power and control, she has much to show us. How does her life contribute to a positive
view of women and of gender today? How does a twelfth-century woman
have anything to say to a world seeking to liberate all people?

It is by a sense of humility and obedience that Hildegard finds herself and her calling. It is not self-importance that counts but the importance of what has been entrusted to her as a vessel of God's grace, a
feather on the wind. By letting go of control and worldly desire in her
own life and by counseling this to others (as we have clearly seen in her
Letters) we achieve what the Living Light gives us the *viriditas* to do. We
are all here to see to the "greening" of the world. Roles and titles mean
nothing if they are hollow: how else would she dare berate popes and an
emperor with a notoriously bad temper? Although it is clear that she, as
a woman, would have to forgo traditional roles of power and authority,
her expression of her visionary experiences in whatever form gave her
more authority and recognition than many of the "authority" figures of
her time. We have seen that this is not her intent, as her notions of a

world with stable hierarchies and class systems is one she counts on. She is not flouting the system for personal gain but calling the system to account for its failures, and only as she believes she is directed to do. This is why it is crucial to note that it is *I Who Am* that speaks: Hildegard believes herself an instrument of God's design. Hildegard reminds us that anything is possible with God, regardless of what has been determined by the artificial world created by humanity. She chides us for seeking control when what we need is fulfillment and purpose. She had influence because of her faith in its source, in herself alone. And perhaps she, unlike some of the other women mystics, shows us what one woman can do when she possesses enormous creativity within a supportive community life. Hildegard's view of women and men is often based on outmoded ideas of biology or literalist readings of the Bible, yet she emphasizes continually their complementarity. In her personification of the divine virtues in female form, her use of *Caritas* and *Sophia,* she offers us visual pictures of the feminine divine. Nowhere is this more apparent than in her praises of the Virgin Mary and the virginity of women in her community as signs of the coming of the heavenly kingdom. Her references to the Living Light have the advantage today of a genderless term for an inexpressible reality we name God.

Given over to the religious life as a child, called upon to be strong when she felt weak, to express herself when she wanted to remain silent, Hildegard challenges us today to reinterpret our own situation. As a prophetess emerging from a life lived mystically, she reminds us that our own situation is not the individual, standing alone, but the individual in the setting of a community and society. By considering all of her talents, works, and trials we have tried to show the depth of the challenge she presents to us. She calls us to look beyond the everyday but to value it at the same time. She calls us to see that order in the world is a good idea, but it has to be reflective of a virtuous order, a life lived rightly in community. She calls us to see that in times of turbulence we cannot give up but must stand up for what is central to our very being. She challenges our preconceived notions of gender in the divine and human spheres. She asks us to love life even when it is hard to bear. She gives us her example and her tools. Now it is our turn to figure out, singly and together, how to bring *viriditas* more fully into the world of today and tomorrow.

Notes

1. See Barbara Newman on Matthew Fox and Bear & Co. (his publishing house) and also other "uses" made of Hildegard by contemporary writers who take her out of context: "Sibyl of the Rhine: Hildegard's Life and Times," in *Voice of the Living Light*, 1 and n. 4. Her ironic summary cannot be surpassed.

2. J.-P. Migne, ed., *Acta inquisitionis de virtutibus et miraculis sanctae Hildegardis, Patrologiae cursus completus: series latina*, vol. 197, 136ff. Hereafter abbreviated as *Acta* and *Patrologia Latina* respectively (the former title is correct but implies that all of the works collected here are for hagiographical purposes; when this is not the subsection, it is referred to as *Patrologia Latina*).

3. Gottfried and Theodoric, *The Life of the Holy Hildegard [Vita Sanctae Hildegardis]*, trans. Latin to German with commentary by Adelgündis Führkötter, and trans. James McGrath from German to English. Eds. for English text, Mary Palmquist and John Kulas (Collegeville, Minn.: The Liturgical Press, 1980) 50. Hereafter abbreviated as *Vita* or *Life*. There are several sources and fragments of the *Vita* available; this is the preferred English translation I will be using. The abbreviation *Vita* rather than *Life* means I have consulted the original Latin. Another excellent English translation taken directly from the Latin but less readily available is that of Silvas, *Tjurunga*.

4. Joanne Ohannneson's *Scarlet Music* (New York: Crossroad, 1997) popularizes the life of Hildegard in a novel and is very popular; however, her representation of a child torn from her parents is clearly a modern rather than a medieval mindset and does justice neither to Hildegard nor to her parents.

5. This is all speculation based on Hildegard's account in the *Vita* and by others in the *Acta*. The date of her enclosure or entry is made even more contradictory by other sources, some recently discovered, that would make her older at the time she entered the monastic life.

6. *Vita domnae Jutta*. Written by an anonymous monk who could have been Volmar, this work is due for translation by Anna Silvas into English in the

near future. I have relied for the information here primarily on the articles by Barbara Newman and John Van Engen in *Voice of the Living Light,* ed. Newman. For dating conflicts between the documents at a significant time in Hildegard's life, see, in particular, note 22. Source cited by the above authors as the original is *"Vita Domnae Juttae Insclusae,"* ed. Franz Staab, *Reformidee und Reformpolitik imspät-salisch-früstufischen Reich* (Mainz, 1992) 172–87.

7. *Vita domnae Jutta.*

8. *Vita/Life,* 51.

9. This primarily makes a difference in the experience the eight-year-old girl would have had. An act of oblation, which is a formal transferal from one custodian and way of life to another, is considerably less traumatic than the ceremonies that accompany the enclosure of an anchoress. Additionally, if she entered at twelve oblation and vows were more likely. It would also account for Hildegard's knowledge of the "outside world" of class distinctions.

10. Hugh White, trans. and introduction, *Ancrene Wisse: Guide for Anchoresses* (London: Penguin Books, 1993) 27–29. This is the most accessible of the English translations of the Anchoritic Rule for most readers, although it is meant to apply to anchorites living in England specifically. Nevertheless, it remains substantially the same as the Latin and other vernacular versions.

11. This is based upon my own personal experience of the ruins and Hildegard's guiding metaphors. Had she been enclosed as the dead, not allowed to leave her room, then her imagery is puzzling. Moreover, when one looks at the site of the enclosure and the ruins of the church, it does not appear to have been directly connected to the church, as was the usual case with anchorages, although some present us with archaeological evidence to the contrary. Certainly the nuns may have provided care as infirmarians, which would account for Hildegard's familiarity with the world outside her cell and with her medical knowledge.

12. Baird and Ehrman, *Letters of Hildegard of Bingen,* vols. 1 and 2; see *Letters* 1, "Introduction," 7. All quotations are taken from the critical and authoritative translation of Baird and Ehrman, who in turn are translating into English the critical Latin text edited by L. Von Acker in the series Corpus Christianorum continuo medievalis, vol. 91. Hereafter referred to as *Letters* 1 or *Letters* 2.

13. *Life,* 55, 56.

14. Newman, "Sibyl of the Rhine: Hildegard's Life and Times," in Newman, *Voice of the Living Light,* 7. See also *Vita Juttae.*

15. *Vita,* 51; translation combined with translations from the *Patrologia Latina.*

16. John Van Engen, "Mother and Teacher," in Newman, *Voice of the Living Light,* 68–69.

17. As Hildegard seems to have little to say about Jutta, and very little that seems emotional in her *Vita,* we could discount Jutta's influence somewhat. We do not know what the tone means: perhaps she is speaking from a great distance of years, perhaps their relationship was private, perhaps formal. It undoubtedly was central to her formation and later abilities. On this issue at greater length, see the work of Schmitt, "Blessed Jutta of Disibodenberg," 170–89, for more details about Jutta's life and influence on Hildegard.

18. Van Engen, "Mother and Teacher," in Newman, *Voice of the Living Light,* 35–36. For an enlightening comparison of the possible influences on Hildegard as a *magistra* of the Benedictine Order, compare his assessment of Jutta's training and influence with that cited in note 16, above.

19. Ibid.

20. Dronke, "Problemata Hildegardiana," 108–17. This is also more emphatically claimed in Emilie zum Brunn and Georgette Epiney-Burgard, eds. and trans., *Women Mystics in Medieval Europe* (New York: Paragon House, 1989) 8.

21. See such diverse sources as Neil Postman's *Technopoly* and Robert Southern's work on the Middle Ages.

22. *Confessions,* chs. 6–8.

23. Nolan, *Cry Out and Write,* 23–24; see also 62–63 for a further defense of this thesis in specific reference to Hildegard. I am deeply indebted to Nolan for phrasing in elegant and passionate prose many of my own convictions about Hildegard and for insight and inspiration regarding an analysis of the importance and meaning of gender in her writing.

24. This is not a minority opinion, although each researcher has an individual twist on the meaning of literacy. Flanagan, for example, suggests that Hildegard's lack of "formal university education" protected her from some of the assumptions and constraints other educated women show, such as Heloise. See her *Hildegard of Bingen, 1098–1197,* 44–50; see also Mews, "Heloise and Hildegard," 20–29.

25. *Letters* 2, 116, as an example. She warns the abbot against those who presume to know "too much by virtue of their own intellect and striving" rather than waiting on the will of God.

26. Newman, *Sister of Wisdom.* Contrast this very well researched, creative, and balanced approach to Hildegard and the feminine with Hildegard as the model for the contemporary feminist or Hildegard as the unjustly persecuted woman because of her gender. Note particularly Newman's emphatic refusal to put Hildegard in a merely feminine, isolated tradition. For a trenchant example, see the preface.

27. Ibid.

28. Nolan, *Cry Out and Write,* 11.

29. Ibid, 19. It is Nolan's idea "feminine poetics" that I am paraphrasing here, although there are similar suggestions in other authors. See, for example, Christel Meier, "Zwei Modelle." See also the persuasive work of Madeline Caviness, "To See, Hear, and Know All at Once," in Newman, *Voice of the Living Light,* 110–24.

30. See Elizabeth Alvilda Petroff, *Medieval Women's Visionary Literature,* introduction (Oxford: Oxford Univ. Press, 1986), for an argument for such a tradition.

31. Newman, *Sister of Wisdom,* vii, 42ff.

32. "Double vision" or dual vision, seems the simplest way to introduce a core reality for Hildegard that is more technically expressed by the terms *synaesthesia* or *polymath,* both of which will be discussed in later chapters. The importance of the simultaneous experience of vision/text, vision/music, vision/art = art/music/text/vision indicates the many layers of Hildegard's everyday experience and, indeed, her polyphonic quality based on her mysticism.

33. This is especially true of her use of melismatic phrases; we will explain this in detail in chapter 3.

34. See *Letters* 1, 52 and 52r (from Tengswich of Andernach and Hildegard's lengthy reply to Tengswich's entire congregation). It has been suggested by Van Engen in VLL 37 that this adaptation of ritual came naturally in a more open community such as Disibodenberg and that Hildegard was comfortable with external demonstrations of what she considered to be orthodox theological positions, such as the virgin as the symbol of return to paradise.

35. Hildegard is doctrinally orthodox on sin and grace, although she often uses other metaphors to convey these ideas, and subscribed to the vision of salvation found in the twelfth century. I take issue with interpretations of Hildegard's theology as meliorist—that is, the world improving—which other authors put forward. More will be said on this subject when we deal with her account of the Virtues and with her prophetic voice.

36. This is from the letters to Guibert of Gembloux in answer to his many questions. I am indebted for my attention being brought to this particular reference to Orthmann, "Hildegard of Bingen on the Divine Light."

37. *Letters* 2, 169r. She writes here to the prelates of Mainz, who have requested a copy of her anti-Catharist sermon.

38. The dating of the Cathar heresy is not precise; it came from the East and gradually made headway throughout the Christian West. Many would more conservatively put its influence in the 1150s and into the 1160s, but its first influence may have been felt as early as the 1140s.

39. See Bowie and Davies, *Hildegard of Bingen: Mystical Writings,* 4–6 of the introduction; also 134, the letter to Pope Anastasius IV.

40. Mother Columba Hart and Jane Bishop, eds. and trans., *Hildegard of Bingen: Scivias,* The Classics of Western Spirituality (New York: Paulist Press, 1990), preface and declaration. This and all subsequent translations from the Latin, unless otherwise noted, are from this version of the *Scivias.* I have followed their use of prose when Hildegard is explaining her visions or views and used italics when it is the voice of God verbatim. At this juncture this work remains the most accessible and reliable of the English translations. Aside from this critical edition, I have learned a great deal from Bruce Hoseski's translation of the *Scivias* (Santa Fe, N.Mex.: Bear & Co., 1986) by comparison, although its translations are on the whole less reliable. My own reading of the Latin has influenced me, as have the fragmentary translations included in collected works by Davies and Flanagan, to name two impeccable sources. It is important for the reader to note that the theological-visionary treatises have not been assigned endnotes for quotations, since the title, chapter, section, and vision number are included in the text. This will be true for all three works, despite different editions and authors.

41. At the end of the last of her visionary works, the *De operatione Dei,* she once again warns those hearing or reading her visionary works to take care with exactly what is written: "For whoever presumes to do otherwise, sins against the Holy Spirit and will not be forgiven in this world or the next." If this is not immediately apparent, this echoes Scripture in the sense of the authenticity of the words

as they are claimed and in the injunction about the sin against the Holy Spirit, considered by the Church to be the only unforgivable sin (including sins such as apostasy). She could not have phrased it more strongly than this—it is almost tantamount to claiming an equal authority with the accepted scriptural texts!

42. *Letters* 1, 1 and 1r (Hildegard to Bernard and his reply).

43. See, for example, Madeline Caviness' argument in her "Gender Symbolism." I appreciate the use of the material in this article in advance after attending Professor Caviness' superb lecture on this subject in 1993.

44. See, as representatives of this view, Peter Dronke, Christel Meier, Kent Kraft, and others.

45. See, as representatives of this view, Nolan, *Cry Out and Write;* Caviness, "Gender Symbolism," and others.

46. This portrayal shows Hildegard with a wax tablet, Volmar listening and recording in writing as he leans toward Hildegard to hear her speak and to see what she has on the tablet. See plate 1 accompanying the preface to the *Scivias*.

47. Madeline Caviness, "To See, Hear, and Know All at Once," in Newman, *Voice of the Living Light,* 124.

48. Hildegard, *Letters* 1, 26 and 49; *De operatione Dei* 3.10; this expression is a favorite of hers in explaining why women must lead when men will not. The Cathars, mentioned in the previous chapter, and the abuses of church office and power were of foremost concern to Hildegard; the state might always be encroaching, though it should be soundly rebuked, but the house of God should stand firmly for the gospel against heretics and also should reform ecclesial laxity and abuse.

49. Interestingly enough, the title *Scito vias Domini* could possibly have been a deliberate attempt to refute the individual rationalism of Abelard, whose treatise *Sci te ipsum* was condemned at the Council of Sens in 1140 just before she began her work. This is initially the suggestion of Berta Widmer, taken up recently in Andrew Weeks, *German Mysticism,* 47. Weeks makes the apt observation that whether or not there is a direct correlation between the two, "it is, in any event, certain that her repeated admonitions against probing into divine matters and asking too many questions in theology placed her in opposition to the dialectician Abelard and firmly on the side of his opponent and her powerful supporter, Bernard of Clairvaux."

50. In its longer version the monk is described as "a living fragrance vowing the way of secret regeneration" *(vivens odor vovens iter secretae regenerationis),* which fully captures the linkage between odor, fragrance, growth, renewal, and greenness. *Viriditas* is, as we have seen, a transforming power of life and regeneration, not just a literal symbol for greening or greenness but also for what this actually *means* to Hildegard—the life-giving power of God. Although most authors treat *viriditas* as a word usage and focal idea unique to her own work, it is interesting to note there may well have been similar contemporary usages, especially in their use of the term as it relates to the world around them. See Kent Kraft, trans., *The Book of Life's Merits* (New York: Garland Press, 1994) xiii–xiv. Quotations cited from the *Liber vitae meritorum* are from this translation unless otherwise noted.

51. The definition of seven official sacraments was only confirmed by the Council of Trent in the sixteenth century, although this number was commonly used in the scholastic debates of the thirteenth and fourteenth centuries. Interestingly enough, Hildegard has little in her writings about the sacraments, although her own vision is highly sacramental in its scope and intent.

52. *Viriditas* is a key term in Hildegard: there is a full column of references to this word alone in the index to the critical Latin edition of the *Corpus Christianorum,* 43:897. See also the cognate words she associates with *viriditas,* such as *virtus* (five columns), *virga* (1/4 column), *virginitas* (full column), *virgo* (Mary—full column; other—3/4 column), etc.

53. The latter seems extremely unlikely; see Kent Kraft, "More Than the Heart Knows," 97, 106. He bases this on mescalin hallucinatory effects or from hallucinatory substances that could have been derived through ergot, a fungus that grows on rye and is common to Hildegard's area of the Rhineland. For arguments, persuasive and otherwise, for the migraine theory, see Flanagan, op. cit.; *Migraine;* Singer, *From Magic to Science;* and Madeline Caviness, "To See, Hear, and Know All at Once," in Newman, *Voice of the Living Light.*

54. Madeline Caviness, in Newman, *Voice of the Living Light,* 113–17. Caviness' theory not only sees Hildegard's perceptions as migraine but actually sees them as part of her creative process as an artist in formulating the pictorial symbolism. Yet she allows for the images of building to also reflect the actual construction surrounding Disibodenberg.

55. Sacks, *Migraine,* 57–59. Hildegard's visions are only a very brief reference in this large, technical book, so it is not Sacks' central concern to debate the origin or authority of her visions. Despite the exhaustive investigation into various modes of hallucinatory drugs, this is essentially the conclusion of Kraft as well (see n. 53, above), although he is more careful to leave room for wider possibilities of how it may have affected the work.

56. See Flanagan, *Hildegard of Bingen,* for this suggestion and also the text of the *Vita.*

57. Nolan, *Cry Out and Write,* 122. He takes the schema further and in greater detail.

58. See Flanagan, *Hildegard of Bingen,* 74, where she notes that the *Liber vitae meritorum* or parts of it were read aloud with appreciation by the Cistercians at Villers and by the Benedictines at Gembloux.

59. This quotation and all others are taken from Kent Kraft's translation of the *Liber vitae meritorum* unless otherwise noted. Slight alterations in the wording are due to my own translations from the Latin text.

60. This title for the work comes from our earliest and most reliable manuscript, which is currently kept in a library in Ghent, Belgium. Although the *Patrologia Latina* includes a version of the work, it is a later copy and translation of more doubtful provenance; its name, however, continues to be used as the more frequent title for this work: *Liber divinorum operum.* The reader should not be confused by the variation in titles—they are, to all intents and purposes, the same work but assume their identity if the title is encountered elsewhere.

61. *De operatione Dei,* Vision 2.1.

62. We are quite sure there is not a direct route to trace back, as far as the illustrations we have from the Bibliotheca Statale di Lucca are concerned. But the images and text go well together, despite their seeming to be at one remove from the source. See Caviness, in Newman, *Voice of the Living Light,* 110–24.

63. Translations from the *De operatione Dei* present many manuscript problems. The available English translation is in Fox, *Hildegard of Bingen's Book of Divine Works.* I have generally followed this translation for the benefit of the interested reader; however, alterations in wording and style occur as a result of my consultation of the original Latin, translations by Flanagan, *Secrets of God,* also in Derolez and in Dronke, *Liber divonorum operum.*

64. *Life,* 71–72, ch. 16.

65. See, for example, the commentary of Kraft, 286ff., who argues that she was influenced by the School of Chartres and thus by medieval Neoplatonism; see also Dronke, "Platonic-Christian Allegories," 381–96.

66. See the arguments in favor of this view in Newman, *Sister of Wisdom,* especially the chapter on the feminine divine; in Sur, *Feminine Images,* in comparing the visions of the *De operatione Dei;* also in the various works of Elisabeth Gössmann.

67. See Gössman, "Hildegard of Bingen's Male-Female Divinity and Macro-Microcosmic Anthropology," *Hildegard of Bingen: Four Papers,* 22–26, on this very subject. She finds many parallels in other cultures, including those contemporary to Hildegard.

68. It is also important to recognize that although Hildegard accepts many of the ideas about what it means to be "male" or "female" in ways prevalent in her time, she also uses these categories creatively. She also departs from tradition by magnifying the role of the Devil in regard to the Fall, thus mitigating the culpability of Woman as embodied in Eve; and she sees the role of the Virgin Mary as the indispensable means in whose womb the Word became flesh. Mary is then pivotal to the presence of the incarnate God in the world and the absolute reversal of Eve's transgressions, by far surpassing them in positive action.

69. *Letters* 1, 52, partial quotation, 127. For a good analysis of this correspondence and its "cleaning up" by scribes and copyists, see Haverkamp, "Tenxwind von Andernach und Hildegard von Bingen," 515–48.

70. Dronke, *Women Writers,* 167. He admires Tengswich but finds this confusing coming from this particular source.

71. *Letters* 1, 52r, partial quotation.

72. Ibid. Also see Dronke's comments on this point as cited in note 70, above.

73. Letter to Guibert of Gembloux, around 1177. Dronke, *Women Writers,* 169.

74. *Letters* 1, 85r, partial quotation.

75. Ibid., 193–94.

76. *Vision* is put out by Angel Records and is a mixture of Hildegard's music and contemporary compositions and interpretations by Robert Souther. *Vox Diadema* is put out by Erdenklang Musicverlag (distributed by Real Music), and the European ensemble Vox, who use modern technologies such as synthesizers to "enhance" and create the "medieval mood" for listening to the melodies of Hildegard. This

is obviously very different from the still-popular work of the ensemble Sequentia, whose attempt is to be as faithful as possible to the original compositions of Hildegard; although debated by other musicians, their complete cycle of Hildegard's *Symphonia* are perhaps the most accessible and available of the "traditional" recordings.

77. Although this was standard Benedictine practice, for a simple yet very compelling picture of the importance of the Divine Office for Hildegard see Barbara (Grant) Lachman, "Feather on the Breath of God," 95–96.

78. *Letters* 1, 23, Hildegard to the prelates at Mainz, 1178–79.

79. Ibid., 78.

80. Ibid.

81. Ibid., 79.

82. In addition to works in the *Symphonia* using this image it is a prominent one in the *Ordo virtutum,* as we shall see.

83. Ibid.

84. Dronke, sleeve notes 9, 1985.

85. Dronke, *Women Writers,* 197.

86. *Scivias,* Vision 13.

87. Dronke, *Poetic Individuality,* 150–79. Dronke has several articles dealing with Hildegard's music in this book; see bibliography for a list of specific references.

88. Newman, "Poet," *Voice of the Living Light,* 185.

89. In addition to these two major manuscripts, there are the songs incorporated in the *Scivias* and a "Miscellany," both of which are in Wiesbaden; and there are several fragments containing songs in libraries in Stuttgart and Vienna. For more intricate detail about the manuscript tradition, discussion of its importance in determining key qualities of the song cycle, and for those musicologically inclined, see the following authoritative sources: *Hildegard von Bingen: Lieder,* ed. Barth, Ritscher, and Schmidt-Görg (Salzburg, 1969); Dronke, "The Composition of Hildegard of Bingen's Symphonia," in *Sacris Eridiri;* and Newman's critical English text and translation, *Symphonia.*

90. We have an account from Hildegard herself, dating the composition of the *Symphonia* from 1151 (after she finished the *Scivias*) to 1158, in the preface to her *Liber vitae meritorum.* As Dronke and Grant point out, however, even were these collected at this time, there is nothing to preclude additions to the song cycle later or incorporations of earlier works.

91. Newman, *Symphonia,* 29.

92. For a contrast with Abelard, see especially Dronke, *Poetic Individuality,* which contrasts words, theological content, and music; for a comparison with the Victorines and the emerging style of polyphony, many sources are available, among them Christopher Page in his album notes to the recording of her songs. Several works compare her pieces to those of Notker, likening them to one another in style.

93. Bent, "Hildegard of Bingen," 554b. Some musicians rightly take issue both with this quote in its accuracy and exactitude and with the article in this dictionary as a whole. It is used here merely as a clarification helpful to the lay reader, as the musicological issues are extremely complex.

94. Davidson, performing edition of the *Ordo virtutum*. Quoted in Boenig, "Music and Mysticism," 69.

95. Newman, *Symphonia*, 29. Phrase in brackets is my own explanation of "strophic" for the uninitiated.

96. Margot Fassler, "Melodious Singing and the Freshness of Remorse," in Newman, *Voice of the Living Light*, 164–65.

97. *O vos angeli*, the final words in the responsory.

98. Boenig, "Music and Mysticism," 60–72. Although the theme of the Alleluias and their melismatic composition and connection with the mystical are made in many places, for a particularly readable and concise account of this and a deliberate link to Hildegard's use of melisma, see 64–65.

99. See all of Dronke's works listed in the bibliography, for he has been Hildegard's most outspoken advocate in this regard. In particular, see his *Poetic Individuality* for a groundbreaking work that concentrates on this theme in Hildegard. Newman later is able to translate the songs into a poetic free verse as well as a direct Latin translation because of the majority acceptance of Hildegard's work as poetic, due to Dronke's suggestions.

100. Dronke, *Poetic Individuality*, 151.

101. See Newman, *Symphonia*, on this subject, particularly in her reworking of a Carolingian antiphon into the way Hildegard might have heard it (34–35) and in comparing her style with that of Adam of St. Victor (33–34).

102. I have created this chart, listing as each section the titles of each chapter of Newman's *Symphonia* with the exception of the songs without music.

103. *A feather on the breath of God: Sequences and hymns by Abbess Hildegard of Bingen*, Gothic Voices, directed by Christopher Page, with Emma Kirkby, Margaret Philpot, and Emily Van Evera. Hyperion A66039, recorded in London, 1981. *Hildegard von Bingen: Symphoniae (Geistliche Gesänge)*, Sequentia, directed by Barbara Thornton. Harmonia mundi D7800, recorded in Freiburg, 1985. *The Lauds of St. Ursula: Hildegard of Bingen (109801179)*, The Early Music Institute, directed by Thomas Binkley. Focus 911, recorded at the Indiana University School of Music, 1991. *The Harmony of Heaven*, Ellen Oak, Bison Tales Publishing, recorded at the Benedictine Monastery in Clyde, Mo. in 1995.

104. This translation is taken from Dronke, *Poetic Individuality*, in juxtaposition with the translations of Barbara Newman and of Hair and Martin, "O Ecclesia," and from other sources, such as Lachman's appendix of Ursula songs in her book *Journal of Hildegard of Bingen*, jacket notes, and my own interpretations. In the literalist Latin translations that follow in the next two songs, the sources are from several translations and my own compilation of them. In each case the poetic translations are Newman's alone.

105. This is taken from the poetic translations in Newman's *Symphonia*.

106. For a superb close look at this piece in both its poetry and its music and the intertwining of the two, see Hair and Martin, "O Ecclesia," 3–63.

107. Dronke refers to it as a sequence. Recordings can be found by Gothic Voices and Ellen Oak, as noted above, and most recently by Sequentia, *Canticles*

of Ecstasy, directed by Barbara Thornton, Harmonia Mundi 05472 77320 2, recorded in St. Panteleon's Church, Cologne, Germany, 1995.

108. Dronke, "Composition of Hildegard of Bingen's Symphonia," 389. He conjectures this based on the fact that although included in full in [R], it is not in [D]; this might place it after 1175.

109. The literalist translation for this song is taken from Dronke, *Poetic Individuality,* in juxtaposition with the translations by Hair and Martin, "O Ecclesia," 3–62, and other sources such as Lachman's appendix of Ursula songs in *Journal of Hildegard of Bingen,* jacket notes, and my own interpretations.

110. This is taken from the poetic translations in Newman's *Symphonia.*

111. Ibid., 276; see her commentary for parallels in the *Scivias* and on the song itself as a whole.

112. See Barbara (Grant) Lachman, "Hildegard and Wisdom," *Anima* 6, 128: the images of the eagle, incense, and light are also this type of symbol.

113. Recordings are made by Sequentia; also by Instrumentalkreise Helga Weber, *Geistliche Musik des Mittelalters und der Renaissance,* directed by Helga Weber, with Almut Teichert-Hailperin. TELDEC 66.22387, recorded in Hamburg, May 1980; and *Hildegard von Bingen und Ihre Zeit (Hildegard von Bingen and Her Time),* Ensemble für frühe Musik Augsburg, Hans Ganser, Heinz Schwamm, Sabine Lutzenberger, Rainer Herpichböhm. Christophorus CHR 74584, recorded in Germany, 1990.

114. These translations are both in Newman's *Symphonia,* literalist and poetic translations.

115. *Scivias,* 3.2. Dronke comments that the circular motion of the wings in the antiphon is a reference to the Neoplatonic World-Soul; he tends to see her work as platonically inclined in general. See *Poetic Individuality,* 156–57.

116. Newman, *Voice of the Living Light,* 268.

117. Dronke, 157.

118. Dronke, "Medieval Lyric," *Poetic Individuality,* 75–76; idem, "Tradition and Innovation," 80ff.

119. Dronke, "Tradition and Innovation," 82–83.

120. For mathematical analyses of the structure and meaning of Hildegard's music, see especially Escot, "Gothic Cathedral," 14–31.

121. I am grateful to Dolores Super for this observation and insight.

122. For considerations of manuscript questions, Davidson, *Ordo Virtutum,* Medieval Institute Publications (Early Drama, Art, and Music Monograph Series, 18) 23–25. In her appendix she lists the sources for manuscript transmission and their commentators.

123. As an example, see Dronke, *Nine Medieval Latin Plays* (Cambridge: Cambridge Univ. Press, 1994). He manages to be particularly ironic on page 155 in recounting this fact: "The range of evidence suggesting that the *Ordo virtutum* was performed is probably the strongest we have for any of the plays in this volume. The 'sociology' of leading performers today, such as Sequentia, cannot be faulted; it is the scholars, not the performers, who at times tend to imitate the action of the . . . ostrich."

124. Ibid. As an example of implied misogyny, see the reaction of Shein-gorn, pp. 44–45, to the same article in the *New Grove Dictionary of Music and Musicians* that Peter Dronke is citing.

125. See Dronke, *Nine Latin Plays,* 154, for a consideration of this question and inclination to its performance as a dramatic piece rather than an oratorio.

126. Davidson, *Ordo virtutum,* 7–8; see also Dronke's commentary in *Poetic Individuality.*

127. Pamela Sheingorn, "Virtues of Hildegard's Ordo Virtutum, in Davidson, *Ordo virtutum,* 52–57.

128. Ibid., 50–52.

129. There were originally eight modes from which chant could be composed, latterly called "church modes." Before developing key signatures this encompassed the tonality and minor or major sound a piece would have by using certain modes and/or contrasting them. The eight modes are the Dorian, Hypodorian, Phrygian, Hypophrygian, Lydian, Hypolydian, Mixolydian, and Hypomixolydian. For a complete explanation with examples, see any good dictionary of music and musical forms.

130. Wiethaus, "Cathar Influences," 192–203.

131. Dronke, *Poetic Individuality,* 174–75.

132. Davidson, *Ordo Virtutum,* 14; idem, *Music and Performance,* 15.

133. In the manuscript *Disciplina* is written and then crossed out. From the words sung it is impossible to identify this personification with any certainty, though she is still conventionally referred to as "Discipline."

134. Davidson, *Music and Performance,* 15.

135. See Sheingorn, "Virtues of Hildegard's *Ordo Virtutum,*" Davidson, *Ordo Virtutum,* 51–55.

136. Translation from the Latin variant, which is found in [R] and [Wr]. The critical Latin edition of the *Epistolae* in the *Corpus Christianorum* by van Acker and the English translation by Baird and Ehrmann do not mention music but choose the variant, which merely says that she utters unknown speech. This letter to Pope Anastasius can be dated easily, as Anastasius' reign lasted little more than a year, between 1153 and 1154.

137. Schnapp, "Virgin Words," 293. Schnapp is one of the few writers in English to even consider the *lingua ignota,* and his interest is primarily semantic. He is interested in the genesis of many "private" languages and their connection with the "public" area or with standard referents by means of which they can be decoded. His observations about Hildegard are of interest because of his grasp of her character in a way we would not immediately expect. For the definitive discussion of the *lingua ignota* it is necessary to go either directly to the manuscripts or to German sources such as M. L. Portmann and A. Ordermatt, *Wörterbuch der unbekannten Sprache (Lingua Ignota)* (Basel: Basler Hildegard-Gesellschaft, 1986). See Schnapp, "Virgin Words," 283, n. 23, for further sources and authentic manuscript traditions.

138. Schnapp, "Virgin Words," 290, n. 37.

139. Ibid., 284.

140. Ibid.

141. Ibid., 286ff.

142. The Proem from Pitra to the Life of St. Disibod appears in *Letters* I, 77r, to Abbot Helenger but does not translate the entire life of the saint himself.

143. See her hymn to St. Rupert, *O Ierusealem,* in which she celebrates these qualities, *Symphonia.*

144. *Commentary on the Rule of St. Benedict,* translation, introduction, and commentary by Hugo Feiss. All of the translations used in this section will be from this version. This particular citation is from Feiss' introduction, pages 11–12.

145. The numbers in parentheses refer to the sections of the document.

146. I am grateful to Thomas Izbicki for this insight in an unpublished paper given at Kalamazoo in 1995, in which he points out the centrality of fire in Hildegard's treatment of Athanasius and its link with the *Scivias;* "Fire, Flame, and Coruscation." The image of fire would be hard to miss here and elsewhere, and the elaborations on the theme are my own. In Hildegard's letter to Eberhard she also uses the image of the tree and the stone.

147. All quotations are my direct translations from the Latin manuscript found in Pitra, *Analecta Sacra Hildegardis,* 1066–80.

148. Note the careful use of *viriditatem* here: for Hildegard, the celestial and temporal worlds were united by the "greening" life force that is, or is from, God.

149. *Letters* 1, 31r, to Bishop Eberhard of Bamberg, 98.

150. These arguments, while important, are too technical to enter into, especially since they are largely speculative on the part of a given author. Notes in most works do not seem adequate to support either of the radical views: that she borrowed everything, or that she was well acquainted and consciously edited in many types of medical literature. See note 141 for some of those engaged in these debates.

151. Hildegard's medical works are considered completely spurious by Widmer, *Heilsordnung und Zeitgeschehen,* 20. She rejects both of them as being Hildegard's work on the basis of content and style; the content is too deterministic and rationalistic for them to be Hildegard's authentic writings. They also were rejected for similar reasons by Singer, *From Magic to Science;* however, his bias is toward a modern empirical view of all of Hildegard's opus. Others note that the lack of their presence in the Reisenkodex along with the other, undoubtedly authentic works of the time argue that they have been compromised at least and are inauthentic at worst; for an argument *for* authenticity plus a list of sources, see Florence Eliza Glaze, "Behold the Human Creature," in Newman, *Voice of the Living Light,* 145–46. Glaze gives much greater credence than the above to Hildegard's knowledge and interpretation of a variety of medical sources.

152. Although the manuscript tradition is riddled with difficulties and its transmission comes from weak sources, we have at least three contemporary lists of her works, which would name them as authentic: her mention of them in the introduction to the *Liber vitae meritorum,* in a letter from Volmar to Hildegard, and a mention in the *Vita.* For the difficulties with the manuscript tradition and why our sources are weak see Dronke, *Women Writers; Problemata Hildegardiana;* Glaze, "Behold the Human Creature," in Newman, *Voice of the Living Light,* 145–46.

153. We have a variety of manuscripts, none before the thirteenth century, and often they are divided and fragmented. For a simple, concise listing of these Latin extracts and the current location of the manuscripts, see Glaze, in Newman, *Voice of the Living Light,* 148. The best English translations, although not complete, are those of Flanagan, *Secrets of God,* 89–118.

154. Glaze, "Behold the Human Creature," in Newman, *Voice of the Living Light,* 135–36, 141.

155. Various authors have commented on the bias toward healing: see Flanagan, *Hildegard of Bingen as Prophet;* Walker-Moskop, "Health and Cosmic Continuity," 19–25; Daaleman, "Medical World of Hildegard of Bingen," 280–89.

156. Daaleman, "Medical World of Hildegard of Bingen," 285.

157. Glaze, "Behold the Human Ceature," 135, and n. 43.

158. Flanagan, *Hildegard of Bingen,* 83. Flanagan has done by far the most translations of the *Physica* in her narrative and considers it much more fully than other books on Hildegard.

159. Ibid. 85.

160. Flanagan, *Secrets of God,* 93–94.

161. Ibid, 102.

162. Flanagan, *Hildegard of Bingen,* 93.

163. The phrase in quotation marks is the one coined by Glaze; see n. 147, above.

164. For an unsuccessful attempt, see either the original German or the English translation of Strehow and Hertzga, *Hildegard of Bingen's Medicine,* and the scathing review it receives from Russell in *Église et Théologie* 20:129, which has the advantage of also describing the medical practice from which this book emerges. It is noteworthy because Russell is himself sympathetic to Hildegard as a person who strove for knowledge of all kinds; his comment on this book ultimately is summed up by the terse and telling statement: "It is unfortunate that what it has produced is a twentieth-century handbook for the practice of twelfth-century medicine." Other homeopathic practitioners are more cautious in the literal use of Hildegard's remedies.

165. See Dronke, *Women Writers,* 171–83, for an extensive discussion and argument for this point of view.

166. See Ulrich, *Hildegard of Bingen.*

167. Newman, *Sister of Wisdom,* 153–54. Newman's discussion of Hildegard's attitude toward sex is a particularly balanced view. For an interesting commentary on Hildegard's theories of physiology and her lack of emphasis on resurrection of the body, see Caroline Walker Bynum, *Resurrection of the Body,* ch. 4, 157–63.

168. *Lunaria* refers to the phase of the moon at the time of conception, which was thought to influence the character and prospects for health of the one born at a given time. See Dronke on this point, *Women Writers,* 177–79.

169. Flanagan, *Hildegard of Bingen,* 104–105. Flanagan and Newman give interesting expositions of these works, the former concentrating on the works as a

whole and the latter concentrating on what it means for Hildegard's idea of the feminine. Dronke is persuasive in his argument for a Manichean strain in Hildegard's thinking about the body, but because she defends an orthodox Christian position against the Cathars and takes a genuine interest in the maladies and cures of the body, the argument may be an attempt to systematize that which is not systematic.

170. Daaleman, "Medical World of Hildegard of Bingen," 287. He bases this view on other sources, which are contained in the citations; it is, however, the way in which many formal treatises concerning "worldly concerns" began, so the inference is a logical one.

171. *Holistic Healing,* 9–10.

172. *Causae et curae,* 36.

173. *Holistic Healing,* xix, 45–52.

174. Flanagan, *Hildegard of Bingen,* 97.

175. *Holistic Healing,* 53; italics mine for emphasis.

176. Newman, *Sister of Wisdom,* 152, 153.

177. From the *Causae et curae,* as quoted and translated by Dronke, *Women Writers,* 175.

178. From the German edition of *Causae et curae,* 51, translation from Daaleman, 289.

179. Translation and wording a combination of my own, the *Vita,* Dronke in *Women Writers,* and Newman in *Sister of Wisdom.* For a different translation, possibly more grammatically accurate, see *Letters* 2, 103r. I have kept this translation for its multiplicity of sources in translation and because these are excerpts.

180. Concerning the issue of the eremeticism of the times, see Kerby-Fulton, "Return to the First Dawn of Justice," 383–407, in her assessment of Hildegard and of the eleventh- and twelfth-century reform movements. For an overview of these reform movements, see the works of Jean Leclerq on the twelfth century in particular.

181. Kerby-Fulton, "Smoke in the Vineyard," in Newman, *Voice of the Living Light* 76ff. I disagree with many of her assumptions about Hildegard's belonging to the German symbolist school (as it has been defined in modern times), since while her rhetorical style may owe much to this movement, her attitudes toward predicting what was to come in the future were based solidly in orthodox twelfth-century thought on predestination and the inevitability of the kingdom, with no hint of "meliorism" in her attitudes. Even Kirby-Fulton acknowledges that *Symbolismus,* as a German movement, is primarily poetic rather than intellectual in content.

182. Kerby-Fulton, "Return to the First Dawn of Justice," for his intent; my judgment here is to the inordinate emphasis on fortune-telling, although Hildegard did stoop to this kind of prophetic utterance at times. See Dronke on this point.

183. Gebeno's popularization, the *Pentachron seu Speculum Futurorum Temporum,* can be found in partially edited form in Pitra, *Analecta Sacra.* For useful commentary on the matter of Gebeno's success see Flanagan, "Hildegard of Bingen as Prophet," 17.

184. Führkötter and Schrader, *Eichtheit des Schrifttums der hl. Hildegard von Bingen,* 30.

185. This is interesting, considering that the symptoms of migraine usually have the painful events concurrent with or preceding any sort of visual or auditory content; and yet she says several times that the weakness came after her revelations.

186. *Letters* 1 78, 172–73.

187. It has been suggested that in addressing the monks of Disibodenberg and the sisters at Rupertsberg, Hildegard's admonitions and homilies are more positive in outlook. It seems to me that, at least in the case of Disibodenberg, this is not true; if anything, she seems unduly harsh because of her disappointment with the community and possibly because of the need for a decisive break with them.

188. Summary of parts of *Letters* 1, 78r, immediately following on pages 173–75.

189. Ibid. 173–74.

190. Colman O'Dell, "Elizabeth of Schönau and Hildegard of Bingen."

191. Barbara Newman, "Visions and Validation," 174–75. Newman reports a struggle between Elisabeth's angel and her abbot in which the abbot was forced to "apologize" liturgically to the petulant angel as the condition for his return to revelations through Elisabeth. See also the correspondence between Hildegard and Elisabeth in *Letters* 2.

192. This frame of reference would have been natural to Hildegard from her education in the Psalter and other sources; I do not think it necessarily implies that she belongs in the German *Symbolismus* movement, although her impenetrable style may have been influenced by her reading of the Old Testament, the Gospel of John, and this contemporary movement.

193. Flanagan, "Hildegard of Bingen as Prophet," passim.

194. For this exchange of letters, see *Letters* 1, 70 and 71r. They were located in the area of Burgundy in what is now France, so this woman had to travel a long distance just to see Hildegard. She chose to make it a penitential journey on foot rather than on horseback and accompanied. Despite all of these factors in favor of the request (the right attitude on the part of everyone involved), Hildegard refused to say that she could do any more than God permitted in the circumstances.

195. *Letters* 1, 30.

196. *Letters* 1, 62.

197. *Letters* 1, 10r.

198. *Letters* 1, 18r. *Letters* 1, 19, is even more vitrolic, although not mentioning the circumstances certainly threatens Heinrich, the archbishop of Mainz at the time.

199. Dronke, *Women Writers,* 155; Flangan's quote on page 180 includes Adelheid in the distress that Hildegard expressed in a letter to Richardis' mother, the Marchioness von Stade; however, this could have been family politics.

200. *Letters* 1, 64.

201. See Dronke's excellent discussion of the Richardis dispute in *Women Writers*, 154–59. See also the views of Flanagan, *Hildegard of Bingen*, 180–84; Newman, *Sister of Wisdom*, 222–25.

202. This is variously interpreted as meaning that Richardis wished to rejoin her former sisters or as the possibility of a visit that would lead to reconciliation with Hildegard but not a permanent return. The language is ambiguous, and the latter seems infinitely more likely, though many commentators (as I suspect Hildegard herself) lean toward the former interpretation.

203. *Letters* 1, 13 and 13r. For an analysis and lengthier discussion of this exchange see the sources cited in the previous note.

204. The *Letters* have only recently received the attention needed to produce a critical edition, first in Latin by Van Acker in the series *Corpus christianorum continuo medievalis* (vol. 26), and subsequently in the English translation and editing of Van Acker's work by Baird and Ehrman in *Letters of Hildegard of Bingen*, vols. 1 and 2. All quotations come from these editions of the *Letters* unless otherwise noted, and will be referred to as *Letters* 1 or *Letters* 2. There will eventually be four volumes in the English translation, as Hildegard wrote about four hundred letters. The organization dictates the content of the letters that are available in translation: Van Acker used the *Reisenkodex* as a model, which classifies the letters first by the rank of the correspondent, then by geographical location. They do not appear in chronological order except within these categories, which can make them difficult for the reader to follow.

205. The *Reisenkodex* contains most of the letters but is very unreliable about the authenticity of the letters. The *Patrologia Latina* (197) is inadequate, and other letters have been found and translated by Pitra (*Analecta Sacra* 8); Dronke (*Women Writers*); and Klaes (*Vita Hildegardis*), which add substantially to the correspondence we find elsewhere. As with most of the manuscript studies and the initial judgment of their authenticity, the groundbreaking work is done in Fürkotter and Schrader, *Die Echtheit des Scriftums der heiligen Hildegard von Bingen*.

206. Of these four hundred letters, the current editions only contains those in the following two classes: class 1, correspondence with popes, archbishops, and bishops; class 2, ecclesiastics associated with a specific location, arranged by place. Future editions will include six more classes. Class 3 are letters to clergy whose names are known but who cannot be identified geographically and are arranged hierarchically; class 4 includes letters to and from the noble laity, notably kings and emporers such as Barbarossa; class 5 are letters to and from the laity associated with a specific place and organized geographically; class 6 are laity whose geographical location is uncertain; class 7 includes letters in which there is no complete evidence of the status of the correspondents; class 8 treats the texts that are of dubious character as letters, which may be either sermons or "fused writings"; class 9 are not letters at all but are included in her miscellaneous works, most of which we will treat below. There is a final class that includes obviously added and falsified materials. For this information I am drawing on the introduction to the English text of the *Letters* 1, 17. For further detail about the letters, their translations, manuscript histories, and technical difficulties see this work or the work of Van Acker, cited at n. 204, above.

207. See for example, *Letters* 1, 11.

208. For a concise but graphic reminder of this, see *Letters* 1, introduction, 10–12.

209. Joan Ferrante, "Blessed is the Speech of Your Mouth," in Newman, *Voice of the Living Light,* 105, 107.

210. See *Letters* 1, comments before 3r.

211. Ibid. 34, partial quotation.

212. *Letters* 1, 8. Partial quotation.

213. This charter is among the artifacts preserved at the original site where the Rupertsberg stood, and it is a very impressive document.

214. Both of these quotations are taken from Nolan, *Cry Out and Write,* 54–55, who has translated them from the German translation by Mariana Schrader.

215. *Letters,* 1, 16r, quoted in part, 66–67.

216. Flanagan, *Hildegard as Prophet,* 23.

217. *Letters* 1, 50 and 50r, complete; 123–24.

218. *Letters* 1, 36.

219. *Letters* 1, 58, to Prior Dimo, without the first paragraph; 136.

220. *Letters* 1, 68, 68r, 69.

221. The entire account is presented in the *Vita* from chapters 20–23; 83–96 in the English translation by McGrath, *Life of the Holy Hildegard.*

222. *Vita* 94, autobiographical fragment.

223. On the issue of hagiographical embellishment and the cure effected here see Dronke, *Women Writers,* 163–64. He is the one who suggests a gradual process of healing, connecting it with the medical and herbal knowledge of Hildegard and her sisters evident from the *Causae et curae.*

224. *Letters* 1, 46, 119.

225. *Letters* 1, 31r.

226. *Letters* 1, 40 and 40r, quoted in part.

227. Führkötter, "Hildegard von Bingen," in Brück, *Hildegard von Bingen 1179–1979,* 49, for a discussion of this particular location.

228. For the specifics of the preaching journeys I am almost entirely dependent on the work of Schmitt, whose article is the only available supplement in English concerning the details of these journeys. See "Leaven of God's Justice," 69–88. All other resources are in German or from the *Vita.* Important German sources include J. Schmelzeis, *Das Leben und Wirken der Heiligen Hildegardis;* J. May, *Die Heilige Hildegard von Bingen* (Munich: 1929).

229. She corresponded with Ruthard, its first abbot (see Letter 81); Eberhard, his successor, before (see Letter 82) and after (see Letter 32) he fled to Rome to become the abbot of St. Athanasius; and with his successor among the ruins, Gebhard and his monks (See Letter 139).

230. Miriam Schmitt, "Leaven of God's Justice," 77.

231. *Letters* 1, 85, partial quote 192. It would be interesting to know exactly what the abbot wrote about to the emperor, but we do not know what the letter concerned.

232. May, 157, and accepted as accurate reporting by Schmitt, 79.

233. Ibid. 156ff.

234. The critical edition of the *Letters* 1, dates this as 1169, quite some time after her visit there. Shortly afterward he resigned the abbacy, and we have no further evidence of her corresponding with the newly appointed abbot.

235. *Letters* 1, 61, 139–40. This letter is dated as "after 1157" in the critical editions, but if I am correct that this was written as an enthusiastic response to Hildegard's preaching and presence in Bamberg, it would have to be after 1158 or 1159.

236. *Vita,* ch. 17, p. 82, for a listing of the sites she visited. Schmitt, 80, for her conjectures about the second preaching journey.

237. *Patrologia Latina* 197:254–58; the quote here is translated by Newman in *Sister of Wisdom,* 27.

238. First paragraph, my translation from *Patrologia Latina,* above. Second, translation from *Patrologia Latina* and Newman, 28.

239. Excerpts from *Letters* 1, 26r.

240. See two of these letters, one to the abbot Ludwig, in Bowie and Davies, *Hildegard of Bingen,* 136, 147. See also Dronke, *Women Writers,* for the friendship between Hildegard and the abbot, also for another letter translated there, 193–95.

241. Newman, *Symphonia,* 300–302 in the commentary. This includes songs written for St. Eucharius, first bishop of Trier, who was the monks' original patron. She may have sent the songs after the preaching tour to Trier; the abbey was reconsecrated to St. Matthias in 1148.

242. Dronke, *Women Writers,* 193.

243. Ibid., 186–88, for a discussion of this correspondence and a translation of the letters.

244. *Patrologia Latina* 197:303; Ep. 81.

245. Flanagan, "Hildegard of Bingen as Prophet," 34, suggests this maternal position is one they decided on, not Hildegard herself. Nonetheless, they rebuke her for the lack of maternal affection and ask for what she sees of their fate in her visions.

246. See *Patrologia Latina* 197, Ep. 116, 366–67. As paraphrased from the account of Schmitt, 82.

247. I have followed Schmitt (82–83) and Schmelzeis in this regard. For alternative locations, see May.

248. *Letters* 1, 15r, copy of the sermon sent to Philip of Cologne; partial quote 59–60.

249. Ibid., 59.

250. Ibid.

251. Ibid., 55. The choice of using the masculine gender here is the translator's and is not easy to rephrase given Hildegard's long and complicated clauses. Because of the number of pronouns in this section, I have let it stand for all humanity as Hildegard surely intended it to.

252. Wiethaus believes the *Ordo virtutum* was specifically written to counter the Cathar heresies through theological discussion of their beliefs. For details see

her article, "Cathar Influences," 192–203. Of particular interest is her summary of the content of the sermon given against the Cathars at Cologne, 196.

253. *Vita* 96. This passage comes from the third part, chapter 26, and Hildegard speaks of her illness being increased by evil spirits. In chapter 27 she speaks of seeing a man in a vision who commanded them to leave, whereupon she recovered her strength. Theodoric tells us she regarded these illnesses as a thorn in the flesh, like Paul, to keep her humble.

254. See these letters in *Patrologia Latina*, 197:283–84, 357–59. See also Schmitt, 85.

255. My translations from Pitra, 521, 549; of course, until these appear in critical edition, we are unsure as to their exact date and provenance.

256. See Flanagan, "Hildegard of Bingen as Prophet," 34. Flanagan contests that about 10 percent of the letters sent to Hildegard acknowledge her directly as a prophet, and in the rest of the correspondence it is implicit. The letters from Zweifalten always consciously acknowledge her prophetic role.

257. *Hildegard of Bingen's Book of Divine Works, with Letters and Songs,* 305. The letters are translated by Ronald Miller.

258. See *Patrologia Latina*, 197:157–297, 313, as cited in Newman, *Sister of Wisdom,* 27, n. 72, also her discussion of this point as it touches on Hildegard and Elisabeth of Schönau. See similar comments and insight into Catharism in Raoul Manselli, "Amiciza Spirituale ed Azione Pastorale nella Germania del Sec. XII: Idegarde di Bingen, Elisabetta ed Ecberto di Schönau contro l'Eresia Catara," *Studi in Onore di Alberto Pincherle,* 302–13.

259. Bowie and Davies, *Hildegard of Bingen,* 141–42.

260. Miller, "Letters," 330–31. The translation here goes on past the Bowie-Davies excerpt to add this note of hope.

261. Dronke, *Women Writers,* 194. Text of the letter on the same page, and commentary continuing to page 195.

Bibliography

Allen, Prudence. "Two Medieval Views on Woman's Identity: Hildegard of Bingen and Thomas Aquinas." *Studies in Religion/Sciences Religieuses* 16:1 (1987) 21–36.

Baillet, Louis. *Les Minatures du Scivias de Sainte Hildegarde.* Paris, 1911.

Bain, Jennifer. "On Hildegard's Perception of Pitch in Her Chants." Unpublished presentation at Kalamazoo, 1995. Forthcoming as an article.

Baird, Joseph, and Radd Ehrmann, trans. *The Letters of Hildegard of Bingen.* Vol. 1. New York: Oxford Univ. Press, 1994.

———. *The Letters of Hildegard of Bingen.* Vol. 2. New York: Oxford Univ. Press, 1998.

Barton, Julie. "Mutual Interplay: Body and Soul in the Theology of Hildegard of Bingen." *Tjurunga* 46 (1994) 3–14.

Beer, Frances. *Women and Mystical Experience in the Middle Ages.* Woodbridge, Suffolk: The Boydell Press, 1992.

Bent, Ian. "Hildegard of Bingen." *New Grove Dictionary of Music and Musicians.* Vol. 8. Ed. Stanley Sadie. London, 1980. 553–56.

Berg, Ludwig. "Die Mainzer Kirche und die heilige Hildegard." *Archiv für Mittelrheinische Kirchengeschichte* 27 (1975) 49–70.

Böckler Maura, trans. "Chorfrau der Benediktinerinnen-Abtei St. Hildegard zu Eibingen." *Wisse die Wege (Scivias).* Salzburg: Otto Müller Verlag, 1963.

Boenig, Robert. "Music and Mysticism in Hildegard von Bingen's O ignis spiritus paracliti." *Studia Mystica* 9:3 (1986) 60–72.

Bowie, Fiona, and Oliver Davies, eds. *Hildegard of Bingen: Mystical Writings.* New York: Crossroad, 1990.

Brück, Anton. *Hildegard von Bingen, 1179–1979; Festchrift zum 800. Todestag der Heiligen.* Mainz: Selbstverlag der Gesellschaft für Mittelrheinische Kirchengeschichte, 1979.

Burnett, Charles, and Peter Dronke. *Hildegard of Bingen: The Context of Her Thought and Art.* London, 1998.

Büttner, Heinrich. "Die Beziehungen der Heiligen Hildegard von Bingen zu Kurie, Erzbischof und Kaiser." *Universitas: Dienst an Wahrheit und Leben (festschrift, band 2).* Mainz: Matthias-Grunewald-Verlag, 1960.

Bynum, Caroline Walker. "'. . . And Woman His Humanity': Female Imagery in the Religious Writing of the Later Middle Ages." *Fragmentation and Redemption: Essays on Gender and the Human Body in Medieval Religion.* New York: Zone Books, 1991.

Caviness, Madeline. "Gender Symbolism and Text Image Relationships: Hildegard of Bingen's *Scivias,*" 71–100. *Translation Theory and Practice in the Middle Ages.* Ed. Jeanette Beer. Kalamazoo, Mich., 1997.

Craine, Renate. "Hildegard of Bingen: 'The Earth Hungers For the Fullness of Justice.'" *Cistercian Studies* 26 (1991) 120–26.

———. *Hildegard: Prophet of the Cosmic Christ.* New York: Crossroad, 1997.

Cunningham, Robert. *Hildegard of Bingen's Book of Divine Works (With Letters and Songs).* Ed. Matthew Fox. Santa Fe: Bear & Co., 1987.

———. "Excerpts from the Book of Divine Works." Ed. Karen Campbell. The German Library 5. *Mystical Writings,* Continuum, 1991.

Daaleman, Timothy P. "The Medical World of Hildegard of Bingen." *American Benedictine Review* 44:3 (1993) 280–89.

Davidson, Audrey Ekdahl. "Music and Performance: Hildegard of Bingen's *Ordo Virtutum.*" Kalamazoo, Mich.: Medieval Institute Publications, 1985.

———, ed. *The Ordo Virtutum of Hildegard of Bingen: Critical Studies.* Kalamazoo, Mich.: Medieval Institute Publications, 1992.

Derolez, Albert. "The Genesis of Hildegard of Bingen's Liber Divinorum Operum: The Codicological Evidence." *Litterae Textuales: Essays Presented to G. I. Lieftinck* 2. Amsterdam, 1972. 22–23.

Despres, Denise. "Redeeming the Flesh: Spiritual Transformation in Marie de France's Yonec." *Studia Mystica* 10 (1987) 26–39.

Dronke, Peter. Appendix on the Melodies of Abelard and Hildegard. *Poetic Individuality in the Middle Ages: New Departures in Poetry 1000–1150.* Oxford: Clarendon Press, 1970.

———. "The Composition of Hildegard of Bingen's Symphonia." *Sacris Erudiri* 19 (1970) 381–93.

———. "Hildegard of Bingen as Poetess and Dramatist." *Poetic Individuality in the Middle Ages: New Departures in Poetry 1000–1150.* Oxford: Clarendon Press, 1970. 150–79.

———. "The Text of the Ordo Virtutum." *Poetic Individuality in the Middle Ages: New Departures in Poetry 1000–1150.* Oxford: Clarendon Press, 1970.

———. "Tradition and Innovation in Medieval Western Colour-Imagery." *Eranos Jahrbuch* 49 (1972) 51–106.

———. "Problemata Hildegardiana." *Mittellateinisches Jahrbuch* 16 (1981) 107–31.

———. *Women Writers of the Middle Ages: A Critical Study of Texts From Perpetua (d. 203) to Marguerite Porete (d. 1310).* Chapter 6 and appendix. Cambridge: Cambridge Univ. Press, 1984.

———. "Platonic-Christian Allegories in the Homilies of Hildegard of Bingen." *From Athens to Chartres: Neoplatonism and Medieval Thought.* Ed. J. J. Westra. Leiden, 1992. 381–96.

_____. *Nine Medieval Latin Plays*. Cambridge: Cambridge Univ. Press, 1994.

Eckert, Willhad Paul. "The Vision of Synagoga in the Scivias of Hildegard of Bingen." *Standing Before God*. Ed. Finkel and Frizzell. New York: KATV Publishing House, 1981. 301–11.

Escot, Pozzi. "The Gothic Cathedral and Hidden Geometry of St. Hildegard." *Sonus* 5 (1984) 14–31.

_____. "Hildegard Von Bingen: Universal Proportion." *Sonus* (1992).

Feiss, Hugo. Introduction and translation. "Hildegard von Bingen: Explanation of the Rule of St. Benedict." Toronto: Peregrina Publishing Co. (formerly *Vox Benedictina* 7:2 [1990]).

Flanagan, Sabina. "Hildegard of Bingen as Prophet: The Evidence of Her Contemporaries." *Tjurunga* 32 (1987) 16–45.

_____. *Hildegard of Bingen: A Visionary Life*. London and New York: Routledge Press, 1989.

_____. *Secrets of God: Writings of Hildegard of Bingen*. Boston: Shambala, 1996.

Ford-Grabowski, Mary. "Angels and Archetypes: A Jungian Approach to St. Hildegard." *American Benedictine Review* 41:1 (1990) 1–19.

_____. Fox, Matthew, ed. *Hildegard of Bingen's Book of Divine Works (With Letters and Songs)*. Santa Fe: Bear & Co., 1987.

Führkötter, Adelgundis. *Hildegard von Bingen*. Salzburg: Otto Müller Verlag, 1972.

_____, ed. *The Miniatures from the Book of Scivias: Know the Ways*. Turnhout, Belgium: Fabrieken Brepols, 1977.

_____, ed. *Kosmos und Mensch aus der Sicht Hildegards von Bingen*. Mainz: Verlag der Gesellshaft für Mittelrheinische Kirchengeschichte, 1987.

Führkötter, Adelgundis, and Marianna Schrader. *Die echtheit des schrifttums der hl. Hildegard von Bingen*. Cologne and Graz, 1956.

Gies, Frances, and Joseph Gies. "An Abbess: Hildegarde of Bingen." *Women in the Middle Ages*. New York: Thomas Y. Crowell Co., 1978.

Gössman, Elisabeth. "Hildegard von Bingen." *Mittelalter I*. Ed. M. Greshact. (1983) 224–37.

_____. "Das Menschenbild der Hildegard von Bingen und Elisabeth von Schönau vor dem Hintergrund der frühscholastischen Anthropologie." *Frauenmystik im Mittelalter*. Ed. P. Dinaelbacher. Oatfildern: Schwabenverlag, 1985.

_____. "The Image of the Human Being According to Scholastic Theology and the Reaction of Contemporary Women." *Ultimate Reality and Meaning: Interdisciplinary Studies in the Philosophy of Understanding* 11 (1988) 183–95.

_____. *Hildegard of Bingen: Four Papers*. Toronto: Peregrina Publishing, 1995.

Gouguenheim, Sylvain. *La Sibylle du Rhin: Hildegarde de Bingen, Abbesse et Prophétesse Rhénane*. Paris, 1996.

Grant, Barbara L. "Hildegard and Wisdom." *Anima: An Experimental Journal of Celebration* 6 (1980) 125–29.

_____. "A Feather on the Breath of God." *Parabola: The Magazine of Myth and Tradition* 9:2 (1984) 94–98.

Hair, Greta Mary, and Janet Martin. "O Ecclesia: The Text and Music of Hildegard of Bingen's Sequence for St. Ursula." *Tjurunga* 30 (1986) 3–62.

Haverkamp, Von Alfred. "Tenxwind von Andernach und Hildegard von Bingen: Zwei 'Weltanschauungen' in der Mitte des 12. Jahrhunderts." *Institutionen, Kultur, und Gesellschaft im Mittelalter: Festschrift für Josef Fleckenstein.* Sigmaringen: Jan Thorbecke Verlag, 1984. 515–48.

Hertzka, Gottfried. *Das Wunder der Hildegard-Medizin.* Stein am Rhein/Schweiz: Christiana-Verlag, 1984.

Hildegard of Bingen. *Scivias.* Trans. Bruce Hozeski. Santa Fe: Bear & Co., 1986.

———. *Scivias.* The Classics of Western Spirituality. Trans. Columba Hart and Jane Bishop. New York: Paulist Press, 1990.

———. *Three Antiphons.* Bryn Mawr, Penn.: Hildegard Publishing Co., 1990.

———. *The Book of Life's Merits.* Trans. Kent Kraft. New York: Garland Press, 1994.

———. *Book of the Rewards of Life.* Trans. Bruce Hozeki. New York, 1994.

———. *Holistic Healing [Causae et curae].* Trans. Patrick Madigan. Collegeville, Minn.: The Liturgical Press, 1994.

Hildegard of Bingen. *Liber Divinorum Operum.* Ed. Albert Derolez and Peter Dronke. CCCM 90. Belgium: Turnhout, 1995.

Izbicki, Thomas. "Fire, Flame, and Coruscation: Hildegard of Bingen's Explanation of the Athanasian Creed." Unpublished paper, 1995.

Jeskalian, Barbara J. "Hildegard of Bingen: Her Times and Music." *Anima: An Experimental Journal of Celebration* 10 (1983) 7–13.

Kerby-Fulton, Kathryn. "A Return to 'The First Dawn of Justice': Hildegard's Visions of Clerical Reform and the Eremetical Life." *American Benedictine Review* 40:4 (1989) 383–407.

Kraft, Kent. *The Eye Sees More Than the Heart Knows: The Visionary Cosmology of Hildegard of Bingen.* University Microfilms: Ph.D. diss. Univ. of Wisconsin-Madison, 1978.

———. "Five Songs by Hildegard of Bingen." *Vox Benedictina* 1 (1984) 257–63.

———. "The German Visionary: Hildegard of Bingen." *Medieval Women Writers.* Ed. Katharina Wilson. Athens, Ga.: Athens Univ. Press, 1984. 109–30.

Lachman, Barbara (Grant). "Five Liturgical Songs by Hildegard von Bingen." *Signs* 5 (1980) 557–67.

Lachman, Barbara. *Journal of Hildegard of Bingen.* Bell Tower Publications, 1994.

Lagorio, Valerie. "The Continental Women Mystics of the Middle Ages: An Assessment." *The Roots of the Modern Christian Tradition.* Series on the Spirituality of Western Christendom, 2. Ed. Roxanne Elder. Kalamazoo: Cistercian Publications, 1984.

———. "The Medieval Continental Women Mystics: An Introduction." *An Introduction to the Medieval Mystics of Europe.* Ed. Paul Szarmach. Albany: SUNY Press, 1984.

Lauter, Werner. *Hildegard-Bibliographie.* 2 vols. Alzey: Der Rheinhessischen Druckwerkstätte Verlag 1970, 1984. Third volume forthcoming.

McGrath, James, trans. The monks Gottfried and Theodoric. *The Life of the Holy Hildegard.* Collegeville, Minn.: The Liturgical Press, 1995.

Meier, Christel. "Zwei Modelle von Allegorie im 12. Jahrhundert: Das allegorische Verfahren Hildegards von Bingen und Alans von Lille." *Formen und Funktionen Der Allegorie.* 70–89. Ed. Walter Haug. Stuttgart, 1979.

_____. "Virtus und Operation als Kernbegriffe einer Kinzeption der Mystik bei Hildegard von Bingen." *Grundfragen chrislicher Mystik*. Series Wissenschaftliche Studientaugung Theologia Mystica. *Mystik in Geschichte und Gegenwart, band 5*. Stuttgart-Bad Cannstatt, Weingarten, Ravensburg, 1985.

Mews, Constant J. "Heloise and Hildegard: Re-Visioning Religious Life in the Twelfth Century." *Tjurunga* 44 (1993).

Müller, Gerhard. "Charisma und Amt: Die heilige Hildegard von Bingen in der Auseinandersetzung Mit Dem Kirchlichen Amt." *Catholica* 34:4 (1980) 279–95.

Newman, Barbara. "Hildegard of Bingen: Visions and Validation." *Church History* 54 (1985) 163–75.

_____. "Divine Power Made Perfect in Weakness: St. Hildegard on the Frail Sex." *Distant Echoes*. Vol. 2 of Peaceweavers. Kalamazoo: Cistercian Publications, 1987. 103–22.

_____. *Sister of Wisdom: St. Hildegard's Theology of the Feminine*. Berkeley: Scholar's Press, 1987.

_____. "Some Medieval Theologians and the Sophia Tradition." *The Downside Review* 108 (1990) 111–30.

_____. *Symphonia: Critical Edition*. Rev. ed. Ithaca: Cornell Univ. Press, 1998.

_____, ed. *Voice of the Living Light: Hildegard of Bingen and Her World*. Berkeley, UCLA Press, 1998.

Nolan, Edward Peter. *Cry Out and Write: A Feminine Poetics of Revelation*. New York: Continuum Press, 1995.

O'Dell, M. Colman. "Elizabeth of Schönau and Hildegard of Bingen: Prophets of the Lord." *Distant Echoes*. Vol. 2 of *Peaceweavers*. Kalamazoo: Cistercian Publications, 1987. 85–102.

Olds, Linda. "Metaphors of Hierarchy and Interrelatedness in Hildegard of Bingen and Mary Daly." *Listening* 24 (1989) 54–66.

Olson, Robert. "The Green Man in Hildegard of Bingen." *Studia Mystica* 15:4 (1992) 3–18.

Orthmann, James. "Hildegard of Bingen on the Divine Light." *Mystics Quarterly* 11:2 (1985) 60–64.

Pernoud, Régine. *Hildegarde de Bingen: Conscience inspirée de VII siecle*. Monaco, 1994.

Pfau, Marianne Richert. "Hildegard von Bingen's *Symphonia Armonie Celestium Revelationum:* An Analysis of Musical Process, Modality, and Text-Music Relations." Ph.D. diss. SUNY at Stony Brook, 1990.

_____. "Mode and Melody Types in Hildegard von Bingen's Symphonia." *Sonus* 11 (1990) 53–71.

Pitra, Joannes Baptista Cardinal, ed. *Analecta Sanctae Hildegardis. Analecta sacra*. Vol. 8. Includes *Expositiones Evangeliorum,* 145 *Epistolae,* and other works. Monte Cassino, 1882.

_____. *Analecta Sanctae Hildegardis Opera*. Republished ed. Vol. 8 (all Hildegard). England: Gregg Press, 1966.

Porcile, Maria Teresa. "Solitude and Solidarity." *The Ecumenical Review* 38:1 (1986) 35–47.

Pretsch, Hermann Josef. "Die Kontakte des Benediktiner-Doppelklosters in Zweifalten mit Hildegard von Bingen und Abt Berthold Konflikt mit Seinem Konvent." *In Archiv für Mittelrheinische Kirchengeschichte.* Ed. A. Dell. Speyer am Rhein, 1986. 147–73.

Raoull Manselli. "Amicizia spirtuale ed azione pastorale nella Germania del sec. XII: Ildegarde di Bingen, Elisabetta ed Ecberto di Schönau contro l'eresia Catara." *Studi e Materiali di Storia Delle Religioni* 38 (1967) 302–13.

Riethe, Peter, trans. *Naturkunde (Liber simplicis medicinae).* Salzburg: Otto Müller Verlag, 1959.

Rose, C., and M. Gawel. *Migraine: The Facts.* Oxford: Oxford Univ. Press, 1979.

Russell, Kenneth. "Matthew Fox's Illuminations of Hildegard of Bingen." *Listening* 24 (1989) 39–53.

———. Book Review. *Église et Theologie* 20:1 (1989) 129.

Ryan, Hildegard. "St. Hildegard and St. Bernard." *Tjurunga* 42 (1992) 16–28.

Sacks, Oliver. *Migraine: The Evolution of a Common Disorder.* Berkeley: UCLA Press, 1970.

Schipperges, Heinrich. "Antike und Mittelalter." *Krankheit, Heilkunst, Heilung.* Series Institut für Historische Anthropologie, Veroffentlichungen des Instituts für Historische Anthrolpologie, Band 1. Ed. Schipperges et al. (1978) 229–70.

———. *Hildegard of Bingen.* Trans. Eva Jauntzems. New York, 1989.

———. trans. *Welt und Mensch* (De operatione Dei). Salzburg: Otto Müller Verlag, 1965.

Schmitt, Miriam. "Hildegard of Bingen: Feather Carried by the Wind, Borne Up to God." *Sisters Today* 58 (1986) 71–78.

———. "Hildegard and Prophecy." *Benedictines* (1986) 31–41.

———. "Blessed Jutta of Disibodenberg: Hildegard of Bingen's Magistra and Abbess." *American Benedictine Review* 40:2 (1989) 170–89.

———. "St. Hildegard of Bingen: Leaven of God's Justice." *Cistercian Studies* (1989) 69–88.

Schnapp, Jeffrey. "Virgin Words: Hildegard of Bingen's Lingua Ignota and the Development of Imaginary Languages Ancient to Modern." *Exemplaria* 3:2 (October 1991) 1994.

Sharp, Michael David. "The Diabolic Feminine: Woman and Evil in Three Works of Hildegard von Bingen." Unpublished paper. Ann Arbor. 1992.

Shipperges, Heinrich, trans. *Der Mensch in der Verantwortung: Liber Vitae Meritorum.* Salzburg: Otto Müller Verlag, 1972.

Silvas, Anna, trans. "Saint Hildegard of Bingen and the Vita Sanctae Hildegardis." *Tjurunga: An Australasian Benedictine Review* (1985–86) 29, 30, 31, 32.

Singer, Charles. *From Magic to Science.* New York: Dover Publications, 1958.

Strehlow, Wighard and Gottfried Hertzka. *Hildegard of Bingen's Medicine.* Folk Wisdom Series. Santa Fe: Bear & Co., 1988.

Sur, Carolyn. *The Feminine Images of God in the Visions of Saint Hildegard of Bingen's 'Scivias.'* New York: Edwin Mellen Press, 1993.

Ulrich, Ingeborg. *Hildegard of Bingen: Mystic, Healer, Companion of the Angels.* Collegeville, Minn.: The Liturgical Press, 1990.

Walker-Moskop, Ruth. "Health and Cosmic Continuity: Hildegard of Bingen's Unique Concerns." *Mystics Quarterly* 11 (1985) 19–25.

Weeks, Andrew. *German Mysticism from Hildegard of Bingen to Ludwig Wittgenstein: A Literary and Intellectual History*. Albany, N.Y.: State Univ. of New York Press, 1993.

Widmer, Berthe. "Zum Frauenverständnis Hildegards von Bingen." *Theologische Zeitschrift* 45 (1989) 125–41.

_____. *Heilsordnung und Zeitgeschehen in der Mystik Hildegards von Bingen*. Basel, 1955.

Wiethaus, Ulrike. "Cathar Influences in Hildegard of Bingen's Play 'Ordo Virtutum.'" *American Benedictine Review* 38 (1987) 192–203.

_____. "In Search of Medieval Women's Friendships: Hildegard of Bingen's Letters to Her Female Contemporaries." *Maps of Flesh and Light: The Religious Experience of Medieval Women Mystics*. Syracuse, N.Y.: Syracuse Univ. Press, 1993, 93–111.

Zueltz, Monica. "Hildegard of Bingen." *Sisters Today* 58 (1986) 66–70.

Select Discography:
Briefly Annotated for the Listener

Gothic Voices, dir. Christopher Page. *A Feather on the Breath of God: Sequences and Hymns by Abbess Hildegard of Bingen*. Hyperion CDA 66039. 1984.

> One of the earliest accessible recordings of Hildegard's music, noted for its ethereal quality, and consisting of sequences and hymns written by Hildegard for the Divine Office.

Anonymous 4. *11,000 Virgins: Chants for the Feast of St. Ursula*. Harmonia mundi 907200. 1997.

> A superb ensemble of four voices, this is a wonderful recording for hearing the melodies and modes used by Hildegard.

Early Music Institute, dir. Thomas Binkley. *The Lauds of St. Ursula*. Focus 911. 1991.

> This disk has six ensemble singers, who manage to sound like they are on the journeys of St. Ursula, especially capturing the innocence of the initial songs, if not the technical perfection of the recording of Anonymous 4.

Ellen Oak. *Hildegard of Bingen: The Harmony of Heaven*. Bison Tales 0001. 1995.

> An unusually moving recording of Hildegard. One voice, in a range lower than one usually hears her pieces sung. Very evocative for the modern listener, without sacrificing Hildegard's sense of her compositions.

Ensemble für frühe Musik, Augsburg. *Hildegard of Bingen und ihre Zeit: Geistliche Musik des 12 Jahrhunderts*. Christophorus 74584.

> An interesting disk because it contains the work of Hildegard, her contemporary Abelard, and some anonymous works of the time. Very useful for

comparing Hildegard's and Abelard's styles and for the use of male as well as female voices.

Oxford Camerata, dir. Jeremy Summerly. *Hildegard von Bingen: Heavenly Revelations*. Naxos 8.550998. 1994.

A very different disk, in that it alternates between men and women as groups, at times individual male and female voices, usually on different songs. The timbre of the voices is quite different from many early music groups. Worth hearing 'O viridissma virga" sung by men in a baritone range.

Schola der Benediktinerinnenabtei St. Hildegard, dir. M.-I. Ritscher. *Gesänge der bl. Hildegard von Bingen*. Bayer 100116. 1979.

Recorded at the Abtei St. Hildegard, this has a full and lovely sound to it, with the Choir of the Sisters of St. Benedict recording the pieces of their foundress.

Sequentia, dir. Barbara Thornton. *Symphoniae: Geistliche Gesänge*. Deutsche Harmonia mundi 770-2-RG. 1985.

These spiritual songs are vocally etheral, with a mixture of pieces and styles, recorded in a cathedral with the resonance this gives them.

Sequentia, dir. Barbara Thornton. *Canticles of Ecstasy*. Deutsche Harmonia mundi 05472-77320-2. 1994.

This is the first in a series of albums (which follow) put out by Sequentia in honor of the 800th anniversary of Hildegard's birth. Every care has been taken to record the cycle of her songs in order and with faithfulness to their interpretation of her musical notation.

Sequentia, dir. Barbara Thornton. *Voice of the Blood*. Deutsche Harmonia mundi 05472-77346-2. 1995.

The second in the series. Very expressively done.

Sequentia, dir. Barbara Thornton. *O Jerusalem*. Deutsche Harmonia mundi 0542-77353-2. 1997.

The third in the series. Evocative of the prophetess, especially in some pieces.

Sequentia, dir. Barbara Thornton. *Ordo virtutum*. Two disks. Deutsche Harmonia mundi 77051-2-RG. 1982. Re-recorded on one disk in 1998. Deutsche Harmonia mundi 05472-77378-2.

The final entry in the series is a re-recording of an earlier performance of Hildegard's morality play in song, *The Order of the Virtues*. Magnificent, though the listener is warned that lulled by the Virtues, female voices singing sublimely, the spoken voice of the Devil (the only male part) comes as a rude shock, yet shows the power of the piece.

Sequentia, dir. Barbara Thornton. *Saints*. Deutsche Harmonia mundi 05472-77378-2. 1998.

One more entry in the attempt to give a complete account of Hildegard's opus by Sequentia, the title summarizes the content.

Schola und Chor der Benediktinerinnenabtei St. Hildegard, Eibingen. *Zum Fest der Heiligen Hildegard von Bingen: Gregorianische Gesänge aus Messe und Offizium.* Deutsche Harmonia mundi 882586-907. 1990.

Interesting because it is the Choir of the Abtei St. Benedict in Eibingen, it also contains pieces in honor of their foundress. Otherwise, the songs are Gregorian chant of the Mass and the Office, but using many of Hildegard's compositions.

Richard Souther. Original compositions, arrangements and interpretations. *Vision: The Music of Hildegard von Bingen.* Angel Records 7243-5-55246-2-1. 1990.

A very different, popularized piece, but the only experimental or "new age" recording of Hildegard worth listening to at all. The composer has attempted to intertwine his compositions with Hildegard's, more as a tribute than an exploitation, and this popularized form of Hildegard's work sent many out to find the original recordings made by specialized ensembles not familiar to the general listening public.

Erdenklang Musicverlag, dir. Ulrich Rützel. *Vox Diadema.* Real Music RM8999. 1990.

An example of how truly awful Hildegard's music can be when exploited for other purposes. She is utterly unrecognizable in this recording.

Index

Disibod, St., 121–23
Disibodenberg, conflicts with, 31, 50, 146–49; formative influence, 5–10, 14; women in, 4–5, 11–15
doctrinal issues. *See* authority, theology
double vision *or* dual vision, 18–20, 60–61, 190–91, 195–96, 201n32; *see also synaethesia*
Dronke, Peter, 12, 76, 91–92, 99–103, 106, 134, 139, 191–92, 205n63, 207n99, 207n104, 208n123

Eberhard of Bamberg, bishop, 126, 153–54, 178
Ecclesia, 33, 37–41, 45–47, 83, 95–99
education, Hildgard, 9–14, 147–48, 158–60
"effeminate age," 24, 74, 116, 196
Ekdahl, Audrey Davidson, 112, 208n122
Elisabeth of Schönau, 98, 149, 213n191
eternity, 51, 54–56, 62–63, 65
Eugenius III, pope, 28–29, 161–62
Eve. *See* Fall
evil, 19, 21, 31, 42, 44–47, 55–58, 160; personified by the devil, 19, 21, 82–83, 107, 110, 112, 205n68; *see also* Fall, sin
exteriority. *See* bipolarities

Fall of humanity, 18–20, 33–37, 134–36, 205n68; *see also* evil, grace, and Incarnation
feminine, in the divine & personifications, 32–33, 53, 66–71, 74, 76, 102; in style of writing, 15–16, 53, 74; in humanity, 74, 148–50, 167–69; all, 196–98, 201nn 23, 26, 205nn 66, 67, 68
fire. *See* imagery
Flanagan, Sabina, 135, 152, 201n24, 211n153, 211n158, 211n169

gemstones. *See* imagery

God. *See* Incarnation, Living Light, Trinity
Gottfried and Theodoric, 3
greeness. *See viriditas*
Gregory VII, pope, 163
Guibert of Gembloux, 77–78, 143–44, 158, 194–95

Hartwig, archbishop of Bremen, 155, 157
healing, advice about, 127–41; miraculous, 172–74; source of, 48, 111–12,
heaven, 38–41, 81–85, 101–4, 117–20; as final end, 55, 71, 98–99, 120; source and purpose of visions, 18–20, 26–27, 52, 86
Heinrich, bishop of Liege, 172
Helenger, abbot, 123, 147, 154–55
Henry IV of Germany, 160, 163
Henry V, 21
Hildebert, 2–4
Hildegard of Bingen: creativity of, 13–16, 28–30, 79, 197–98; formative influences, 1–24; illness and health, 3–4, 24, 28, 48–49, 67, 74, 139–40, 146–47, 187–88; *magistra*, 14, 17, 24, 128, 146, 196; orthodoxy and church teaching, 20–23, 127, 150–53, 166–69, 184–86; preaching tours, 177–90; *see also* specific topics and works
holiness, 31, 69, 77, 112; of Jutta, 4, 10
humanity, 19–20, 33–36, 62–63, 140–41, 197
humility. *See* virtues
humors, bodily, 69, 130, 132–33, 137–40

ignorance, claims of, 11–13; "indocta", 11; modesty topos, 13
imagery, examples of: fire, 6–7, gemstones, 130–31; *see also* art, feminine, light, music, personifications, theological-visionary treatises